Henry Augustus Willis

Fitchburg in the War of the Rebellion

Henry Augustus Willis

Fitchburg in the War of the Rebellion

ISBN/EAN: 9783337116255

Printed in Europe, USA, Canada, Australia, Japan

Cover: Foto ©ninafisch / pixelio.de

More available books at **www.hansebooks.com**

FITCHBURG

— IN THE —

WAR OF THE REBELLION.

BY HENRY A. WILLIS.

"But these are deeds which should not pass away,
And names that must not wither."

FITCHBURG:
PUBLISHED BY STEPHEN SHEPLEY.
PRINTED BY J. GARFIELD & CO.
1866.

To The
FATHERS AND MOTHERS
WHO HAVE GIVEN THEIR NOBLE SONS;

TO THE WIDOW WHO HAS OFFERED UP HER HUSBAND;

TO THE SISTERS AND BROTHERS OF THE DEAR ONES FALLEN;

AND TO THE ORPHAN, WHO ONLY KNOWS THAT ITS FATHER WENT TO THE WAR AND NEVER MORE RETURNED;

TO THESE, AS A TOKEN OF HEARTFELT SYMPATHY,
THE WRITER DEDICATES THIS BOOK.

FITCHBURG, OCT. 1ST, 1866.

INTRODUCTION.

Many Histories of the Great Rebellion have been written; many others will be, and perhaps the best and truest record of the perilous times through which we, as a Nation, have just passed, will be written many years hence. These will be general in their character, and will not descend to the details of the part which states, cities, towns and communities had in the great contest. Our present purpose is to put upon record in a concise form *our* share as a Town in the great work of vindicating the Constitution, the establishing of universal freedom, and preserving unsullied the glorious "flag of the Republic."

Justice, alike to the living and the dead of the actors in the great drama, demands that their deeds shall be embalmed in the memories of posterity through all coming time. Gratitude to the living and precious memories of the dead prompt us to the welcome task before us.

A community which has sent nine companies into the field during the war, which has promptly filled its quotas under all calls and has now to its credit seventy-five men surplus above all demands upon it, has certainly a record of which it may well be proud, and one well worth preserving.

The personal experiences of these our sons and brothers and fellow-citizens if they could be related — "the story of their lives from year to year: the battles, sieges, fortunes they have passed; the most disastrous chances; the moving accidents by flood and field; of hair breadth 'scapes in the imminent deadly breach; of being taken by the insolent foe, and of their redemption thence, and portance in their travels' history:"— these would fill with intense interest many a volume.

Our purpose in the present volume is to give an account of the early action of the town in the first weeks and months of the Rebellion; the organizing of the various companies and the circumstances of their departure, and a history in brief of the operations and adventures of each regiment with which they were connected, following them through the whole term of service, and noticing particularly the principal engagements in which they bore a part.

Also, an account of the various enterprises organized and carried on by our citizens for the relief of the soldiers and their families. Our "patriot dead" will be appropriately noticed, and accounts will be given of the various public funerals of the martyrs whose precious remains have been borne to our midst from the places where they fell. Also, narratives of our citizens who suffered and perished in Southern prisons. A complete list will be given of every soldier who enlisted from Fitchburg, with his rank, company and regiment, when and for what discharged, deaths, wounds, &c. Also, a full account of the two drafts with lists of men drafted, &c. Also, correspondence of soldiers—incidents—and various matters of interest.

In short, it will be our effort to make the book as complete a record as possible of who our soldiers were, what they did, and what befel them during their term of service.

With thus much for introduction, we enter upon our work fully conscious of our inability to do the subject full justice, and humbly craving the kind consideration and gentle criticism of the reader.

OPENING SCENES & EARLY ACTION OF THE TOWN.

The opening scenes of the Rebellion are fresh in our minds; the Presidential Election of 1860, the secession of State after State, the imbecility of the wretched old "functionary" who encumbered the Presidential Chair, the occupation of Fort Sumter by Major Anderson, the attempt to provision the Fort, and the final attack upon it.

On Saturday, the 13th of April, 1860, news came to our town that Fort Sumter had been attacked and was gallantly holding out. On Sunday evening, the 14th, the writer in company with the telegraph operator and another gentleman, visited the Telegraph Office for news. So much had been said and written of the "impregnability of Fort Sumter" that we were ill prepared for the message which soon clicked off to us as follows:

"CHARLESTON, APRIL 13TH, 1861.

Fort Sumter has unconditionally surrendered. The news has just come. Gen. Chestnut (Ex-Gov. and Commander-in-Chief,) has just landed and marched to Gov. Pickens' residence followed by a great crowd with great joy. It is said that ten men of Fort Sumter were killed, and that the Federal Flag was shot away by the Palmetto Guards on Morris Island. In all, two thousand shots have been fired. No Carolinians hurt. Maj. Anderson and men under guard were conveyed to Morris Island. The bells are ringing out merry peals. Our people are engaged in every demonstration of joy. It is estimated that there are eight thousand men on the Island and in the neighborhood. I have just returned from a visit to Fort Sumter and I am assured that no one was killed at the Fort — this is reliable and puts to rest all reports about Sumter. Maj. Anderson has reached the city and is the guest of Gen. Beauregard. Our people sympathize with Major Anderson, but abhor those who were in the steamers off our bay and in sight of our people, and did not even attempt to re-enforce the Fort. Judge Magrath has just returned from the Fort and reports that the wood work and officers' quarters are all burned; none of the officers were wounded. The Fort will be taken possession of to-night by the Confederate troops.

LATER. Lieut. Worden of the Federal Navy has been taken prisoner of war and his despatches from Lieut. Slimmer to Washington seized. Fort Pickens was reinforced last night. Great rejoicing in this city."

Such was the sad story as first communicated to Fitchburg. The ball had fairly opened, and the rebels had achieved the first victory. What would be the result? Where would it end? No one then could predict. But we who survive have learned too well the sad history of the last four years of bloody war and can rejoice over the final glorious consummation.

The sad news was fully confirmed by Monday morning's papers, which gave all the details.

The call of President Lincoln for seventy-five thousand Volunteers opened our eyes to the fact that war, so long feared, so much to be deplored, so uncertain in its duration and consequences, was at last upon us. We can well remember the excitement of that memorable day; the prompt response of Gov. Andrew to the President's call, and his order for several regiments of the Militia to proceed at once to Washington to the defence of our National Capitol.

We had at that time two companies of Militia in town: the "Fitchburg Fusiliers," Capt. John W. Kimball, and the "Washington Guards," Capt. Edwin Upton, both of the old Ninth Regiment, which then had but three other Companies. The commanders of these Companies, in response to "General Orders, reported their companies in condition to go forward at once, if called upon. But it appeared that enough *whole* regiments to meet the present emergency had been offered and accepted. Meantime the Third, Fourth, Fifth, Sixth and Eighth Regiments were hurriedly started for the scene of action.

All was excitement; little business was done; people gathered on the street corners with saddened hearts, but with determined looks, discussing what might next occur.

Tuesday, Wednesday, and Thursday passed, and Friday, the ever memorable 19th of April came. Late in the afternoon the telegraph flashed to us the news of the attack in Baltimore as follows: "The Sixth Mass. Reg't. is now fighting its way through Baltimore; four men have been killed, many wounded, and the fighting still going on." Who that remembers those days can ever forget the shock? What patriotic heart does not remember its impulses as the terrible truth burst upon him that our own Massachusetts soldiers had indeed become the first victims of this wicked outbreak? The impulse to rush to arms and descend like an avalanche upon the accursed city which had permitted this thing to come to pass, was only a feeling shared in common with the whole North. The next morning's papers gave full particulars, and a meeting of our citizens was held the same afternoon to see what this town would do towards sustaining our government in its trial hour. Alvah Crocker, Esq. presided and opened the meeting with a few eloquent and patriotic remarks, and was followed by various other gentlemen, after which the following resolutions were presented and unanimously adopted.

"*Resolved*, That we respond cordially to the Proclamation of the President of the United States; that we declare our unflinching resolution to support our government in its struggle to maintain its honor, integrity and existence.

Resolved, That we will use our utmost endeavors to secure a vote of the town whereby the sum of ten thousand dollars shall be raised by direct tax, which sum of money shall be appropriated to provide for the support of the families of any of the soldiers who may be called out during the present war, and for fitting out and equipping such men."

The excitement had become intense and almost painful. Men met and grasped each other's hands in silence; in tears; with hearts too full for utterance but with *looks* which meant *war*.

All felt that there was now one duty above all others devolving upon every loyal man; to give personally a full and hearty support to the Government by all the means within our power. The next day was Sunday, the first Sabbath in "war time." How unspeakably sad it was! Our good people wended their way to church with altered feelings and under circumstances greatly changed from what had been their wont. The beautiful "flag of the Republic" floated sadly over the street in the gentle breeze of that Spring morning—but its stars seemed dim, its stripes only suggested blood. Whether it was longer to be the symbol of a free, united, happy country, or only to exist as a relic of a "fallen Republic" was a question that no one could answer that morning—and yet, as we gazed upon it we seemed to gather strength and confidence, for we remembered that it also represented power which properly put forth by loyal hands could bring us out of all our difficulties, and we thanked God that the departments of Government, at least, were in honest, loyal hands.

The services in the churches were of a patriotic nature and our National Hymn, "America" which never before seemed of particular significance, was sung with a pathos and a meaning which reached all hearts. Thus passed the quiet Sabbath. It was not however, altogether a quiet one. It being expected that our companies might be ordered forward the next morning the "busy notes of preparation" were heard, and many of our ladies were engaged through the day in preparing clothing for the brave fellows who, like the minute men of the Revolution stood ready to move at a moment's warning. But, as will be seen they were not called upon for several days.

On Saturday, April 27th, a Town Meeting was held at which the resolutions adopted at the Citizens' meeting April 20, were carried into effect by appropriating by *unanimous vote* the sum of ten thousand dollars for the benefit of the soldiers and their families. The following were chosen a committee to take charge of the same: Ebenezer Torrey, Moses Wood, C. Marshall, William Woodbury, Levi Downe, Alpheus P. Kimball, Timothy S. Wilson. A committee was also appointed to ascertain what reduction might be made in the expenses of the town for the current year, to report at an adjourned meeting one week later.

The "Fusiliers" and "Guards" had recruited their companies, and this day, April 27th, had witnessed a grand parade and drill of both, joined also by Capt. Rockwood's company, of Leominster, which had marched up from that town to show us their skill in drilling and for the purpose of getting into "marching trim." All three of these companies were ready and anxious to be called upon to join the "fray." But their time had not yet come. Patriotic, impetuous, brave hearted young men; they feared the struggle would be ended and they might have no part in it. Would to God it might have been so. But alas! it was destined that the war should go on, and before it ended room should be found for *all* who desired to enlist to do battle in the cause of their country and for freedom.

The zeal of our citizens suggested various measures, not all of which were of practical value.

One of these was that every soldier that we should send to the field should be armed with a revolver and a bowie-knife. Accordingly one hundred and fifty revolvers were purchased and brought into town for the use of our two organized companies, and at the same time Messrs. Whitman and Miles with characteristic liberality, offered to manufacture the same number of *bowie-knives*. Suffice it to say, that before the troops were called upon to march, it was decided that neither of the above mentioned articles would be much needed for *ornament* or use. The revolvers were sold to go to a Western State which believed in "arming to the teeth," and the *bowie-knives*, we *hope*, were put to some good use. Meantime, preparations went forward, for it was felt that our "boys" would soon be called upon to march.

The ladies took hold of the sad but patriotic work and held meetings at the armories of the soldiers to prepare bandages, clothing, &c. At these meetings might be seen the soldiers with their female friends together winding the bandage or scraping the lint that might ere long be used to bind up their own wounds. Sad thoughts! but far from deterring any man they only served to fix more firmly the determination to do their whole duty at whatever cost.

On Saturday, May 4th, the adjourned town meeting was held, at which the committee on retrenchment recommended a reduction of five thousand dollars in the town appropriations for the current year, which recommendation was adopted—two thousand dollars being taken from the schools, two thousand from highways, and the balance from the public library and other departments of town expenses. Every one deplored the reduction of the amount appropriated for schools, and many thought the necessity for it did not exist, but the general feeling at the time was that the war would completely paralyze business, that great distress would follow, that the raising of money necessary for carrying on the war would bear very heavily upon all, and while great liberality should be practised in granting money for war expenses, the most rigid economy should be observed in all other directions, even though the cause of Education should in the mean time suffer. But it may be proper to add in this connection that through all the other years of the war our *schools* at *least* were sustained with the accustomed liberality of our people.

At the town meeting of the 4th of May, the chairman of the committee having in charge the ten thousand dollar appropriation read a note signed by the various physicians of the town offering their professional services gratis, to all families of soldiers engaged in suppressing the rebellion, which we believe they continued to do until the war had closed. The following is a copy:

" *To the Military Relief Committee: Gentlemen;*

The undersigned, Physicians of Fitchburg, members of the Massachusetts Medical Society, through you, hereby tender gratuitous professional services, when desired, to the families of the soldiers of this town, while engaged in the war to defend the Government of the United States against the present Southern Rebellion.

THOMAS R. BOUTELLE,
JONAS A. MARSHALL,
ALFRED HITCHCOCK,
JAMES R. WELLMAN,
GEORGE JEWETT,
GEORGE D. COLONY.

" Fitchburg, May 1st, 1861."

Thursday, May 16th, was a great day with us. The High School and the Day Street Schools had procured flags which were thrown to the breeze amid the booming of cannon, music, and speeches by several of the young men of the schools, the teachers, and other citizens. The two military companies paraded on the occasion and united in the ceremonies. The same evening witnessed an interesting scene at the Town Hall; the presentation to the Fusiliers and Guards of two beautiful silk flags which the ladies had procured at an expense of eighty dollars.

The Hall was densely crowded. Hon. J. W. Mansur presided and opened the meeting, in well chosen remarks defining our duties as citizens in the present crisis. At the conclusion of his remarks Miss Emily Twichell stepped forward with one of the flags, and addressing Capt. Kimball of the Fusiliers, presented it to his company, expressing the hope that they might never be called upon to bear it to the field; but if otherwise, that they would stand by it to the last. Capt. Kimball responded eloquently on accepting the flag in behalf of his command. He caused his men to swear that it should *never* trail in the dust while a single arm was left to uphold it. He spoke of the scenes through which the banner of the Republic had been borne in times past; of the Revolution;

and of the victories and defeats of that and subsequent wars. "Emblem of liberty: if struck down now, the hope of men for free government would be forever extinguished."

Miss Eliza Trask then, in a clear voice and appropriate language, presented the other flag to Capt. Edwin Upton, who received it in behalf of his command with a few appropriate remarks.

We now propose to give a history of the recruitment and organization of each of the nine companies sent out from this town, taking them up in their regular order and following out the record of each in connection with the regiment to which it was attached. The circumstances attending the formation of each will be given—accounts of public meetings held for the purpose of stimulating recruiting—amount of bounties offered, and paid, if any. The original roll of each company will be given which will contain the names of all belonging to the same, whether residents of Fitchburg or not.

Also, the ceremonies and parades attending their departure for camp where any occurred. We commence with Capt. James Savage's company, of the Second Regiment.

HISTORY OF THE SECOND REGIMENT.

The first company actually raised and accepted from this town under the call of the President for three years troops, was recruited by Capt. James Savage Jr., who opened his office about the 1st of May, and recruited his company in about a week. Capt. Savage was from Boston, but well known to many of our citizens. Educated at "Harvard," brought up amid all the luxuries wealth could afford, he was one of the first to respond to the call of our country. His record is a short but noble one. His company was attached to the Second Regiment. He was promoted to Major in June, 1862, wounded at Cedar Mountain August 6th, and died in a Richmond prison on the 19th of September following. The following is a list of members of this company:

ROLL OF COMPANY D, SECOND REG'T MASS. VOLS.

OFFICERS.

Captain, JAMES SAVAGE, JR., Boston.
1st *Lieut*., WILLIAM D. SEDGWICK, Lenox.
2d *Lieut*., HENRY L. HIGGINSON, Boston.

NON-COMMISSIONED OFFICERS AND PRIVATES.

SERGEANTS.
Parker Theodore K., Winchendon.
Crocker Harry A., Winchendon.
Cheney Harry A., Ashburnham.
Miller Adam, Lee.
Snow, George W., Nashua, N. H.

CORPORALS.
Newton George B., West Boylston.
Kendall Charles W., Ashburnham.
Thurston Thomas B., Fitchburg.
Maynard Frederick, Winchendon.

Moulton Ansel A., Fitchburg.
Cobb Horatio S., Lee.
Palmer William, West Boylston.
Fay Benjamin F., Ashburnham.
Thompson Jed. C., Marlboro'.

MUSICIANS.
Taylor James H., Winchendon.
Booth Alvin C., Fitchburg.

WAGONER.
Webster George W., Bedford.

PRIVATES.

Anthony Webber F., Tyringham.
Alden George H., Templeton.
Allen Charles, Boston.
Anderson John E., West Boylston.
Balcom Muron E., Marlboro'.
Barry Patrick, Northampton.
Bartlett Anson B., Clinton.
Beach Wm., West Boylston.
Bickford Walter, Gardner.
Billings Alfred, Lunenburg.
Billings Amos, Lunenburg.
Bishee Charles E., Fitchburg.
Boston George H., Winchendon.
Bliven Arthur, Lenox.
Blunt William H., West Boylston.
Brooks Albert E., Westminster.
Bruce George A., Winchendon.
Cahill John, Northampton.
Cassady William, Leominster.
Chase Wm. P., West Boylston.
Clapp Cyrus J., Rindge, N. H.,
Clapp Samuel B., Gardner.
Cleaves Charles, Dayton, Me.
Cheney Gilbert A., Newton U. Falls.
Childs Isaac, West Boylston.
Cobb Horatio S., Lee.
Colman Michael, Hinsdale.
Colvin Frederick, West Boylston.
Conant Alphonzo, Fairhaven, Ct.
Curtis George S., Lunenburg.
Derr John, Stockbridge.
Eager William O., Westminster.
Farewell Abel, Jr., East Boylston.
Farewell Charles B., Northbridge.
Fielding Gersham W., Tyringham.
Fitzgibbon James C., Ashby.
Hadley Isaac C., Winchendon.
Harris William L., Shirley.
Hayward Horace P., Fitchburg.
Heald Charles H., Ashburnham.
Himes James P., Gardner.

Holmes Theodore D., Tyringham.
Hosmer Geo. B. T., West Boylston.
Houghton Albert, Leominster.
Houghton Roscoe, Lee.
Hyde Wm., West Boylston.
Ingram Gilbert B., Tyringham.
King Ossian M., Fitchburg.
King Wm. J., Tyringham.
Kinsman Frederick, Fitchburg.
Lakin J. C., Bennington, Vt.
Lakin Crosby, Fitchburg.
Largler Thomas, Lunenburg.
Litchfield Charles D., Lunenburg.
McComber Elijah, Fairhaven, Ct.
Newton Winsor, West Boylston.
Nason Edwin F., Fitchburg.
Nutting Allen A., Ashburnham.
Orne David, J., Clinton.
Palmer Wm., West Boylston.
Partridge Henry J., Westminster.
Parkhurst William, Springfield.
Peterson John, Boston.
Pierce Henry O., Fitchburg.
Pierce Henry S., Winchendon.
Phillips George R., Leominster.
Phillips James M.,
Priest M. A., Marlboro'.
Pollard Edwin R. Winchendon.
Prescott James M., West Boylston.
Rafferty Thomas, Lee.
Reed William H., East Boston.
Shattuck Danforth, Pepperell.
Sweet George H., Tyringham.
Tarbox Charles, Fitchburg.
Toombs Wm. D., West Boylston.
Tichenor George, Tyringham.
Wilcox Franklin, Westminster.
Walker Charles C, Lunenburg.
Wetherbee Joseph A., Westminster.
Whyte Alfred A., West Boylston.
Woodward Melvin A., Lee.

It will be observed that most of the men were from other towns but it must be remembered that we already had two full companies ready to go, and as the prospect was now good that they would be accepted, the young men who had enlisted in them did not feel like leaving to join Capt. Savage.

But his company though not mainly of our own citizens,

still went out from us and was known as the "Fitchburg Company" and as such, we propose to give its record here.

The fortunes of the Second Regiment were the fortunes of this company, and we give in brief its history. This regiment was mustered into the United States service May 11th, 1861, and left the State July 8th, and at once joined the command of Maj. Gen. Patterson on the upper Potomac, and remained in that neighborhood engaged in picket duty until about the 1st of March, 1862. It led the column of Gen. Banks up the valley of the Shenandoah, was engaged at Front Royal, and participated in the celebrated "retreat of Gen. Banks," and sustained a loss of seventeen killed, forty-seven wounded, eighty-four missing. On the 6th of August occurred the disastrous battle of Cedar Mountain. This regiment was in the thickest of the fight; at one time being alone, nearly surrounded by rebel troops, but after pouring a terrible volley into the enemy, succeeded in retreating in good order. The loss of the regiment in this action was five officers killed, six wounded, three taken prisoners, among the latter Major Savage who died in the enemy's hands. About half the non-commissioned officers were killed or wounded, and one-third of all the privates. Total, thirty-four killed, one hundred twenty wounded, thirty-one missing.

During the retreat down the valley this regiment was engaged in a midnight encounter with the enemy in which four companies only were engaged, but which made so obstinate a resistance that three rebel regiments were brought up one after another, before they gave way. We give below an account of the affair written by Col. Quincy, supported by "rebel" testimony.

"THE SECOND MASSACHUSETTS.

NEW ORLEANS, JULY 1, 1866.

To the Editors of the Boston Daily Advertiser:—

To the survivors of the old regiment who were present at its first 'baptism of fire' in the midnight skirmish of Bartonsville, where as rear guard, it covered Banks's retreating column, the following account of the affair in Dabney's 'Life of Stonewall Jackson,' page 375, will be of interest:—

'But as it (the column) approached Barton's Mills, five miles from Winchester, the enemy, posted on both sides of the road, again received it with so severe a fire that the cavalry advance retired precipitately out of it, carrying the General and his attendants along with them, and riding down several cannoneers who had been brought up to their support. So pertinacious was the stand of the Federalists here that the 27th, 2d and 5th Virginia Regiments were brought up, and the affair grew to the dimensions of a night combat before they gave way.'

The 'Federalists' engaged as above described, consisted of four companies of the Second Massachusetts, deployed as skirmishers on either side of the pike, the rear of the battalion being in column by platoon in the road. The skirmish line was commanded by our brave and lamented Maj. Wilder Dwight. The company most hotly engaged, and whose losses were heaviest, was Company I, commanded by Captain, since Brevet Major-General Adin B. Underwood. The regiment was unsupported by any other troops. Its friends cannot but be satisfied with the enemy's account of this its first achievement under fire. — three confederate regiments being brought against our skirmish line of four companies, and the affair growing to the dimensions of a night combat, before the well remembered 'cease firing' and 'retreat,' at last rang out from Major Dwight's bugler and was repeated in varying cadence along the line.

Whether the 'Federalists' would have received so much credit for their "pertinacity," had the historian known who they were, may be a question. A few pages further on, General Banks is depicted as deserting his army long before the conclusion of the next day's battle. Should it be desired, however, to specify in the next edition the particular body of 'Federalists' by whom Jackson's column was checked at Bartonsville, the facts here stated may be relied on as the truth of history.

S. M. Q."

From this time until the 17th of September, the Regiment had the usual experience of marching and countermarching, and performing picket duty. September 17th, 1862, occurred the battle of Antietam. In this action the Regiment sustained itself most gallantly, and captured a flag from the enemy. Their loss was thirteen killed, fifty-four wounded, two missing. The accomplished Lieut. Col. Wilder Dwight was mortally wounded in this engagement. After this battle the Regiment was assigned to picket duty on the Potomac where it remained until nearly the close of the year, when it was marched to Fairfax Court House, in which vicinity it remained in winter quarters until April 27th, 1863, when the whole army broke camp and started on the Chancellorsville campaign. May 3d, 1863, occurred the disastrous battle of Chancellorsville, in which the Regiment was hotly engaged for one hour and a half, and suffered a loss of five officers and one hundred twenty-three enlisted men in killed and wounded. On the 9th of June the Regiment was engaged in an attack on Stuart's cavalry at "Bearly Ford" which was driven back with small loss to our army, the Second losing but one killed and two wounded. On the 2d and 3d of July, 1863, the Regiment was engaged at Gettysburg and its record there was a most honorable one. We copy from the Official Report:

"At about seven o'clock A. M., July 3d, orders were given to the Second Regiment and one other regiment to advance across the open meadow and take the enemy's position. It seemed certain destruction, but such were orders, and Lieut. Col. Mudge gave the commands—'Rise up, over the breastworks double quick.' With a cheer, with bayonets unfixed, without firing a shot, the line advanced as rapidly as the swampy ground would allow. Col. Mudge fell dead in the open field as on foot and sword in hand, he was cheering on the men. Three color-bearers were shot in going two hundred yards — but the colors kept on — into the enemy's line, over the breastwork, and the Regiment holds the old line. But from behind every tree and rock the rebel fire is poured in. Another color-bearer is shot dead waving the colors. The regiment on the right falls back in disorder. Ten of the officers of the Second are killed or wounded, and a regiment of the enemy is flanking it. Major Morse gives the order to fall back just in time to prevent it from being surrounded. Slowly and sullenly it retires to the other side of the meadow, and taking position behind a ruined stone wall, opens fire on the enemy wherever they show themselves. In that advance of four hundred yards, and in twenty minutes time, the Regiment had lost out of twenty-two officers and two hundred ninety-four men, one hundred thirty-four killed and wounded."

Immediately after the battle this Regiment joined in the pursuit of the retreating enemy which (as is well known,) was without important result.

After considerable marching and countermarching, with an occasional skirmish, until the 27th of September, it took passage in the cars from Bealton Station for the West to re-enforce Gen. Rosecrans. It arrived at Stevenson, Alabama, October 4th, having travelled one thousand one hundred seventy-eight miles by rail, and finally settled down at Elk River Bridge, Tennessee, where it remained until the end of the year.

The marches of the Regiment during this year were eighty-one in number, making eight hundred sixty-five miles, and its travel by railroad and steamboat one thousand three hundred ten miles. Its losses during the year were two hundred ninety-eight killed, wounded, and prisoners.

During the last few days of December, 1863, a portion of the Regiment numbering one hundred fifty-five re-enlisted, and on the 10th of January, 1864, left for Boston on a furlough of thirty days. On the 22d of February, it started on its return and joined its corps in Tennessee, March 1st. Active operations were at once resumed and from this time until September 2d, the "campaign of Atlanta" was carried on, in which the Regiment took a prominent part, engaging in several battles and skirmishes, and suffering a loss of forty-six in killed and wounded. From September 2d, to November 16th, the Regiment remained on provost duty at Atlanta, and at the end of that time commenced "Sherman's grand march to the sea." Space will not allow us to give a detailed account of this great campaign. This march of three hundred miles through the enemy's country without a base or line of supplies, will ever be a grand historic event. It resulted in the fall of Savannah and the virtual union of Grant's and Sherman's forces. The troops had only half rations of coffee, sugar, and salt, and one-sixth rations of bread—making up the deficiency from the sweet potatoes, corn meal, beef-cattle, sheep, poultry, and other provisions of the country, of which there was an abundance. The losses of the Regiment in the campaign were nine prisoners and three wounded.

The Regiment arrived near Savannah, December 22d, and remained there until January 17th, 1865, at which time the march into South Carolina commenced. From this time until the 24th of March, when the army reached Goldsboro', N. C., the Regiment was almost daily on the march, and during the time engaged in some fighting, losing about thirty in killed and wounded.

Here a few days rest was obtained, when the march was again resumed (April 9th,) for Raleigh, which place was reached on the 13th, and about which time hostilities ceased. On the 30th the march to Washington was commenced, and on the 19th of May Alexandria was reached.

It took part in the grand review of the whole army May 24th, after which it performed provost duty in the vicinity of Washington until July 14th, 1865, when it was mustered out of the service and started for Boston, and had a fine reception in New York as it passed through the city. On the 26th the Regiment was finally discharged having seen a service of four years, two months and fifteen days.

Such in brief, is the history of one of our earliest and best regiments. Its record is indeed a brilliant one.

THE FUSILIERS AND THE FIFTEENTH REGIMENT.

On the 11th of May the Fusiliers voted to volunteer for the war. Posters were issued for recruits to fill up the company to the maximum. The "Guards" also commenced filling up for the same purpose and it was hoped that the old Ninth Regiment might be filled up and accepted as the old Ninth. But for some reason unknown, its claims were ignored at "Head Quarters" and a regiment of foreigners recruited in Boston and vicinity, was assigned its number. In the meantime other regiments were being organized, and at last the Fusiliers were ordered into camp at Worcester and assigned to the Fifteenth Regiment. This Company left us on the 28th of June and their departure was made the occasion of quite a demonstration. The company turned out at about ten o'clock A. M. They were escorted by a large company of "old Fusiliers" composed of men from forty to sixty, who had served in its ranks in "bye gone days," being officered for the occasion as follows:

Captain, JONAS A. MARSHALL.
Lieutenant, IVERS PHILLIPS.
Ensign, ALFRED R. ORDWAY.
Orderly Sergeant, ALFRED WHITE.

These "veterans" presented a very creditable appearance, being accompanied by a portion of the "old Fitchburg Brass Band" composed of the following: Jonathan Farnsworth, Cyrus Thurston, Ebenezer Thurston, Jeremiah Kinsman, Charles Derby, J. K. Gibson, the first three of whom paraded with the company at its first appearance forty-five years before. One of these who commonly was obliged to walk with one cane and sometimes with two, was so inspired by the influence of the occasion that he threw away his staff and marched erect and vigorous as of old. Following these was a "Second Edition" of the Fusiliers composed of younger men, who had more recently served in the ranks, and who, from various causes were prevented joining their old comrades for service in the field. These were commanded by Captain E. T. Miles and wore the uniform of the old Fusiliers and escorted the company to camp at Worcester.

After a short march the procession entered the Town Hall at 10½ o'clock A. M., where a large number of their friends and fellow citizens had met to say "good bye." Remarks were made by Hon. Alvah Crocker and others. Captain Marshall of the *ancient* Fusiliers addressd the company who were about to leave for the seat of war, counselling them to do their whole duty in every emergency, and to sustain the honor of the "old Fusiliers" and their native town wherever duty called them. Captain Kimball in behalf of his command responded eloquently. Each member of the company was then presented with a New Testament from the clergymen of the town and the following note was read.

"*To Captain J. W. Kimball and command:*

GENTS: The undersigned feeling a deep interest in you, as a portion of that mighty host now being marshaled into the greatest conflict of our age, (that between liberty and despotism) tender to you all our warmest sympathy, and offer for your highest welfare our earnest prayers; and we ask each of you to accept from us as a token of our friendship for you personally a copy of the New Testament. It is of small pecuniary value, but priceless in its permanent worth. It will occupy but a small place in your knapsack, but may it fill with its principles of love to God and man, the widest, warmest chambers of your hearts, and mould all your activities to its own ideal of Christian manhood. May its divine light shine upon your path; and amidst all the possible scenes before you, in health and in sickness, in rest and in conflict, in life and death, may its peace be your's through the noble Captain of our Salvation, the Lord Jesus Christ.

      (Signed)   ELNATHAN DAVIS,
                WILLIAM P. TILDEN,
                KENDALL BROOKS,
                ALFRED EMERSON,
                HENRY M. LOUD,
                ANDREW J. WEAVER."

The soldiers were then vaccinated gratuitously by Drs. Hitchcock and Jewett.

Prayer was offered by Rev. Mr. Emerson, after which the company was escorted to the Fitchburg Hotel to partake of a dinner provided for them by the citizens, subsequent to which the procession was again formed and marched to the Worcester R. R. Depot followed by an immense crowd of citizens. Here many affecting scenes took place—the tender parting of the soldiers with their friends, (alas! to how many the last on earth)—the affectionate heartfelt God speed of many of the comrades of the soldiers, sad even to tears some of them, that they could not join them—the final starting of the train amid the hearty huzzas of the multitude, made the occasion one long to be remembered.

Before the departure Captain Kimball in a few earnest words consigned to the care of that portion of the company remaining at home the flag presented to his command a short time previous by the ladies of Fitchburg. As the train moved slowly away the Band played sadly and slowly the old familiar air of "Auld Lang Syne." And so left us our first company of Fitchburg men for the war.

Oh, ye who witnessed that scene, and had no son, no brother, no husband or father there, did you then understand the full force of its meaning? Did it then occur to any of us that this noble company of young men, the pride of our hearts and homes, were leaving us for three long years of hardship and suffering, and that ere their return should see thirty-three of their number killed or dead from disease contracted in the service, while two-thirds of the remainder should have been wounded, many maimed for life? Such was the tale, and such is war; cruel, heartless war.

Below is given the list of members of the company.

COMMISSIONED OFFICERS.

Captain, J. W. KIMBALL, Fitchburg.
1st *Lieut.*, CLARK S. SIMONDS, Fitchburg.
2d *Lieut.*, J. MYRON GODDARD, Fitchburg.

NON-COMMISSIONED OFFICERS AND PRIVATES.

SERGEANTS.

Eager C. H., Fitchburg.
Spooner Henry A., Fitchburg.

May James, Fitchburg.
Murkland John, Fitchburg.
Rich Harrison, Fitchburg.

CORPORALS.

Taylor Geo. C., Fitchburg.
Monroe Chas. D., Fitchburg.
Sibley Fred. H., Fitchburg.
Hildreth Francis A., Fitchburg.
Brown Cyrus, Fitchburg.
Fisher Andrew, Winchendon.
Hunkings Harrison M., Fitchburg.
Daniels Geo. T., Fitchburg.

MUSICIANS.

Harwood Geo. A., Fitchburg.
Pierce Daniel R., Fitchburg.

WAGONER.

Scott Abraham, Winchendon.

PRIVATES.

Adams George, Fitchburg.
Bruce Abel Jr., Fitchburg.
Brown Frank A., Fitchburg.
Benjamin Geo. F., Westminster.
Bailey Wm. E., Winchendon.
Boss Geo. L., Fitchburg.
Britton Fred. H., Fitchburg.
Bonney Daniel, Sterling.
Bruce Robert, Winchendon.
Beaudry, Anable, Winchendon.
Bowen Roland E., Millbury.
Cunningham Geo. H., Fitchburg.
Church Alfred B., Woonsocket.
Carpenter Daniel, Fitchburg.
Carpenter George, Cambridgeport.
Clark Benj. F., Fitchburg.
Chase Edwin, Winchendon.
Campbell John, Fitchburg.
Carpenter Henry M., Southbridge.
Eames Walter A., Fitchburg.
Elliott Robert J., Ashburnham.
Eaton Calvin J., Worcester.
Farnum John R., Fitchburg.
Farmer Chas. H., Fitchburg.
Fletcher Philander H., Fitchburg.
Gilchrist Geo. S., Fitchburg.
Gibson Artemas H., Fitchburg.
Gibson Wm., Fitchburg.
Griswold Wm. T., Fitchburg.
Griswold Chas. E., Fitchburg.
Harwood Kilburn, Fitchburg.
Hosmer Granville, Fitchburg.
Hosmer Henry J., Fitchburg.
Hosmer Joel K., Fitchburg.
Houghton Joseph R., Westminster.

Howard N. Porter, Westminster.
Hartwell Rollins E., Winchendon.
Holman Wm. H., Winchendon.
Johnson Marcus R., Bradford.
Joslin Henry L., Fitchburg.
Kendall Edward S., Westminster.
Kendall Chas. W., Winchendon.
Kendall Oscar A., Winchendon.
Lowell Henry C., Winchendon.
Litchfield Albert, Fitchburg.
Lawrence Amos W., Fitchburg.
Loud Francis H., Winchendon.
Marshall Joseph A., Fitchburg.
Morse John E., Fitchburg.
Moody Jos. L., Fitchburg.
Matthews Jos. B., Winchendon.
Marshall Frank S., Fitchburg.
Maynard Winthrop, Winchendon.
Nichols Lyman, Westminster.
Nichols Frederic, Westminster.
Nichols Francis, Westminster.
Osborne Ai D., Fitchburg.
Pope Horace T., Fitchburg.
Pope Chas. F., Winchendon.
Phillips Geo. W., Fitchburg.
Pratt Joel, Fitchburg.
Plaistead Amos C., Fitchburg.
Prichard John H., Fitchburg.
Ring John R., Fitchburg.
Riley Andrew, Winchendon.
Simonds George B., Fitchburg.
Simonds Altan A., Fitchburg.
Sheldon Henry L., Fitchburg.
Scott Frank, Fitchburg.
Scott D. Walter, Winchendon.
Scott Elijah M., Winchendon.
Stewart Frederic C., Winchendon.
Safford Stillman, Winchendon.
Stevens Charles A., Winchendon.
Stone Luman W., Fitchburg.
Taylor Thos. P., Fitchburg.
Taylor Wm. E., Winchendon.
Whittemore Henry F., Fitchburg.
Wetherbee Orlando, Fitchburg.
White Lowell C., Westminster.
Walker John K., Ashburnham.
Wyman Horace H., Winchendon.
Whitcomb Gilman W., Princeton.

JOINED AFTER REG'T LEFT MASS.

Bliss David, New Salem.
Bruce Napoleon B., Winchendon.
Davis Samson, Ashby.

Edgell Stillman W., Fitchburg.
Fisher Seth R., Winchendon.
Flagg Augustus, Royalston.
Gibson Lemuel W., Fitchburg.
Leach Flavel, Royalston.
Marsh John, Fitchburg.
McIntire Herbert D., Fitchburg.
Newton Silas M., Royalston.
Wheeler Chas. A., Fitchburg.
Whitcomb Benjamin, Winchendon.

This Company was at once incorporated into the Fifteenth Regiment. Capt. Kimball was promoted to Major, and Lieut. Simonds to Captain, before leaving the State.

This Regiment was mustered into the United States service July 12th, 1861, under the command of Col. Charles Devens, Jr., and left the State for Washington August 8th following, where it arrived August 11th. August 15th it was ordered to march to Poolesville, Md., distance thirty-five miles, and arrived there August 27th. It became a part of the "Corps of Observation," under command of Gen. Charles P. Stone. The Regiment was occupied with camp and picket duty until October 21st, 1861, when occurred the unfortunate affair at Ball's Bluff. The events of that disastrous day are familiar to all; the morning attack, the obstinate resistance of our troops to superior forces from morning till night; the retreat to the river, the lack of facilities for crossing, the scenes of murder and drowning in the dark waters of the Potomac. Suffice it to say that the Fifteenth Regiment sustained itself nobly in this its first trial under fire, but lost most heavily. Of the six hundred and twenty-five men of the Regiment who crossed the river in the morning, but three hundred and thirteen returned uninjured at night. The loss was twenty-six killed, sixty-six wounded, and two hundred and twenty-four missing, mostly taken prisoners.

The Regiment remained at Poolesville until Feb. 25th, 1862, when it marched for Harper's Ferry, reaching there the 26th. Remained in this vicinity until March 22d, when the Regiment started to join the Army of McClellan, on the Peninsula, arriving at Hampton April 1st. Soon after this Col. Devens was promoted to Brigadier General, and the command of the Regiment was at once assumed by Lieut. Col. Kimball, Col. Ward being absent from the Regiment on account of wounds received at Ball's Bluff. Under Lieut. Col. Kimball's command, the Regiment took an active part in the siege of Yorktown and the various battles fought during the occupation of the Peninsula by McClellan, being actively engaged at the battles of "Fair Oaks," "Savage Station," and "Nelson's Farm;" we give below the

OFFICIAL REPORT OF COL. KIMBALL AT FAIR OAKS.

"HEADQUARTERS FIFTEENTH MASS. VOL'S.
In Camp at Fair Oaks, Va., June 3d, 1862.

CAPT. DANIEL HEBARD, A. A. G. :

I have the honor to report that on Saturday, the 31st ult., I received orders for my regiment to be ready to march at a moment's notice, and in light marching order. At three o'clock I left camp and took my position in brigade line, which was the extreme left of said line. At this time and for an hour previous, very heavy firing was heard on the south side of the Chickahominy creek. The brigade was immediately put in march, and we crossed the stream at the Corduroy bridge, and found the plain upon the south side partially overflowed, and we were obliged to wade through it, the water in some places coming up to the waists of the men; but they rushed through without hesitation, cheering as they went. The roads were very heavy from the recent rains, but the men pressed forward with alacrity, and a portion of the way at 'double quick' time, and I arrived on the field at about five o'clock, bringing in all my men. I immediately formed in line of battle in the rear of the 82d New York volunteers. I had scarcely given the order to rest when a sharp fire of musketry commenced upon Kirby's battery stationed a short distance to my right. I was ordered to go to the support of that battery, thereby relieving the 6th Massachusetts, Col. Russell. I immediately formed in line of battle in the rear of the battery, and remained in that position some time. My men stood up manfully to the work and three several times rushed forward and helped work the guns, by extricating them from the mud into which they settled at each discharge. At this time, after the fire had slackened somewhat, I was ordered to move by the left flank and to come into the rear of the 82d New York volunteers, and then to move forward at 'double quick' passing their line to the front, and to occupy and hold the wood from which the enemy were being driven. My orders were promptly obeyed, the men charging bayonets into the woods with a terrible yell.

I established my line by your command near the edge of the wood, throwing out pickets to the front. The men rested upon their arms until morning without sleep, ready and anxious to renew the conflict at daybreak, if necessary.

I desire to remark that my regiment behaved with great coolness and bravery during the entire action, obeying my orders as promptly as at dress parade. There was no one officer or private that showed any signs of trepidation or fear, but instead, a fixed determination of all that their bayonets should drink deep of rebel blood before they should take the battery, which they attempted to do three several times but were repulsed each time with great loss. As to the behavior of my command during this portion of the engagement I would respectfully refer you to Lieut. Kirby commanding the battery. It gives me great pleasure to speak approvingly of the conduct of Major Philbrick, who had just assumed the duties of that position, showing conclusively that our confidence in him had not been misplaced; also of my entire staff. Surgeons Bates and Haven were indefatigable in their attendance upon the wounded. Chaplain Scandlin labored incessantly bringing the wounded from the field, often exposing himself to imminent danger by so doing. Too much praise cannot be awarded to Adjutant Baldwin, who got up from a sick bed against my express wishes, to render me what service he could. He was scarcely able to sit upon his horse, but he remained with me during the entire battle, conveying my orders with great promptness and precision.

When all did their duty so well, it would be manifestly unjust to particularize any one or more of the line officers for individual notice, and I will therefore say that their behavior, without exception, during this engagement, meets with my entire approbation and approval. I have the honor to remain,

Very respectfully, your obedient servant,

JOHN W. KIMBALL, Lieut. Col. Commanding."

In this connection we give below a copy of a *private* letter from Gen. Gorman to Gov. Andrew, complimentary to the Fifteenth, which will be read with interest and pride. We are not aware that it has ever before been published. It is more valuable because the spontaneous tribute of an officer of large experience, and who knew whereof he affirmed. He commanded the Brigade of which the Fifteenth was a part.

"HEADQUARTERS GORMAN'S BRIGADE,
Fair Oaks, near Richmond, Va., June 13th, 1862.

His Excellency JOHN A. ANDREW,

SIR: Now that the smoke of the battle-field has cleared away, I cannot forbear taking the opportunity to testify to the gallant, soldierly conduct of the Fifteenth Regiment of your troops in our late contest—the bloodiest of the war. It was their fortune to be participants in a *real*, not imaginary bayonet charge made upon the most intrepid and daring of the rebel forces, at a critical moment for our cause. Most nobly and gallantly did they honor themselves and their gallant State, and most proudly may she feel over them. With such troops in the field we are invincible, and the result of this contest with an unholy rebellion cannot be doubtful. I ask, sir, in conclusion, that the history of the Fifteenth Mass. Volunteers may be made part of the history of the State, as associated with one of the most brilliant exploits of the war, which the official reports will soon disclose to your Excellency, to which I refer with pride and satisfaction.

I have the honor to be your Excellency's obedient servant,

W. A. GORMAN, Brig. Gen'l U. S. V. Com'g."

On the 22nd of August the Regiment arrived at "Newport News" and took passage for Alexandria, where it arrived August 28th. Left the next day for Chain Bridge, and from there marched to Centreville in time to cover the retrograde movement of the army from the "Second Bull Run" towards Washington. Nothing of great importance occurred to the Regiment until the 17th of September, 1862, when was fought the memorable battle of Antietam. We quote from Lieut. Colonel Kimball's official account of the fight.

"On the morning of September 17th the great battle of Antietam commenced, and at nine o'clock General Sumner's corps was ordered to the front to follow up the success already achieved by the troops under General Hooker. It has been the subject of much remark that troops never went into battle more cheerfully than did ours that morning, so confident were all that the shattered enemy would be driven ere night across the river. At half past ten o'clock, the Fifteenth in the front line of the Division became engaged, and for twenty minutes sustained a terrific fire from the enemy, at the expiration of which time the disheartening order to fall back was given. We have neither time, space, or heart to record in detail the disasters to the Fifteenth on that day. It was repulsed in common with all other regiments attached to our Division. In the history of our State we claim to be mentioned as having fought a good fight; as an evidence of which we ask only that the list of casualties occurring in the Regiment that day may always be coupled with the report of the commanding officer. The record stands thus: Twenty-four officers and five hundred eighty-two enlisted men went into the fight; five officers were killed, six were wounded (one mortally,) sixty enlisted men left dead on the field, two hundred forty-eight wounded, twenty-four missing—total, three hundred forty-three killed, wounded and missing. The National and State colors, hardly to be recognized as the same once so bright and beautiful, were brought off in safety by hands other than those who had borne them into the fight, together with a battle flag of the enemy.

The enemy held in check by the artillery, did not follow up his success, but evacuated the position during the night, and the terrible battle-field fell into our hands the next morning."

Our Company B lost heavily in this engagement, among them Captain Simonds who was instantly killed while conversing with Colonel Kimball after the battle was nearly over.

The following is an extract from a letter of Major General Sedgwick, who commanded the Division of which the Fifteenth was a part at Antietam, to Gov. Andrew.

"I have already forwarded through the military channels a list of officers and soldiers who were distinguished for gallantry and good conduct, recommending them for promotion, and I would again commend to your Excellency Colonel Lee of the Twentieth, Colonel Hinks of the Nineteenth, Lieut. Colonel Kimball of the Fifteenth, and Lieut. Colonel Palfrey of the Twentieth. Great credit is due these officers for the splendid condition in which these regiments took the field. The Fifteenth and Nineteenth are in my opinion *fully equal to any two in the service.*"

The following is Lieut. Colonel Kimball's official report of the engagement:

"HEADQUARTERS FIFTEENTH REG'T MASS. VOL'S.
Camp near Sharpsburg, Sept. 20th, 1862.

CAPT. DANIEL HEBARD, A. A. G.:

I have the honor to report that on Wednesday, the 17th inst., at seven o'clock A. M., I was ordered to hold my command in readiness to move at a moment's notice. At half past seven o'clock we took up our line of march, with five hundred eighty-two muskets, including First Co. Andrew's Sharp Shooters, Captain J. Saunders, attached to this command, being the third in the Brigade line. We moved in a direct line towards the ground held by the forces under command of General Hooker, fording in the march Antietam creek. On reaching the field a line of battle was formed in which my command occupied the position of third regiment of the first line. We then moved forward in line of battle about a mile over the ground gained by General Hooker, passing fences, fields and obstacles of various description, eventually occupying a piece of woods directly in front of which and well covered by the nature of the ground, fields of grain, haystacks, buildings, and a thick orchard, were the enemy in strong force. At this time we were marching by the right oblique in order to close an interval between my command and that of Colonel Hudson, Eighty-Second New York Volunteers, and as we gained the summit of a slight elevation my left became hotly engaged with the enemy (covered as before mentioned) at a distance of not more than fifteen yards. A section of the enemy's artillery was planted upon a knoll immediately in front and not more than six hundred yards distant from my right wing. This was twice silenced and driven back by the fire of my right concentrated upon it. The engagement lasted between twenty and thirty minutes, my line remaining unbroken, the left wing advancing some ten yards under a most terrific fire of infantry. Meanwhile, the second line of the Division which had been halted some thirty or forty yards in the rear advanced, until a portion of the Fifty-ninth Regiment New York Volunteers, Colonel Sidball had closed upon and commenced firing through my left wing on the enemy. Many of my men were by this manoeuvre killed by our own forces, and my most strenuous exertions were of no avail either in stopping this murderous fire or in causing the second line to advance to the front. At this juncture General Sumner came up and his attention was immediately called by myself to this terrible mistake. He immediately rode to the right of the Fifty-ninth Regiment and ordered the firing to cease and the line to retire, which order was executed with considerable confusion. The enemy soon appeared in heavy columns advancing on my left and rear, pouring in a deadly cross fire on my left wing. I immediately and without orders ordered my command to retire, having first noticed the same movement on the part of the second and third lines. We retired slowly and in good order, bringing off our colors and a battle flag captured from the enemy, re-forming by the order of General Gorman in a piece of woods some five hundred yards to the rear and under cover of our artillery. This position was held until I was ordered to support a battery planted upon the brow of a hill immediately in our rear, the enemy having opened again with artillery. His fire being silenced, the position was held throughout the day. I desire to say that my entire regiment behaved most gallantly during the engagement, evincing great coolness and bravery as my list of casualties will show. Although suffering terribly from the fire of the enemy, it was with great surprise that they received the order to retire, never entertaining for a moment any idea but that of complete success, although purchased at the cost of their lives. The order forbidding the carrying wounded men to the rear was obeyed to the very letter. Of my line officers without exception, I cannot speak in too high praise. They were all at their posts bravely and manfully urging on their men and equally exposed with them; those wounded refusing all assistance, ordering their men to return to the rank and do their duty. I desire to call your particular attention to Major Philbrick and Adjutant Hooper. They were with me during the entire engagement in the thickest of the fight, receiving and executing my orders with great coolness and promptitude.

I have the honor, Captain, to remain your most obedient servant,

JOHN W. KIMBALL, Lieut. Col. Com'g Fifteenth Reg't."

After the battle of Antietam the Regiment was engaged in a campaign in the Shenandoah Valley until about December 1st; was engaged at Fredericksburg, Dec 12th 1862, and went into winter quarters at Falmouth about December 20th. Three hundred ninety-one recruits were received by this Regiment from the State during the year. Nothing of note occurred until the spring campaign under General Hooker. The first movement was made on the first of May, 1863, and from this time the Regiment was engaged in reconnoissances and picket duty on the Rappahannock until the 25th of June, when the forced march commenced which ended at Gettysburg. The march was a most trying one, but how these men stood up under it is best shown by the following order which was read to them June 27th.

"HEADQUARTERS 2D DIVISION, 2D CORPS,
June 26th, 1863.

GENERAL ORDERS, No. 105.

The Fifteenth and Nineteenth Mass. Volunteers for marching to-day in the best and most compact order, and with the least straggling from their ranks, are excused from all picket duty and outside duty for four days.

By command of

BRIG. GEN'L GIBBON.

On the 2d, 3d and 4th of July, 1863, the Regiment was hotly engaged at Gettysburg; that terrible battle which rolled back the rebel tide of invasion, and proved the turning point in the fortunes of the war. It was indeed *our* Waterloo, and to have been engaged in it and survived it, is an honor which any man may well be proud of, and death *there*, was better than many years of grovelling life. The record of the Fifteenth here is very brilliant, and we extract from the Official Report an account of the second day's battle:

"On Friday, July 3d, the rebels opened on our lines with a hundred pieces of artillery, at about one P. M. This terrific fire was continued for about two hours; but, though the air seemed filled with fragments of bursting shells, but comparatively little damage was done. At three P. M., the rebel infantry moved to the assault. Our men sprang promptly to meet them, glad at a prospect of work—relieving them from their painful recumbent position, which a boiling sun rendered the more intolerable. The contest lasted an hour or two, during which both armies showed a determination to hold its ground regardless of results. A slight wavering of the rebel line was detected, and, at the suggestion of Colonel Hall, commanding Third Brigade, the colors of the Fifteenth were ordered to advance, when the remnant of the Regiment rallied promptly around them, and the whole line moved as if by one impulse, marched forward, and carried the position. The Regiment was sent out to picket the field; and at daylight on the 4th, skirmishing commenced and continued until the Regiment was relieved at eight o'clock. The Regiment went into action with eighteen officers and two hundred and twenty-one enlisted men. During the three days it lost three officers (Col. Ward, Capt. Murkland of Fitchburg, and Lieut. Jorgensen,) killed, eight officers wounded, nineteen inlisted men killed, eighty-five wounded, many of them mortally. Saturday, July 4th was spent upon the field."

After this battle, the Regiment moved into Virginia, and was engaged in the neighborhood of the Rappahannock and Manassas, on picket duty, occasional reconnoisances and skirmishes with the enemy, until about the 1st of December, 1863, losing at various times four officers and about thirty enlisted men in killed, wounded and prisoners.

Dec. 5th, the Regiment moved to Strasburg, Va., where it went into winter quarters, and remained until the first of May, 1864.

The Spring campaign of 1864 opened about the first of May. At that time the Fifteenth had present about three hundred officers and men. In the battles of the Wilderness it lost about *one-half* this number in killed and wounded. The simple statement, that in all the marches and battles from the Rapidan to Petersburg in which the Second Corps was engaged, the Fifteenth bore its part, is of itself sufficient history.

On the 22d of June, the Regiment (dwindled down to *five officers and seventy muskets*) confronted the enemy near the Jerusalem plank road before Petersburg. A break, or gap in the line of battle allowed the enemy to throw a large force on the flank and in rear of the Second Division, Second Corps. Hidden from view by the dense undergrowth, the manœuvre was not comprehended until too late.

The first intimation of the position of affairs was a demand from the enemy to surrender. Taken by surprise, and overwhelmed by numbers, the remnant of the Regiment was captured almost entire. Four officers and sixty-five men were marched off prisoners of war; one officer and five men escaped to tell the story. This officer being wounded the same day, the few remaining, increased somewhat by the arrival of convalescents, were placed for a few days in another command, until officers and more men on their way from the hospitals should arrive. On the 12th of July, 1864, the Regiment was ordered to proceed to Worcester, Mass., to be mustered out of service, its term of three years having expired, and left immediately, arriving there July 21st, about one hundred and fifty strong. The Regiment had a splendid reception by the State and city authorities, and the remnant of our Co. B, (only about twenty men) were given a public reception the same evening at Fitchburg.

During the year, but one officer of the Regiment was killed,

Lieut. Simonds, of Fitchburg, who went out as a private in the Company. He was a brave soldier, and a pure man, and much esteemed and beloved by his comrades and all who knew him.

This ends a brief narrative of the Fifteenth's three years service. To give in detail the varied experiences of this gallant Regiment through these weary years, would make a good sized history of itself. It may truthfully be said that no regiment has a prouder record; none will live longer in history.

THE WASHINGTON GUARDS AND THE TWENTY-FIRST REGIMENT.

The "Guards," although ready and anxious to go into the Fifteenth Regiment, with the Fusiliers, for some reason were not permitted so to do. The Company was finally ordered into Camp at Worcester July 19th, 1861, and became a part of the Twenty-First Regiment. Their departure was the occasion for a public demonstration. The "Home Guards," Capt. J. B. Proctor, "Home Fusiliers," Capt. E. T. Miles, and Engine Company No. 2 turned out for escort. A meeting was held at the Town Hall, at which prayer was offered in behalf of the departing soldiers, by Rev. Mr. Trask, and addresses pertinent to the occasion were made by various citizens. A nice dinner was served the soldiers at the American House. During the afternoon the Ashburnham and Templeton Companies arrived, also on their way to Camp at Worcester, when a grand parade of the three Companies took place through our principal streets, finally taking the cars for Worcester late in the afternoon. The occasion was a very enthusiastic one, and they left amid the wildest cheers, and with the blessings of the crowd assembled.

So passed into the line of their country's defenders our second band of heroes. Their subsequent history, until the expiration of their term of service, is contained in the narrative of the Twenty-first Regiment, which we now proceed to give in brief.

COMPANY D, TWENTY-FIRST REGIMENT.

COMMISSIONED OFFICERS.

Captain, THEODORE S. FOSTER, Fitchburg.
1st *Lieut.*, CHARLES BARKER, Fitchburg.
2d *Lieut.*, EBEN T. HAYWARD, Fitchburg.

NON-COMMISSIONED OFFICERS AND PRIVATES.

SERGEANTS.

Beckwith Henry A., Fitchburg.
Goodrich George E., Fitchburg.
Whitney Julius D., Fitchburg.
Cummings Israel, Fitchburg.
Hill George C., Shirley.

CORPORALS.

Skinner Orrin E. Fitchburg.
Goodrich I. B., Fitchburg.
Stewart William M., Fitchburg.
Jaquith Azro B., Fitchburg.
Whitney Charles M., Fitchburg.
Whitney, James D., Grafton.
Brock Andrew M., Fitchburg.
Crosby Charles C., Waltham.

MUSICIANS.

Whitcomb Charles A., Fitchburg.
Lamb Levi L., Fitchburg.

WAGONER.

March Addison, Charlton.

PRIVATES.

Adams Ephraim, Fitchburg.
Abbott Henry S., Fitchburg.
Albee Seth,
Aldrich F. W., Westmoreland, N. H.
Atherton Galen P., Harvard.
Bigelow Orlando, Wolcott, Vt.
Battles Harrison W., Fitchburg.
Boynton, William S., Fitchburg.
Barker Horace R., Fitchburg.
Bailey Alonzo A., Wolcott, Vt.
Bigelow Frank W., Fitchburg.
Bronson, James, Fitchburg.
Carter Rufus H., Fitchburg.
Childs George H., Greenfield.
Davis Charles F., Bangor, Me.
Delany Dennis, Fitchburg.
Delany John, Fitchburg.
Delharty James F., Templeton.
Donahue Edward, Shirley.
Doherty Thomas A., Worcester.
Elmer Orin, Shirley.
Eastman Amos S., Ashby.
Fay Charles E., Fitchburg.
Fiske Dwight G., Greenfield.
Flint Samuel W., Fitchburg.
Grant Charles M., Northfield.
Goodrich Charles E., Fitchburg.
Gleason Amos W., Lunenburg.
Green Charles T., Fitchburg.
Dean Nathaniel C., Fitchburg.
Graves, William R., Lunenburg.
Goodfellow Daniel W., Fitchburg.
Horton Charles L., Southbridge.
Howe, Edward A., Grafton.
Hodgman William, Shirley.
Haskell Henry, Winchendon.
Hardy George H., Harvard.
Hastings Lewis T., Deerfield.
Ingerson William W., Harvard.
Jaquith Asa S., Fitchburg.
Kempton Elias J., Fitchburg.
Lamb Ansel H., Hartford, Conn.
Lynaugh John, New Ireland, Conn.
Matthews George H., Winchendon.
Marsh Alphonso, Fitchburg.
Marsh Timothy S., Fitchburg.
Marshall Joseph F., Fitchburg.
Montjoy Charles F., Fitchburg.
Murry James M., Worcester.
Millett Henry B., Oakham.
Montgomery James, Harvard.
March Harry, Charlton.
May Simeon, Fitchburg.
Nelson Henry O., Wales.
Newell John D., Greenfield.
Osborne P. E., Westmoreland, N. H.
Owen Benjamin, Leominster.
Prentice Henry O., Grafton.
Patch Henry J., Fitchburg.
Parkhurst Emmons M., Fitchburg.
Pratt Lewis G., Shelburne.
Rugg Daniel W., Fitchburg.
Rickett William J., Wales.
Roth Gilbert, Wales.
Stearns Albert C., Worcester.
Smith George S., Lunenburg.
Sands Harrington W., Shirley.
Safford Frank, Burlington, Vt.
Swift John, Fitchburg.
Tolman Calvin E., Fitchburg.
Wheelock Samuel, Fitchburg.
Whitcomb George A., Fitchburg.
Warren Thomas, Fitchburg.
Warren Preston, Fitchburg.
Warren Henry A., Fitchburg.

Weeks Frank W., Northfield.	Wright Walter S., Fitchburg.
Warren John G., Harvard.	Willis George, Stowe.
Ward George, Brookfield.	Waitt Erastus F., Deerfield.
Williams Jonathan, Wales.	Wood Charles, Sunderland.

The Twenty-first Regiment left Worcester for the seat of war on the twenty-third of August, 1861, with full ranks, under Col. Augustus Morse. It was at once ordered to Annapolis, Md., to become a part of an Expedition fitting out by Gen. Burnside. From this time until about the first of January the Regiment was engaged in perfecting itself in discipline and drill, the ordinary duties of the camp, and picketing the Annapolis railroad. The Regiment left with the Expedition to North Carolina, Jan. 6th, 1862, under Lieut. Col. Maggi, Col. Morse remaining (*at his own request*) at Annapolis, in command of that post. And it may be proper to add in this connection, that Colonel Morse never again joined the Regiment, but was honorably discharged the following May. On the 8th of February, 1862, occurred the battle and victory at Roanoke Island, in which the Regiment was for the first time under fire, acquitting itself most nobly, capturing a battle flag from the rebels, and planting its own flag on the battery, the first Union flag inside the works. The loss of the Regiment in this battle was fifty-seven killed and wounded. No higher tribute to the gallantry of the Regiment in this action could be paid than the following letter, which explains itself.

"HEADQUARTERS 21ST REG'T M. V.,
CAMP BURNSIDE, DEP'T N. C.
Roanoke Island, Feb. 10th, 1862.

TO CAPT. THEODORE S. FOSTER,

Dear Captain:—The day before the battle of the 8th inst., the aid-de-camp, Lieut. Frank Reno, told me that he would present a flag to the company of the Second Brigade who would fight most bravely. The day after the battle in which our Regiment comported itself so gallantly, he gave the flag to me, saying, 'Give it to the company which has fought the best in your Regiment.'

But at a meeting of the officers of the Twenty-first Regiment, presided over by me, it was decided that the flag be given to you *alone*, as a small token of the great coolness, bravery and intelligence which you displayed on the 8th instant.

You may inscribe on the flag these words: *The Officers of the Twenty-first Regiment M. V., to the brave Capt. T. S. Foster, of Co. D.*

I am your sincere friend,
A. C. MAGGI, Lieut. Col. Com'g."

The flag alluded to was sent home by Capt. Foster to be deposited in the Public Library. The following note accompanied it:

"CAMP BURNSIDE, ROANOKE ISLAND,
March 4th, 1862.

To THE CHAIRMAN OF THE FITCHBURG LIBRARY COMMITTEE:

Enclosed I send a flag, together with a letter accompanying it, which has this day been presented to me by the officers of the Twenty-first Regiment Mass. Volunteers. As it has been my honest endeavor to faithfully serve my country and its flag, I have tried to win, not glory for myself, but for the town which I have the honor to represent. Therefore I feel it my duty to present the flag to the town of Fitchburg, to be preserved in the Public Library, as a memento of the gallant services of Company D, Twenty-first Regiment, Feb. 8th, 1862.

Very truly yours,
THEODORE S. FOSTER,
Capt. Co. D, 21st Regt. Mass. Vols.

On the 14th of March the Regiment was again engaged at the battle of Newbern, and was highly commended in the official reports for the dash and bravery which it displayed in this action, and was presented by General Burnside with the first gun taken by them from the enemy, (a brass field piece,) "as a monument to the memory of a brave man," referring to the gallant and youthful Adjutant F. A. Stearns, of Amherst, who was killed early in the action.

The total of the Regiment's loss in this action was three officers and fifty-four enlisted men killed and wounded. April 17th the Regiment took passage from Newbern to Elizabeth City, landing the 19th, and after a forced march of twenty miles, took part in the spirited battle of Camden, in which a victory was achieved. Their loss in this engagement was fifteen in killed and wounded. The Regiment then returned to Newbern, remaining in that vicinity performing the ordinary camp and picket duty until July 6th, 1862, when it took passage for Newport News, arriving July 9th, and became a part of the Army of the Potomac. Here it remained until about the 2d of August when it took passage aboard steamers for Aquia Creek, Va., arriving on the 4th, and immediately proceeded to Fredericksburg, where it went into camp. The Regiment took part in the unfortunate campaign of General Pope and participated in his retreat from the Rapidan, suffering, in common with the rest of that army, all the hardships incident to a disastrous retreat. Says another:

"Without shelter from the elements, exhausted by long and distressing marches, suffering frequently for want of food, for three weeks they constantly stood to their arms with undiminished courage."

The battles of "Second Bull Run" and Chantilly soon followed, in both of which this Regiment bore its share. In the latter the Regiment suffered a greater loss than any it had before met with, owing to being drawn into an ambuscade of rebel regiments. Its loss was as follows: Officers killed, wounded and prisoners, eleven; enlisted men, one hundred thirty-three.

Among the killed were the brave Lieut. Colonel Rice, and Lieut. H. A. Beckwith, of this town. At South Mountain the Regiment was again engaged, losing five wounded; and again on the 17th of September, bore their full share in the bloody battle of Antietam. The Regiment was in the left wing of the army.

"The brigade to which they belonged charged across the bridge over the 'Antietam' and held their ground upon the other bank, for more than an hour of the time without ammunition, against an attacking force far superior in numbers."

Their loss was large in proportion to the number (about one

hundred fifty,) taken into the action, and was as follows: One officer killed, two wounded; six men killed, thirty-four wounded.

After this battle, and until about the first of November, the Regiment was encamped in the vicinity of Pleasant valley, Md., when it again crossed the Potomac into Virginia. On the 13th of December, 1862, occurred the great battle of Fredericksburg, and the Twenty-first was again hotly engaged. We extract from Colonel Clark's account of the battle the following:

"The Second Brigade was ordered to the front, and forming in double line of battle, most gallantly and steadily moved across the plain, swept by the destructive fire of the enemy. When about sixty rods from the city, Color-Sergeant Collins of Company A was shot, and fell to the ground. Sergeant Plunkett of Company E instantly seized the colors and carried them forward to the farthest point reached by our troops during the battle, when a shell from the rebels was thrown with fatal accuracy at the colors and brought them to the ground, wet with the life blood of the brave Plunkett, *both of whose arms were carried away.* The glorious flag was then raised by Color-Corporal Olney of Company H, and carried by him during the remainder of the day. Color-Corporal Barr of Company C was shot while carrying the State Colors, and the post of honor and danger was quickly filled by Color-Corporal Wheeler of Company I. The whole number of casualties in this battle is sixty-nine, viz.: eight killed, fifty-six wounded, five missing. After expending their ammunition, the Twenty-first fell back into the line of support and remained until dark, when they returned to their position near the bridge, where they passed the night and next day."

Soon after the battle of Fredericksburg, the regiment moved to Falmouth and went into winter quarters, remaining until Feb. 9th, 1863, on which day the regiment left for Newport News, arriving there on the 11th, and remained there until March 26th, when it started for the West. It reached Paris, Ky., April 1st, 1863, and went into camp; on the 5th was marched to Mount Sterling, Ky., where it remained engaged in camp and picket duty for three months, gaining the highest encomiums from the people of that rebellious neighborhood. From there it went to Camp Nelson, Ky., and remained two months. Sept. 12th it started for Knoxville, Tenn., marching one hundred and eighty-five miles via Morristown, arriving about 1st October. On the 22d of Oct. the Regiment was engaged at "Elk Springs," where the enemy was driven from his position and pursued twenty-six miles. From this time to November 14th, 1863, the Regiment marched and countermarched, exposed to the severe storms of that season, without tents, upon half or quarter rations, all of the time poorly clothed and badly shod. Many men marched and did duty all the time who were *completely barefooted*. The Twenty-first was a part of the besieged force which for several weeks was shut up at Knoxville. It made one of the most brilliant charges of the seige on the 24th of Nov., when, in company with another picked regiment, it attacked the sharp-shooters of the enemy and drove them (twice their own number) entirely out of North Knoxville, and took and held possession of all the fortified ground in that part of the city. During the entire siege, the regiment was constantly on duty. The men were fast wearing out, when on Dec. 5th the siege was raised. The Twenty-first, with others, was ordered to follow the retreating enemy. From that time, the regiment saw weary marches and constant exposure, and was reduced to such an extremity that *two ears of raw corn* per day were issued to each man as his ration. Thus situated, in the woods of East Tennessee, on the 29th of Dec., 1863, the proposal was made to the regiment to re-enlist for the new term of three years, and in *thirty-six hours all but twenty-four of the regiment had re-enlisted*. Surely here was heroism of which we may well feel proud. Could any one "despair of the Republic," when our soldiers showed such courage, such patriotism, such fidelity to the holy cause in which they had engaged? On the 8th of January, the Regiment started for home on a "veteran furlough," and arrived at Worcester during the same month, where it had a public reception by the citizens.

At the expiration of its furlough, the regiment again left Worcester for Annapolis, to join its old corps (the Ninth) which was getting ready for another movement, and on the 23d of April,

1864, moved into Virginia. It took an active part in the battle of the Wilderness, and its official record of that bloody day we give below.

"Early in the morning of May 6th, the Regiment left 'Germania Ford,' and hearing afar off the rattle of musketry, started for the scene of action. There was not that 'spoiling for the fight' which had once been its experience, but there was in the closed ranks and steady march, an indication that every man appreciated what was before him; what was expected of him, and what might be called for as a sacrifice for Union and Liberty. There is nothing more sublime than the sight of a body of veterans who, hearing the terrible rattle of musketry, and knowing that the death struggle is going on, though yet unseen, prepare to obey the command 'Forward.' The 'Wilderness' of many trees and thick under-brush which formed the battle field of the day is well known, and the Regiment was even within a few yards of the contending parties before any of the troops engaged could be seen. Together with the One Hundredth Penn., the Twenty-first was formed in line of battle on the left of the Second corps, and made subject to Gen. Hancock's orders. Thus situated, the Twenty-first was not at first actively engaged. The Brigade of Gen. Stevenson which assisted in the advance, was composed of new Massachusetts regiments, which did nobly, and took the most advanced position during the day. Their heavy losses were sustained in taking that position and holding it. Afterwards, when a terrible charge was made by the rebels, and the raw troops of the Second Corps gave way before the attack, and rushed across the line of the Ninth Corps, throwing them into confusion and final disorder—then, when they seemed flanked, and only till then, did the Brigade of Gen. Stevenson's Division give way. And then were gallant officers slain while attempting to rally their troops and inspire them with their own spirit of courage. Then fell Gen. Wadsworth. Then was General Stevenson surrounded by rebels and almost captured, or slain, and only saved by his coolness and invincible courage. Then Colonel Griswold fell, and many, many whose valor left them only with breath. While all seemed confusion, and really was so, when the rebels stopped in their charge, we know not why, and when no line of our troops remained, the Twenty-First Mass. and One Hundredth Pennsylvania were deployed and advanced, and by their celerity and gallantry, prevented the rebels reaping any fruits from their temporary success. The rebel line was attacked and the advance repulsed by these veterans, and soon the old lost line was restored in a beautiful manner by General Hancock."

The loss of the Regiment in this battle, was three officers and twelve enlisted men. After this battle the Regiment "fought it out on this line" all the way to Petersburg. On the 10th May, the Regiment was again engaged, making a charge, and losing ten men. May 12th, was also engaged at "Spottsylvania" all day, losing twenty-seven in killed and wounded. Several more were killed and wounded in skirmishes of May 31st and June 1st. On the 2d of June, while protecting the rear of the Corps, the enemy suddenly charged upon them. The Regiment fell back slowly, engaging him fiercely, when the whole corps soon became actively engaged, thus bringing on a general battle of the whole army. In this action the Regiment lost seven killed, twenty-six wounded, thirteen missing.

After a few days of rest, interrupted by an occasional skirmish, the Regiment marched for Petersburg, arriving there June 16th. On the 17th the Regiment was engaged in a brilliant charge upon the enemy's works. We give the account of it from the official report of the commanding officer:

"The charge was ordered at about five o'clock P. M. The Twenty-First arose, but sunk almost immediately beneath the withering fire which met them. There was need of all the courage which they possessed. They rose again, and this time with a patriotic hurrah. The colors were swung aloft gloriously by Color-Sergeant Frank Peckham; brave officers went ahead, among whom was Captain Charles Goss, who, in that terrible moment of trial, brought out all the resources of his soul, proved and tempered in more than twenty battles of the war. A noble courage filled him. He seemed to forget the times when he had been wounded "nigh unto death," and when the line was well formed and advancing nobly, he fell never to rise again till a louder trumpet summoned him than that which was sounded for that advance. In that moment of sublime patriotism which few can know, his soul passed from a body before pierced in many places, but now become unworthy to claim any longer such a noble spirit. Captain Sampson again renewed his courage in leading the Regiment up even to the rebel lines, whence we drove the occupants.

The lines were ours. Darkness settled around—our ammunition was entirely exhausted. Repeated requests were sent for supplies, or for relief;

but none came to our aid. Immediately a rebel charge was made. Nothing was there with which to resist it, and the whole Division fell back in confusion, and the lines so gallantly taken were again lost. The next morning came, but the rebel army had withdrawn, and we advanced without opposition, to works we had conquered and lost the day before."

In this last action, the Regiment lost three officers and twenty four enlisted men killed and wounded; missing, four. From this date to July 30th, the Regiment was constantly at the front, in the rifle pits, and exposed to the fire of the enemy, occasionally losing a man. On the 30th occurred the explosion of the mine, and this Regiment was in the Division which rushed into the "crater" only to be repulsed with severe loss.

Of the causes of the failure of that fatal day much has been said and written, but we have no space to discuss it here. It is sufficient for us to know that the difficulty lay *above* the officers and men actively engaged, than whom, none could have done their duty nobler or better. The Twenty-First lost in this most unfortunate affair, five officers and twelve men killed and wounded, and seven missing.

This was the last action in which the Twenty-First was engaged, and on the 18th of August, it was decided that the Regiment was not a "veteran regiment," because, of the three-fourths that had re-enlisted, fifty-six had been rejected for various reasons, and it was ordered that the Regiment be broken up, and the officers and non-enlisted men proceed home to be mustered out. They accordingly left August 19th, for home, arriving at Boston the 22d. They were furloughed until August 30th, 1864, when they assembled at Worcester and were mustered out of the service.

The re-enlisted men of the Twenty-First were organized with the Thirty-sixth, and their subsequent history will be found in that regiment's history, which we propose to give in its proper place. It was a great disappointment to those men, as well as to all those who have ever been connected with the Regiment, that it could not be continued as an organization until the close of the war, but it has a history of which they, and all of us, may well be proud, and indeed it would have been difficult to *add* anything to the glory of its record. Its deeds from Roanoke to Petersburg are prominent in the history of the war, while the memories of its Stearns, its Rice, its Goss, its gallant Sergeant Plunkett, and scores of others, will live in the hearts of their countrymen to the latest posterity.

HISTORY OF THE TWENTY-FIFTH REGIMENT.

Authority to raise the Twenty-Fifth Regiment was granted on the 9th of September, 1861.

Col. Edwin Upton, of this town, and formerly of the old Ninth Reg't. M. V. M., was designated as its Colonel. This was considered a most excellent appointment. Col. Upton had been for years one of the very best officers in the Militia, and a regiment raised, disciplined and drilled under his directions could not fail of being a most efficient body. The Regiment was mainly composed of the very "flower of the youth" of Worcester County. The company from this town of which the old Washington Guards again formed the nucleus, was raised by Charles H. Foss who was commissioned its Captain.

This Company was recruited under circumstances such as had not existed when the previous ones were sent to the field. The terrible disaster and slaughter at Bull Run had, for the time, dampened the ardor of our young men, and they saw more clearly the probability of a long war. But although recruits came more slowly, they were of splendid material—earnest, courageous, patriotic young men, who considered long and well the step they were taking when they resolved to give up all, aye, even life for the sake of their country. The time seemed to have arrived when it was a most serious question with every young man of spirit, whether it was not his duty first and foremost, to enter the service of his country. "Death, or an honorable life,"—To many an honorable life could only seem to be attained by exposing themselves to an honorable death by following the clear path of duty. This spirit was manifest through all classes and conditions. The sturdy husbandman left his farm; the mechanic his shop; the clerk his desk; the student his books, for what they knew must be a hard and probably a perilous service. Yes, it was now stern, relentless war, and because they loved their country more than wife or child, home or friends, they were willing to leave all and to throw their energies into the great struggle for the Nation's existence. Not more credit is due the soldiers of this recruitment than those who gallantly came forward at the first, it may be, but this much is certain, that those who now entered the ranks saw plainly before them (what the earlier volunteers could not see,) three years probably, of hard service, even if the bullet, or disease spared them so long. They shrank not from it—the prize was worthy of the sacrifice. They helped to win it, we enjoy the fruits of their victory—Blessings on them forever. During the recruitment of this Regiment, a war meeting was held of which the following is an account:

WAR MEETING.

A large meeting of the citizens was held at the Town Hall on Monday evening, Sept. 23d, 1864, for the purpose of helping recruiting in our midst; D. H. Merriam, Esq., presiding. Rev. H. M. Loud opened the meeting with a strong appeal to the young men to rally with more zeal in support of the government. He was followed by Hon. G. F. Bailey, in an eloquent address, in which he reminded the citizens of Fitchburg of a meeting held here *ninety* years before, at which it was *Resolved*, " to stand by Boston in her opposition to tyranny," in an hour when our infant country was exposed to perils as great as those which now threatened us. He urged upon the citizens that they should be true to the blood and fame of those revolutionary fathers, and send forth speedily more of our young men, and offer more freely of our means to carry on this war with vigor.

Gen. Wilson, of California, was next introduced, and addressed the meeting at length on the present condition of the country, its dangers and its necessities, and closed with an earnest appeal to the young men to fill up the ranks.

At the close of the meeting, a subscription paper was started for funds to assist the new Worcester County Regiment, and was headed by Dea. S. A. Wheeler and Dr. C. W. Wilder, with one hundred dollars each.

The effects of the meeting were very salutary, and several recruits were added to Capt. Foss' Company.

The Company was speedily filled, and started for Worcester about the first of October, 1861, and was honored in leaving by an escort of the "Old Guards," from whose organization it had in one sense sprung; the officers, and many of the men having been members of the same. After parading the streets, the Company marched to the American House, where a dinner had been provided for them through the liberality of Charles T. Crocker, Esq., who was present and addressed the men briefly in words of encouragement. Addresses were also made by Amasa Norcross, Esq., and Rev. Geo. Trask.

The company finally left amid great enthusiasm and the hearty God-speeds of their friends and fellow citizens.

It was sad indeed to see our young men continually going out from us to certain danger and death, but it was also inspiring to see their enthusiasm and the noble motives which actuated them. Accepting with all its hardships the service they had chosen, they resolutely turned their backs upon home and friends, and steadfastly set their faces toward the field of their future sufferings and privations—toils and victories.

The following is the roll of Capt. Foss' Company:

COMMISSIONED OFFICERS.

Captain, CHARLES H. FOSS, Fitchburg.

1st *Lieut*. LEVI LAWRENCE, Fitchburg.

2d *Lieut*. J. Henry Richardson, Fitchburg.

NON-COMMISSIONED OFFICERS AND PRIVATES.

SERGEANTS.

Farwell Artemas S., Fitchburg.
Upton Charles E., Fitchburg.
Wilder Oliver D., Ashburnham.
Simonds John, Fitchburg.
Hall Charles, Fitchburg.

CORPORALS.

Rockwood S. A., Ashburnham.
Graham James, Fitchburg.
Proctor George B., Fitchburg.
Barnes Dwight W., Orange.
Lowe George, Fitchburg.
Sawtelle, Walter H., Westminster.
Spaulding John A., Ashburnham.
Putnam Thomas F. Fitchburg.

MUSICIANS.

Brick Charles A., Fitchburg.
Peckham Samuel H., Westminster.

PRIVATES.

Alger Edward, Winchendon
Andrews Frederic A., Fitchburg.
Adams Wm. F., Townsend.
Brooks Benjamin V., Fitchburg.
Boss Orlando, Fitchburg.
Battles Wm. E., Fitchburg.
Bassett Frank J., Ashburnham.
Brown Octavus, Ashburnham.
Brown Alonzo F., Westminster.
Brown, John L., Westminster.
Ball George V., Lunenburg.
Clark Luther, Ashburnham.
Clark Harvey, Ashburnham.
Cotting George P., Fitchburg.
Collins Richard, Fitchburg.
Davis Frank A., Ashburnham.
Dadmun Frank S., Fitchburg.
Elleck Edward W. D., Leominster.
Ellenwood Artemas W., Fitchburg.
Esty Francis, Westminster.
Flagg Warren A., Orange.
Fitzgibbon Michael, Ashburnham.
Fenno Frank B., Westminster.
Gilchrist John A., Lunenburg.
Gardner John F., Fitchburg.
Gird Joseph W., Fitchburg.
Gibson Appleton, Fitchburg.
Gates Francis, Gardner.
Gates Hiram, Gardner.
Henshaw Dexter, Fitchburg.
Howe Wm. B., Princeton.
Howe Luther B., Princeton.
Hartwell Chas. W., Westminster.
Hartwell Samuel, Lunenburg.
Haynes Sylvester, Fitchburg.
Hunter Charles H., Fitchburg.
Holden Ethan W., Westminster.
Hagar William S., Fitchburg.
Jenkins George E., Holliston.
Kinsman George W., Fitchburg.
Maynard Charles H., Princeton.
Morton Orrin, Ashburnham.
Morton Francis H., Ashburnham.
McIntire Parley, Ashburnham.
Minott Edwin M., Westminster.
Miller Charles A., Westminster.
Nixon Nahum, Fitchburg.
Nichols George, Westminster.
Phillips George W., Westminster.
Phelps W. W., Fitchburg.
Phelps Phineas, Fitchburg.
Partridge Wm. H., Fitchburg.
Page George H., Westminster.
Rice George W., Fitchburg.
Roach William, Fitchburg.
Smith Charles E., Ashburnham.
Stockwell James A., South Gardner.
Savaria Louis, Fitchburg.
Spaulding J. Calvin, Fitchburg.
Sylvester George F., Fitchburg.
Sylvester Atwood G., Fitchburg.
Southie Elmer G., South Gardner.
Sanderson Calvin D., Lunenburg.
Stowell Joshua T., Ashburnham.
Scollay John, Westminster.

Simonds Putnam, Fitchburg.
Stratton Charles H., Winchendon.
Thompson Michael, Ashburnham.
Upton Thomas, Fitchburg.
Wiley David D., Ashby.
Whittemore Oliver H., Fitchburg.
Winn Noah, Lunenburg.
Wetherbee Silas, Ashby.
Wallis Lincoln, Ashburnham.

Willis William M., Fitchburg.
Ward Carlos P., Rindge, N. H.
Walker James L., Ashburnham.
Walker Edward P., Gardner.
Whiting Alonzo, Lunenburg.
Wait Milan B., Fitchburg.
Whitney Charles H., Fitchburg.
Ware G. F., Fitchburg.
Whitman Edward, Westminster.

PRESENTATION.

A few of the many friends of Colonel Upton, who had received the appointment of Colonel of the "Twenty-Fifth," being desirous of showing their regard for him as a citizen, and their appreciation of his patriotism, united in the presentation to him of a fine horse and set of equipments.

The presentation took place at the American House on Thursday evening, October 10th, and the occasion was one of great interest.

The meeting was organized by the choice of Amasa Norcross, Esq. as Chairman, when a committee was sent to wait upon Col. Upton, the whole party withdrawing to the front of the Hotel, where in charge of a groom the horse fully equipped awaited them. Mr. Norcross then addressed the Colonel as follows:

"Col. Upton: In behalf of several of your friends and neighbors, I have the pleasure of presenting to you this horse with equipments fitting him for military service. It is not in the gift itself they would have you find the measure of its value, but as a memorial of friendship, an expression of esteem and confidence, they present this token. From your own resources this necessity could easily have been supplied, but the sentiments of friendship and regard, of which this gift is but the symbol, no money can measure or purchase. This expression comes from those who have for many years observed your course in private as well as public life, and now on the eve of your departure to join the forces now marshalled in defense of all on earth we most highly prize, they would give you assurance that you have not failed that good name which is rather to be chosen than great riches, and that loving favor which is better than silver or gold. Accept then, this expression of their regard, with the full assurance that wherever in the defense of your country, you may be found, your personal welfare, and the success of the great cause of government and humanity shall be alike near and dear to their hearts.

The donors tender their earnest hopes and strongest wishes for your personal safety, and, when the safety of the country may permit, for your return to your native town to enjoy once more among your friends the blessings of peace."

To this Colonel Upton replied as follows:

"Mr. President, gentlemen, fellow townsmen, friends and neighbors: For this beautiful horse, and these splendid equipments, accept my thanks, and allow me to assure you that my earnest endeavor shall be to use them to the best advantage while I shall be spared to assist in putting down the most wicked rebellion that ever cursed a people on the face of the earth; and in conclusion, I say again accept my thanks."

At the conclusion of his remarks the Colonel invited his friends to partake of a bountiful collation after which several hours were spent in social intercourse. The intellectual entertainment was opened by Hon. Moses Wood, who, in a spirited speech, congratulated the Colonel that he had been placed in a position where he could be of so much service to his country. He was followed by Hon. J. W. Mansur in an earnest and eloquent speech upon the times, who closed with the following sentiment:

"The Worcester County Regiment of the Revolution, and the Worcester County Regiment of to-day, and their commanders Bigelow and Upton; may the laurels won by the former be brightened by the courage and patriotism of the latter."

John J. Piper, Esq., followed in defence of the militia system of Massachusetts which enabled her to respond so promptly and efficiently, to the sudden emergencies of the country.

Remarks were also made by Messrs. Crocker, Stone, Sabin, Ruggles, Blood, and others, and at a late hour the company separated with many fond wishes for the welfare and safe return of their honored host.

Colonel Upton was subsequently presented by his brother officers at the Custom House, with a complete set of regimentals as an expression of their regard during his short term of service with them.

The Twenty-Fifth left the State for the seat of war, Oct. 31st, 1861, and proceeded at once to Annapolis to join Gen. Barnside's expedition. Here the time was occupied until January 7th, 1862, in acquiring proficiency in the duties of soldiers. And it may be added that this Regiment during that time became, and was complimented by the General Officers as one of the best of the large number gathered at that post. On the date last mentioned the Regiment took passage for North Carolina, arriving at Hatteras Inlet on the 14th of January, 1862. Here for three weeks they underwent great hardships in common with the rest of the expedition, the gales preventing a passage through the Inlet into the Sound until the first week in February. During this time, the "Zouave" aboard of which were two companies of this Regiment, foundered, but all were providentially saved. On the 5th the fleet got under way for Roanoke Island, arriving the 7th. On the 8th occurred their first battle ("Roanoke Island.") In this engagement the Twenty-Fifth "had the advance," being at first thrown forward as skirmishers, and then forming in line of battle and pressing forward to within two hundred yards of the rebel works. They were actively engaged for three hours, when, their ammunition being exhausted, they were ordered to the rear. A lodgment being effected by our troops at another point of the works the rebels left this fort, and the Twenty-Fifth, in company with several other regiments, advanced and occupied the works.

The loss in this battle was six killed; forty-two wounded.

We subjoin Colonel Upton's Official Report of the battle:

"HEADQUARTERS TWENTY-FIFTH REG'T MASS. VOLS.
Roanoke Island, February 16th, 1862.

CAPT. SOUTHARD HOFFMAN, A. A. G.

SIR: At about daybreak on the morning of Saturday, February 8th, by order of Brigadier General Foster, my regiment left the bivouac it had occupied the night previous at Hannon's house, and advanced accompanied by General Foster, in its position on the right of his brigade. Arriving at the ford about one-half mile from Hannon's house, the advance was fired upon by the enemy's pickets. I was immediately ordered by General Foster to throw forward skirmishers. I ordered Company A, Captain Pickett, to deploy, supported by Company E, Captain Thomas O'Neil. The enemy's fire was returned, and his pickets retired rapidly to, and down the main road, followed by the skirmishers. Advancing to about a mile from the ford, they reported having discovered the enemy in position, apparently about two thousand strong. Gen. Foster at once ordered me to form the Regiment in line of battle across the road, the right resting on a clearing commanded by the guns of the enemy, the left extending into the woods and thicket. Fire was opened by both parties, our artillery shortly after getting into position supported by the right wing of my Regiment. I was ordered to press steadily forward, bringing our lines within about two hundred yards of the enemy's battery. Fire was kept up by us without intermission, for about three hours, until about half past ten A. M., when our ammunition being exhausted, I was ordered to form in column by company, in rear of our right, which was done in good order. The men rested on their arms waiting for a fresh supply of ammunition, until the enemy having left his works, I was ordered to advance in company with the remainder of General Foster's brigade. Arriving at the upper end of the Island, I was ordered by General Foster to quarter in the camp then in possession of the Twenty-Third and Twenty-Fourth Regiments Mass. Volunteers.

Appended is a list of killed and wounded, amounting to six killed, and forty-two wounded. I would express my great satisfaction with the conduct of the Regiment, both officers and men. It was, throughout the engagement, of the bravest kind, standing as they did for hours, in the water to their knees, exposed to an incessant fire of musketry, grape and shell, with no disposition on the part of any man to waver. The skirmishing of Company A, Captain Pickett, was performed in a manner that would have done credit to regulars. I can but express my particular satisfaction with the manner in which Lieut. Colonel Sprague, Major McCafferty, and Adjutant Harkness performed the duties devolving upon them, and the support rendered me by them, throughout the engagement.

  (Signed)   EDWIN UPTON,
           Col. Twenty-Fifth Reg't Mass. Vols."

The Regiment remained on the Island until March 7th, 1862. On that day it embarked for Newbern, arriving at Slocum's Creek on the 12th, and on the 13th marching to the city. The capture of Newbern occurred on the 14th, and we give from the pen of Colonel Upton the following modest and straight forward account of the part his Regiment had in the same.

LETTER FROM COL. UPTON TO THE "SENTINEL."

HEADQUARTERS TWENTY-FIFTH REG'T MASS. VOLS.
Newbern, N. C., March 8th, 1862.

FRIEND GARFIELD:— Ere this you are aware that the Burnside expedition, which many prophesied would be a failure, has made another strike, and one too, that has been felt by the enemies of our country. After leaving Roanoke Island, we arrived in the Neuse River, about twelve or fifteen miles from this place, on Wednesday afternoon of last week. On Thursday morning our gunboats commenced to throw shells along the bank of the river, and the transports to land their troops at the entrance of a creek which runs into the Neuse River. This entrance the enemy, in anticipation of our landing at that place, had driven spiles into, but our tug-boats soon opened a way for landing by pulling them out, though it caused us a little delay. Early in the afternoon our forces, some ten or twelve thousand men, were landed, and we took up our line of march towards this place. Finding no opposing force we passed along some three miles, when we found some deserted barracks that had been occupied, as the natives told us, by cavalry who left about eleven A. M., in great haste. We passed some two or three miles further on and reached the main road, and soon came to a clearing and discovered a breastwork thrown up, and a battery commanding the road. This breastwork was nearly a mile in length, and well constructed, with a deep ditch in front. But the enemy had run and left it. We passed some five miles further on through mud beneath, and rain above, Generals Foster and Parke's brigades taking the country road, and Gen. Reno's the railroad. It was now about seven P. M., and we turned into the woods to the right and bivouacked for the night. We built camp fires, sent out our pickets, partook of a lunch from our haversacks and, after making a reconnoisance down to the river, prepared to spend the night on the ground already very wet, and rain still falling in torrents. Some of our men lying down and some standing up, we generally, passed a sleepless night. At a little past four o'clock in the morning I heard the rumbling of a railroad train, for some distance approaching, and come to a halt. I then supposed it had brought reinforcements to the enemy, and afterwards learned from a prisoner we took, that such was the fact, and was also told by him that trains came later from Goldsboro with troops. We had our lunch early, and were ready to move at seven o'clock. We passed along nearly a mile, and discovered an earthwork thrown up, with the enemy in position, and batteries commanding the road. We were accompanied by the Twenty-fourth Mass. Regiment, Col. Stephenson, and were ordered by Gen. Foster to form a line of battle on the right of the road. We flanked off to the right, and had hardly cleared the road before they opened their batteries, throwing their shot and shell in a very careless manner. We continued on, entered a thick woods and advanced to the right and front toward the edge of the woods; halted and sent out scouts to ascertain their exact position. We found a long line of breastworks, which proved on examination afterwards, some two miles in length, terminating in a fort at the river on our right, with a battery of thirteen heavy guns—both for water and land service (twenty-four and thirty-two pounders,) and on account of its extending to the water, it was impossible to outflank them. Their shot and shell flew all around us, as did also the shell from our own gunboats, their men being hidden from view behind their earth works and fortifications. We were then ordered to flank to the left and support the Twenty-Seventh Mass. Regiment, Colonel Lee, which was located upon the left of our field howitzers. We found our howitzers unsupported, and were ordered to remain and support them, which we did, the battle still raging in all its fury. After holding that position some little time, I was ordered to deploy my Regiment into line of battle and prepare for a charge, as the enemy's batteries were replying less frequently than they had done. Now came the order to charge! and the Twenty-Fifth sent up a hideous yell and sprang forward in double quick time, leaped over the breastwork and drove the enemy out, our State color being the first on the work. I think there was one United States color on the right before ours. We found five horses attached to one field piece when we entered, some being shot and lying in the mud, and some headed one way and some another, the piece having its pole broken. The horses were probably just being hitched for the purpose of retreating, but they were obliged to leave all. I could think of nothing else but the lines written after the battle of Plattsburg, which run something like this:

> "Provost Scott so he left all behind,
> Powder, ball, cannon, teapot and kettle—
> Some say he catch a cold and perish in the mud,
> Cause he eat so much raw and cold vittle."

We immediately formed our Regiment and were ordered to proceed on the road, taking the position for street firing. The battle was still going on on the left with the other brigades. We took a direction into the left of the road, and were ordered by General Foster to move cautiously, as there was danger of coming in contact in the woods, with our own men, some of them having overcoats resembling those worn by secesh. We were told that General Parke's brigade was on our left and front, and General Reno was expected round the enemy's right flank and approaching our front. After getting into position we sent out the two flank companies as skirmishers into the woods, to see what was there, as the balls were flying all around us. They advanced some little distance and discovered that a portion of the enemy were there, and opened fire upon them, as did also the regiment. They soon surrendered, were taken prisoners, and placed in charge of Company H, Captain Moulton, who was detailed to guard them. They numbered about one hundred and fifty men. Their Colonel, who delivered his pistol to me, showed a bullet hole through his cap, which just cleared his head, and said he would rather it had gone through his head than to have surrendered. He was in the fight at Big Bethel, and is a tough customer. We immediately took up our line of march down the railroad towards Newbern. About two miles on the way a large clearing was made, and another breastwork. We were now in full view of the city which seemed all a-blaze; the resin and turpentine works, with the railroad bridge over the Trent river, nearly two thousand feet long, being all on fire. Cheer after cheer went up from the Twenty-Fifth as we approached the city. Our gunboats had already arrived, as well as some of the transports, and we were taken from the abutment of the bridge by them and were the first regiment in Newbern.

We are now favored with very good accommodations, being quartered in good houses that have been vacated by their owners; and, although the keys were not left for our benefit, we found a way to open them, and are now more comfortably situated than at any time since leaving Annapolis. They tell a story about a Colonel Jordan who lives here, whom we took with the prisoners at Roanoke Island. They say he told them that unless they had a strong force and were ready to fight like h–ll, they had better pack up and leave. From the best information I can obtain, the rebels had some ten thousand men here. I had no means of knowing what their loss was, as they had a train of cars standing on the track with four engines and took the most of their dead and wounded away.

Many of the people have left the town, and there are plenty of houses and stores empty, and *rents low*.

We were extremely fortunate in our loss in this battle; indeed, it seems almost a miracle that we have escaped with so small a loss, there having been but four killed, and sixteen wounded.

Enclosed you will please find a list of our killed and wounded, also, General Burnside's and General Foster's official orders.

     EDWIN UPTON. Col. Twenty-Fifth Reg't M. V."

The Regiment remained Newbern until May 9th, and then left for picket duty in the vicinity. During the hot summer months but little was done in this Department. During the month of November the Regiment was a part of an expedition to Washington, N. C. occupying about two weeks, but it was without important results. On the 11th December the Regiment started with the army on the march to Kinston, Whitehall and Goldsboro, and was engaged in the actions of each of those places, but suffered only a few casualties, returning December 21st, 1862. From this time until about the first of December, 1863, the Regiment remained principally at Newbern and vicinity, enjoying what the *boys* term "a soft thing," varied only by an occasional reconnoisance and now and then, a small skirmish, but at the end of this time they were ordered to Newport News, Va., and from that day forward *their's* was no "holiday" experience.

Colonel Upton had been obliged on account of his health to tender his resignation on the 28th of October, 1862, much to the regret of his command, and all who had the welfare of the Regiment at heart. On his retiring he was presented by the *enlisted men* of the regiment, with a beautiful sword, belt and sash costing one thousand dollars. He was succeeded by Col. Josiah Pickett, a brave and efficient officer.

The Regiment remained at Newport News until the 14th of February, 1864, when (four hundred thirty-two of the men having re-enlisted,) it was allowed to proceed to Massachusetts on a "veteran furlough." They reached Boston on the 19th, and were honored with a most cordial reception by the State and City authorities, and also, at Worcester where the regiment was enrolled, they had a most hearty and enthusiastic welcome.

On the 21st of March, 1864, the Regiment again left Boston for the field, arriving at Portsmouth, Va., on the 24th. On the 22d of April the Regiment was ordered to embark for Plymouth, N. C. then besieged by the rebels, but upon arriving in Albemarle Sound found our forces had surrendered, and at once was ordered back to Portsmouth. On the 25th of April the Regiment was assigned to the Eighteenth Corps, Heckman's Division, and immediately sent to Yorktown, remaining there until May 4th, when it sailed for "Bermuda Hundreds," arriving on the 5th. On the 6th of May it was engaged at "Port Walthal Station," where our forces were repulsed, the Regiment losing three killed; fourteen wounded. On the next day the attack was renewed, and the railroad taken and destroyed for some distance. On the 9th the Regiment was again engaged on the Richmond Turnpike. It was on this occasion that the Twenty-Third, Twenty-Fifth and Twenty-Seventh Massachusetts Regiments were immediately opposed to the Twenty-Third, Twenty-Fifth and Twenty-Seventh South Carolina Regiments, and we give in the words of an officer of the Massachusetts Twenty-Seventh, an account of the fight.

"The three last named regiments by a singular coincidence corresponded to the Massachusetts regiments opposing them, Massachusetts versus South Carolina; "mudsills versus "chivalry." The enemy came rushing forward four lines deep with their own peculiar yell. They presented a front and charged with an impetuosity worthy of a better cause until within fifteen or twenty yards of our line, when their column began to waver, our fire being too hot for them. A few arrived within ten yards of our line, but very few ever got back to tell the tale. At a distance of within fifty yards our two regiments, (the Twenty-Fifth and Twenty-Seventh,) forming the front line, opened a deadly fire on them at "right and left oblique," and literally piled up the dead and wounded. A portion of the Twenty-Seventh Mass., and Ninth New Jersey Regiments now made a counter charge, and the audacious foe was soon driven behind his works.

The loss of the Twenty-Fifth in this action was one officer and eleven men killed; two officers and forty-seven men wounded. The officer killed on this occasion was First Lieutenant Charles E. Upton of this town. His patriotism, his courage and his social qualities had endeared him to all of his comrades, while his tender youth rendered more attractive the conduct of his life, and increased the sorrow and sympathy at his death.

On the 11th the Regiment was moved towards Richmond, and on the early morning of the 16th, was attacked by the rebels, who, under cover of a dense fog, had massed their forces and gained the rear of our troops, almost before they were aware of the movement. Says the Report: "The Twenty-Fifth fought splendidly, holding their ground with the utmost tenacity, inflicting on the charging columns of the enemy the most terrible slaughter until surrounded, and with ammunition exhausted, they were ordered to face by the rear rank and charge the rebel line in the rear, thereby throwing the enemy into such confusion as to enable the Regiment to extricate itself from one of the most perilous positions troops were ever placed in; and completely checking the advance of the enemy."

The casualties in the Regiment in this engagement, were eleven killed; one officer and fifty-two men wounded. On the 3d of June occurred the battle of "Coal Harbor." Here it was the fortune of the Regiment to undergo an ordeal which tried its heroism more than any previous experience had ever done. We again extract from the official record.

"On the morning of the 3d of June we were ordered to assault the enemy's works. The movement was made in columns by divisions, the Regiment charging gallantly some distance through a most galling fire, until within a few yards of the entrenchments, where they were met by a storm of bullets, shot and shell that no human power could withstand. Checked in their attempt to break the rebel line, and with two-thirds of their number killed, or disabled, the Regiment still determinedly held the position gained, protecting themselves as best they could by the nature of the ground, until dark, when with their *hands and tin cups*, rifle pits were constructed, thus rendering the position tenable. In this assault the Regiment displayed the most daring heroism and bravery."

Here fell the gallant Captain O'Neill, asking as he died, to have "his face turned towards the enemy." Here fell the brave and accomplished Adjutant McConville, and Lieutenants Matthews, Pelton, and Graham; the last from this town, a brave, impetuous, generous hearted young soldier, who was worthy of the promotion he had so recently received.

The whole loss of the Regiment was four officers and twenty-three men killed; eleven officers and one hundred twenty-eight men wounded, two officers, and forty-seven men missing. On the 13th of June the Regiment was moved to "Point of Rocks," on the Appomattox river, and on the 15th made another assault on the works carrying the position, and capturing two "Napoleon" guns with caissons complete, with a loss of one killed, and eighteen wounded. On the 18th another charge was made without success, with a loss of six killed, and thirteen wounded. Nothing of note occurred until September 4th, when the Regiment was again ordered to North Carolina, reaching Newbern on the 10th.

On the 5th of October, 1864, that portion of the Regiment whose term of service had expired, was ordered to Worcester, Mass., and on the 20th, mustered out of the service of the United States. The balance of the Regiment was consolidated into a battalion of four companies, remaining during the winter and spring in North Carolina, being a part of General Carter's Provisional Division, and marching into the interior during the month of March, making a junction with General Sherman's army at Goldsboro, March 23d, and thence proceeding with it to Raleigh and Charlotte, at which place it remained until July 13th, 1865, when it was ordered to proceed to Massachusetts to be mustered out. The Regiment took part in but one engagement during the year, at Wise's Forks, having one officer and four men wounded.

Thus closes the record of the gallant "Twenty-Fifth." Few regiments have a more brilliant one.

HISTORY OF THE THIRTY-SIXTH REGIMENT.

In July, 1862, under the call of the President for three hundred thousand men, authority was given for the raising of the Thirty-Sixth Regiment. Our quota was found to be ninety-seven, and it was at once decided to send out another company from Fitchburg, and Captain Barker of the "Old Guards," was designated as the proper man to raise the company. The enthusiasm of our people was by no means diminished by the results of the summer campaign. The defeats on the "Peninsula," the reverses of the Second Bull Run and Chantilly, and the decimated ranks of our Fifteenth and Twenty-First Regiments, while they saddened their hearts, also filled them with a determination never to abandon the struggle until the object for which the "appeal to arms" was made, (the preservation of the Union of these United States,) was secured. Our young men came forward nobly, and the company was soon filled up. The following is an account of a public meeting held by our citizens immediately after the President's call was issued, taken from the Fitchburg *Reveille* of July 17th, 1862.

"CITIZENS' MEETING, SATURDAY, JULY 12, 1862.

At the hour appointed on Saturday evening, the Town Hall was crowded with patriotic citizens, who assembled to take some action about raising the ninety-seven men required at this time from Fitchburg, as her portion of the three hundred thousand troops called for by the President.

The meeting was called to order by D. H. Merriam, Esq. Alvah Crocker, Esq. was chosen chairman, and T. K. Ware, secretary. Eloquent remarks were made by Mr. Crocker, Hon. Alfred Hitchcock, T. K. Ware, D. H. Merriam, Esq., Hon. J. W. Mansur, H. L. Read, Amasa Norcross, Esq., Hon. Nathaniel Wood and others.

The following resolutions were presented by T. K. Ware, Esq., and were unanimously adopted:

Resolved, That, as citizens of the town of Fitchburg, we are desirous of giving an earnest and practical response to the appeal of His Excellency, the Governor of Massachusetts, to the several towns of this Commonwealth, and of taking effective measures to do our share in the support of the Administration of the United States in its renewed efforts for the suppression of the rebellion.

Resolved, That, in order to the more rapid enlistment of the quota of recruits allotted to this town, we request our selectmen to call a Town Meeting on as early a day as possible, to take measures for offering a bounty of seventy-five dollars a man to all recruits who shall enlist themselves for the war, from this town.

It being desirable that recruiting should commence at once, the selectmen were authorized to pay each and every recruit, seventy-five dollars as soon as he is enlisted and accepted. The following gentlemen signed a bond agreeing to hold themselves responsible to the selectmen for the money paid out: Hon. Moses Wood, Hon. Alvah Crocker, Hon. Ebenezer Torrey, Hale W. Page, Hon. Alfred Hitchcock, L. H. Bradford, Otis T. Ruggles, Dr. Jonas Marshall, C. J. Billings, George E. Towne, Dea. S. A. Wheeler, D. H. Merriam, T. K. Ware, Charles T. Crocker, Amasa Norcross, Dr. T. R. Boutelle, Dr. Thomas Palmer, John P. Sabin, H. F. Coggshall, Lyman Patch, J. H. Fairbanks, James P. Putnam, Charles W. Wilder, H. A. Willis, Gardner Farrar.

The chairman then announced that they were ready to receive recruits as soon as the papers for enlistment should be prepared. Dr. F. A. Makepeace was the first man who came forward to enlist, and was followed by W. H. Signor and George E. Keyes.

The meeting was conducted, and the business transacted in the same spirited and patriotic manner that has characterized the action of our citizens whenever they have been called upon to furnish men and means to put down this rebellion. A committee of one from each district, and six from the centre district, was chosen to canvass for recruits."

In accordance with the request contained in the Resolutions of the Citizens' Meeting, a Town Meeting was called for July 19th, and we give below the preamble and resolutions adopted providing for the payment of one hundred dollars bounty to each recruit.

This was the commencement with us of the system of paying bounties, which was carried to such a pernicious extent before the war closed. Other communities were doing it, and we were obliged to, or our men would go elsewhere to enlist. And our citizens were only too glad to tax themselves with the burden, feeling that it was due the patriotic young men who were going forth to peril their lives for their country, that their pecuniary compensation should be liberal.

PREAMBLE AND RESOLUTIONS ADOPTED IN TOWN MEETING, JULY 19, 1862.

Whereas, the President of the United States has recently called for three hundred thousand additional volunteer troops, for the suppression of the Southern Rebellion, and, in compliance with that call, the Governor of this Commonwealth has by Proclamation, called upon patriotic and law abiding citizens of every city and town in the State, again to show their hatred of treason, and their loyalty to the Constitution and Union, by furnishing men and money for the Nation's defense.

Therefore, *Voted*—unanimously, that we, the loyal voters of Fitchburg, in town meeting assembled, this 19th of July, 1862, hereby authorize, and instruct our Selectmen to appropriate and pay one hundred dollars, as a bounty, to each, and every acceptable recruit, when he shall have been mustered into the United States service and shall have joined the Volunteer Company now forming in this town, or either of the three companies from this town, now at the seat of war; not to exceed in all, the sum of ten thousand and one hundred dollars."

The departure of the Company for camp, which took place August 1st, was made the occasion for another demonstration.

The Fitchburg Fusiliers turned out to escort the new company and accompanied them to the camp at Worcester.

The men departed as four other companies had before left us, amid the cheers, and followed by the good wishes of their friends and fellow citizens. As they passed from among us we fondly hoped that it might be the last draft upon us; that our troubles might end without exposing the lives of yet more of our able bodied youth. But it was not thus to be. The following is a copy of the Original Roll of this Company:

ROLL OF CO. A, THIRTY-SIXTH REG'T MASS. VOLS.

Captain—THADDEUS L. BARKER.

1st Lieut.—GEORGE L. CHIPMAN.

2d Lieut.—JOSEPH A. MARSHALL.

ENLISTED MEN.

Alexander J. M., Blackstone.
Ames T. J., Leominster.
Arnold Geo. T., Leominster.
Barber Chas. H., Fitchburg.
Brown John, Fitchburg.
Bixby A. B., Fitchburg.
Bacon John, Blackstone.
Bachelder J. H., Blackstone.
Burlingame W. H., Blackstone.
Bradley O. L., Blackstone.
Brooks L. W., Leominster.
Burrage Henry S., Fitchburg.
Beal Foster E. L., Lunenburg.
Bruce L. O., Lunenburg.
Battles F. C., Fitchburg.
Cook T. G., Fitchburg.
Coyle Andrew, Fitchburg.
Chamberlain L., Holden.
Carter A. H., Leominster.
Carter Solon H., Leominster.
Chase Joseph W., Fitchburg.
Derby Chas H., Leominster.
Damon George R., Leominster.
Emory E. F., Fitchburg.
Foster W. A., Fitchburg.
Frederic E. H., Fitchburg.
Frederic G. H., Fitchburg.
French John A., Fitchburg.
Farrar Chas. E, Holden.
Fuller M., Fitchburg.
Fernald Wm., Blackstone.
Greenman J. H., Blackstone.
Gibson G. P., Leominster.
Goodrich Leonard, Leominster.
Gallop L. R., Leominster.
Gibson A. C., Fitchburg.
Gillis James, Fitchburg.
Hancock Jos., Fitchburg.
Howe F., Leominster.
Hurd C. H., Fitchburg.
Humes Jos., Fitchburg.
Hartwell A. J., Fitchburg.
Hamilton J. R., Fitchburg.
Johnson W. C., Leominster.
Keyes Geo. E., Fitchburg.
Knight Geo. E, Fitchburg.
Larkin M., Fitchburg.
Lamb L. L., Fitchburg.
Lamb C. F., Fitchburg.
Long M., Fitchburg.
Mahan Thomas, Fitchburg.
Morgan L. W., Leominster.
McIntire G. M., Fitchburg.
Mack Geo. W., Fitchburg.
May Thomas, Fitchburg.
Mills H. A., Fitchburg.
Makepeace F. A., Fitchburg.
Murphy P. W., Fitchburg.
Meads L. A., Leominster.
O'Brien Wm., Fitchburg.
Oakes Thos., Fitchburg.
Osborn J. W., Fitchburg.
Osborn A. B., Leominster.
Osborn Samuel, Leominster.
Patch Ebenezer, Leominster.
Pollard Augustus, Fitchburg.
Pitts L. Jr., Fitchburg.
Petts A., Gardner.
Porter L. D., Leominster.
Page C. D., Leominster.
Phelps Charles, Fitchburg.
Perkins F. H., Fitchburg.
Prew A. G., Fitchburg.
Robinson G. H., Leominster.
Siner W. H., Fitchburg.
Smith O. F., Fitchburg.
Smith G. M., Fitchburg.
Stockwell O. L, Fitchburg.
Sullivan E., Leominster.
Sullivan John, Fitchburg.
Stevens Robert, Fitchburg.
Sheridan B., Fitchburg.
Stearns Geo. A., Blackstone.
Smith Charles, Leominster.
Sinclair Geo. A., Leominster.
Smith H. R., Leominster.

Stearns Chas. W., Leominster.
Tucker A. S., Holden.
Thornton J. J., Fitchburg.
Thompson H. A., Fitchburg.
Taylor Henry, Fitchburg.
Webb R. F., Fitchburg.
Wetherbee A. L., Fitchburg.
Whitney C. W., Fitchburg.
Worcester John, Fitchburg.
Winch C., Fitchburg.
Wood F. A., Fitchburg.
Wood A. W., Fitchburg.
Whittemore Charles F., Fitchburg.

This Regiment was organized in August, 1862, and Lieut. Col. John W. Kimball of the Fifteenth Regiment, designated as its Colonel, but as he could not get discharged from the Fifteenth, Major Bowman of the Thirty-Fourth, was subsequently appointed.

The Regiment left the State on the 2d of September, 1862, and arrived at Washington on the 7th, and was immediately ordered to join General Burnside's army at Sharpsburg, Maryland, where it arrived September 20th, just too late to be engaged in the battle of Antietam. It remained in this vicinity until Oct. 11th, when it marched to Frederick, thence on the 15th, to Pleasant Valley; thence to Lovettsville, Va., where it arrived October 26th, and remained till the 29th, when it marched with the remainder of the army to Falmouth, arriving Nov. 19th, stopping one week on the route. On the 12th of December, 1862, the Regiment saw its first battle; the battle of Fredericksburg, but was not actively engaged, being held as reserve, and had only two men wounded. It remained at Falmouth until February 10th, 1863, when it left for Newport News to join the Ninth Corps. At this place six weeks were passed in drill and the ordinary duties of the camp, when the Regiment left for the West with the remainder of the Corps. The Regiment arrived at Lexington, Ky., March 29th, where it encamped a week, during which time it was sent to Cincinnati to guard the polls at the election of Mayor. On the 8th and 9th of April the Regiment marched some thirty miles, and reached "Camp Dick Robinson," where it remained three weeks; thence to Middlebury, remaining until May 23d; thence to Columbia, arriving the 26th, where it remained a few days engaged in reconnoisances, and capturing a large number of guerrillas. On the 4th of June, 1863, the Regiment received marching orders and soon learned that their destination was Vicksburg, Miss. The journey was made by rail and steamboat, and they arrived in the "Yazoo" on the 17th, and took up a position near Milldale, some ten miles in the rear of Vicksburg, the duty of the Ninth Corps being to protect Grant's Army from an attack in the rear by Johnston. Vicksburg surrendered on the ever memorable 4th of July, 1863, and on the same day the Corps started in pursuit of Johnston, who was retreating towards Jackson, Miss. On the evening of the 10th they overtook the retreating foe, who had at this point constructed earthworks, and engaged him, the Thirty-Sixth being in the advance as skirmishers, and losing eight men killed and wounded; after remaining at this point until the 17th, losing several more men, the Thirty-Sixth marched to Canton, Miss., where it tore up several miles of the railroad. It then marched back to Snyder's Bluff, a distance of seventy miles, where it arrived the 23d. The march was a very severe one, and fatal in its consequences to many. Without rations, in the middle of July, under the hot Mississippi sun they were marched till some *dropped dead in the ranks*. On the 5th of August under Major Goodell, the Colonel and Lieutenant Colonel having resigned, the Regiment embarked for Cairo, where it arrived the 10th, where it took cars for Cincinnati, arriving the 12th; crossed the river to Covington, and went into camp. From the effects of this terrible campaign in Mississippi, the Regiment lost more than many battles might have cost them. It is safe to say, that from disease, and exhaustion consequent upon it, they lost by death and discharge, *one hundred and fifty men*. On the 17th of August the Regiment left on the route for Knoxville, where it arrived (after long and tedious marches and halts at different points,) on the 27th of September. On the 3d of October the Regiment, with the Ninth Corps, was marched out to meet an army of the enemy under General Jones, advancing from Virginia. On the 10th the battle of "Blue Springs" was fought, which resulted in the defeat of the enemy and a loss to the Regiment of three officers and three men wounded. Among these was the gallant Lieutenant Colonel Goodell, who was struck by a shell while leading the Regiment, and severely wounded. The retreating army was followed twenty miles and many prisoners taken, but the main body escaped. The Thirty-Sixth was engaged at "Campbell's Station," and lost twenty-four in killed, wounded and missing. During the siege of Knoxville the Regiment occupied a position near Fort Saunders, and were engaged when the Rebels made their last desperate assault before raising the siege; but suffered only a slight loss.

During the siege the men of this, as well as all other regiments, suffered much. They subsisted on quarter rations; many were without blankets and shoes, and nearly all without overcoats. From one-third to one-half the men were kept awake and on watch each night. After the retreat of the enemy the Regiment joined in the pursuit, which was continued for thirty miles, and then returned to the vicinity of Knoxville. On the 16th of Jan. 1864, they marched to "Strawberry Plains," where they remained until the 21st, suffering severely from want of food and clothing, the rations being "*six spoonfuls of flour a day for seven days, and what corn could be picked up from under the feet of mules and horses;*" clothing all tattered and torn, and hardly enough to decently cover them.

We have read of the sufferings and privations of our Revolutionary fathers in their struggle to establish this Government, and little did we think that the present generation would witness those scenes so oft repeated in this our struggle to maintain that government. But so it was to be; and as the trials of those old heroes were only equalled by their patriotic devotion to their noble cause, so have these, our sons and brothers, proved that they were worthy descendants of them.

The Thirty-Sixth remained in Eastern Tennessee from this time until March 21st, engaged in picket duty, frequent reconnoisances, and occasional skirmishes. On the 21st of March, 1864, the Regiment commenced its march over the mountains to Nicholasville, Ky., distant one hundred ninety-eight miles, where it arrived April 1st, thus averaging a march of about twenty miles per day. April 2d it took the cars for Annapolis, where it arrived on the 6th. Here the Regiment was new clothed and well fed, and began to enjoy a little rest after their severe winter campaign; but this was of short duration, for on the 23d it was ordered to march to Alexandria, where it arrived April 25th, thence on the 27th, to Fairfax Court House.

On the 6th of May the Regiment was again called to battle. The "Wilderness" is a name which even now fills us with horror. The Regiment acquitted itself nobly, charging the enemy three times with a loss of two officers, and sixty-two men killed and wounded.

In the battle of Spottsylvania on the 12th, the Regiment was engaged and lost still more heavily. Officers killed, two; men killed, twenty; officers and men wounded, fifty-seven. From Spottsylvania to the Pamunkey river the Regiment was in various skirmishes, but the loss was slight. At "Coal Harbor" on June 3d, a severe battle was fought, and the loss was two officers and forty-five men killed and wounded. On the 12th the Regiment marched for the James River, and arrived before Petersburg June 16th. On the 17th they charged the enemy's works, and captured four cannon, and four hundred and fifty prisoners. The loss was small considering the advantage gained, being nineteen in killed and wounded. From June 18th to August 19th, the Regiment remained in the rifle pits losing some twenty men picked off by the rebel sharpshooters. The Regiment then marched to the Weldon Railroad, and on the 30th of September was engaged at "Poplar Grove Church." The loss was one officer and thirteen men killed and wounded. The Thirty-Sixth remained in that vicinity through the remainder of the year, doing picket duty in the rifle pits at the front.

The Regiment remained in the vicinity of Petersburg constantly on active duty, until April 1st, 1865. On the night of April 3d the rebels evacuated the fortifications around Petersburg, and our army was immediately put in motion in pursuit of the retreating enemy. The Thirty-Sixth marched down the South Side Railroad through Nottaway Court House to Jetters Station, reaching that point on the morning of the 7th, the enemy being some ten to fifteen miles in advance. On the 8th "Rias Station" was reached and the Regiment went into camp. On the 9th the Regiment received orders to proceed to Farmville, ten miles distant, to relieve the provost guard at that place. Arriving there at about noon the Regiment relieved the guards and took charge of the large numbers of prisoners which had been captured.

Lieutenant Colonel Barker was appointed Provost Marshal, and the Regiment remained here until April 27th, when it was relieved, and ordered to rejoin its brigade at City Point. April 27th it started by steamer, for Alexandria, where it arrived on the 28th, and went into camp near Fort Lyons where it remained until June 8th, when it was mustered out of service, and started for Readville, Mass. It arrived in Massachusetts, June 10th, and had a hearty public reception by the citizens of Worcester, June 13th, after which the Regiment was furloughed until June 21st, when it assembled at Readville, where it was paid off and discharged.

HISTORY OF THE FIFTY-THIRD REGIMENT.

The next call upon us for troops was for nine months men. This call was issued in August, 1862. Fitchburg responded with two full companies, which were recruited in a very few days. The excitement was intense, and great interest was manifested by all of our citizens in filling up these two companies.

On Sunday August 24th, after the usual church services, a war meeting was held in the Town Hall to assist in the good work. It was addressed by Dr. Putnam of Roxbury, the clergymen of the town, and others, and a marked effect was produced upon all present. On the afternoon of the next day all places of business were closed, and the citizens generally devoted their energies to the business of recruiting. A procession was formed and marched through the streets to the music of drum and fife to the Common, where patriotic addresses were made by various citizens, and the result of the day's work was the addition of many recruits to the ranks of the two companies which were soon filled to overflowing. A Town Meeting was called August 30th, to see what should be done for these new recruits in the way of bounties, and it was unanimously voted to pay them one hundred dollars, each as will be seen by the following copy of the vote.

"*Voted*, That the Town pay the sum of One Hundred dollars to each of the nine months volunteers who shall be mustered into the United States service, who are inhabitants of this town at the time, but not to exceed in all, the sum of Twenty Thousand dollars."

The two companies left for camp at Groton Junction, the last week in September.

We give below their respective rolls:

ROLL OF CO. A, FIFTY-THIRD REGIMENT M. V.

COMMISSIONED OFFICERS.

Captain, EUGENE T. MILES, Fitchburg.

1st Lieut., GEORGE G. NUTTING, Fitchburg.

2d Lieut., D. W. TUTTLE, Fitchburg.

NON-COMMISSIONED OFFICERS AND PRIVATES.

SERGEANTS.

Bailey George H., Fitchburg.
Chaney William B., Fitchburg.
Farrar Ephraim E., Fitchburg.
Taft Jerome K., Fitchburg.
Tourtellot Albert D., Fitchburg.

CORPORALS.

Bruce John F., Fitchburg.
Connor Charles P., Fitchburg.
Eaton William H., Fitchburg.
Green Andrew J., Fitchburg.
Hale Frederick A., Fitchburg.
Kendall Gilbert B., Fitchburg.
Simonds William H., Fitchburg.
Spencer Edward H., Fitchburg.

MUSICIANS.

Atherton Edwin D., Fitchburg.
Carter Charles W., Clinton.

PRIVATES.

Alvord Francis A., Fitchburg.
Barnum Alonzo P., Fitchburg.
Bartlett Thomas, Fitchburg.
Bemis Daniel W., Fitchburg.
Booth John H., Fitchburg.
Bowen Peer M., Fitchburg.
Brown Joseph W., Fitchburg.
Brown Charles H., Fitchburg.
Bardeen William S., Fitchburg.
Battles Charles P., Fitchburg.
Bartlett James F., Fitchburg.
Carlton Merrill, Fitchburg.
Caldwell Charles H., Fitchburg.
Caldwell William M., Fitchburg.
Churchell Horace M., Fitchburg.
Daley James, Fitchburg.
Daisy Henry H., Fitchburg.
Dinnun Patrick, Fitchburg.
Farrar Francis F., Fitchburg.
Farrar Morris, Fitchburg.
Flynn Patrick, Fitchburg.
Forrester Arthur, Fitchburg.
Farwell Edmund P., Fitchburg.
Gates Edwin, Fitchburg.
Gates Eugene, Westminster.
Green Henry D., Fitchburg.
Griswold Albert, Fitchburg.
Harrington Mason R., Fitchburg.
Harrington Cornelius, Fitchburg.
Harris Charles T., Westminster.
Harris Edwin A., Fitchburg.
Hastings John M., Fitchburg.
Hartshorn George F., Fitchburg.
Hartwell James A., Fitchburg.
Harwood Junius, Fitchburg.
Henry William E., Fitchburg.
Hitchcock Alfred O., Fitchburg.
Hill Francis D., Fitchburg.
Harrington David A., Fitchburg.
Jewett Forestus M., Lunenburg.
Jaquith Isaac P., Fitchburg.
Kempton Alphonzo, Fitchburg.
Kendall J. Henry, Fitchburg.
Lesure Thomas G., Fitchburg.
Livermore Ozro J., Fitchburg.
McIntire Albert, Fitchburg.
Parkhurst Boardman, Fitchburg.
Pratt Henry T., Fitchburg.
Russell Charles T., Fitchburg.
Ray Francis N., Fitchburg.
Roach John, Fitchburg.
Rock Charles, Fitchburg.
Robinson Amory, Fitchburg.
Russell Francis C., Fitchburg.
Sawyer Alvin M., Fitchburg.
Sawyer George A., Fitchburg.
Spaulding Josiah, Fitchburg.
Stickney Alvin O., Fitchburg.
Stewart Charles W., Fitchburg.
Shattuck William H., Fitchburg.

Thomas Orin A., Fitchburg.
Thompson Lysander F., Fitchburg.
Tolman Thomas W., Fitchburg.
Underwood Edward M., Fitchburg.
Upham N. Bradlee, Fitchburg.
Wellington Harvey H., South Adams.
Wetherbee William H., Fitchburg.
Wheeler Horace E., Fitchburg.
Wheeler William C., Fitchburg.
Whitcomb Henry F., Fitchburg.
Whitman Waldo, Fitchburg.
Whittemore Alfred, Fitchburg.
Wiley Robert G., Fitchburg.
Winthrop Hubert W., Fitchburg.
Woodbury Oscar F., Fitchburg.
Woodward Frederick F., Fitchburg.
Works George F., Fitchburg.
Woodbury Henry S., Fitchburg.
Wooldridge William, Fitchburg.
Works Frederick L., Fitchburg.
Winchester George G., Fitchburg.
Wyman Jackson, Fitchburg.

ROLL OF CO. B, FIFTY-THIRD REGIMENT M. V.

COMMISSIONED OFFICERS.

Captain—JONAS COREY, Fitchburg.

1st *Lieut.*—CARLOS B. WILSON, Fitchburg.

2d *Lieut.*—OSCAR A. BATTLES, Ashby.

NON-COMMISSIONED OFFICERS AND PRIVATES.

SERGEANTS.

Belcher Alfred W., Fitchburg.
Eddy Amasa T., Fitchburg.
Gilmore D. Alfred, Fitchburg.
Jaquith Levi L., Fitchburg.
Nutting J. Q. A., Fitchburg.

CORPORALS.

Clark James E., Fitchburg.
Farmer Sherborn B., Fitchburg.
Gill Frank C., Fitchburg.
Gould Alonzo, Fitchburg.
Hosmore Stephen C., Fitchburg.
Leonard Elbridge G., Fitchburg.
Mecorney John L., Fitchburg.
Stevens Samuel, Fitchburg.

MUSICIANS.

Eaton Abel, Fitchburg.
Vanderford James, Fitchburg.

PRIVATES.

Aldrich Nathan H., Fitchburg.
Atkinson Jos. P., Fitchburg.
Arnold Charles F., Fitchburg.
Bigelow Calvin A., Fitchburg.
Browning Silas W., Fitchburg.
Bacon Joseph E., Fitchburg.
Bagley Charles H., Fitchburg.
Bagley Moses, Fitchburg.
Brooks Alfred L., Westminster.
Black Charles K., Fitchburg.
Blanchard Benjamin, Fitchburg.
Bickford Charles, Gardner.
Bickford William O., Gardner.
Boutelle Warren P., Fitchburg.
Brigham Henry D., Fitchburg.
Brown George E., Lunenburg.
Chase Alvin B., Fitchburg.
Cochran Nathaniel I., Fitchburg.
Coburn Manley, Fitchburg.
Cady Franklin O., Lunenburg.
Cushing Charles G., Ashby.
Childs J. Ward, Fitchburg.
Clark Eber F., Fitchburg.
Cochran Edward L. P., Fitchburg.
Demsay John C., Fitchburg.
Drake Jason W., Fitchburg.
Danby John, Fitchburg.
French Increase H., Fitchburg.
Farmer O. Franklin, Fitchburg.
Farrell William H., Fitchburg.
French Leavitt P., Ashby.
Farnsworth John M., Fitchburg.

Foster Ai, Ashby.
Goodrich Harrison, Fitchburg.
Gibson Luther B., Fitchburg.
Gould Austin K., Fitchburg.
Garfield Silas, Fitchburg.
Harris William H., Fitchburg.
Hayward H. Porter, Fitchburg.
Hemenway Frank F., Fitchburg.
Harrington John N., Fitchburg.
Hayward Joel A., Ashby.
Hadley Alvah A., Fitchburg.
Hill Thomas, Fitchburg.
Holt Lyman W., Ashby.
Howard George A., Lunenburg.
Kemp John, Fitchburg.
Kendall George F., Ashby.
Miller Charles E., Fitchburg.
Marshall Benj. F., Lunenburg.
Marsh Thomas, Fitchburg.
Marshall George E., Fitchburg.
Minot Edwin H., Fitchburg.
Morse William G., Fitchburg.
Minot Hiram P., Fitchburg.
Mace Henry W., Fitchburg.
Miller Gilbert F., Boylston.
O'Herne James, Boylston.
Parker Alonzo, Fitchburg.
Partridge Harlan P., Fitchburg.
Powers Frederick W., Fitchburg.
Parker Levi, Lunenburg.
Sabin George F., Fitchburg.
Sawin John, Ashby.
Spooner Solon W., Fitchburg.
Tucker Richard, Fitchburg.
Tileston George F., Fitchburg.
Wallis Samuel, Lunenburg.
Wyman Bradley H., Fitchburg.
Wright Amasa, Ashby.
Wheeler Henry M., Ashby.
Wheeler Erastus O., Jr., Ashby.
Willard Herbert, Ashby.
Wheeler Francis S., Ashby.
Wright Levi S., Ashby.
Wright George W., Ashby.
Wilsey Albert C., Fitchburg.
Wiley Benjamin K., Fitchburg.

We proceed to give the history of the Fifty-Third Regiment, of which these two companies were a portion, and of which Colonel J. W. Kimball of this town, was the commander.

Upon assuming the command of the Regiment, Col. K. was the recipient of a fine horse and set of equipments from a few of his friends, upon the occasion of which the following correspondence took place:

"Col. John W. Kimball:—We, the undersigned, your fellow townsmen and personal friends, on the eve of your departure, with higher rank and added honors, for further service in your country's cause, beg of you the acceptance of the horse and trappings accompanying this letter, not as any measure of our regard for you, but as a slight testimonial of our admiration for those soldierly and manly qualities which have already gained for you an honored name in the history of the war. We know that you will believe us, when we say that this is no empty tribute to position and office, but the expression of a regard as sincere and warm as it is merited. When the courage and glorious conduct of the regiment which you have led through so many trying scenes of patient endurance and bloody conflict have attracted the attention and elicited the applause of a whole nation who knew nothing of it but its name, it would be strange indeed if the hearts of those who have been associated with the gallant men of that regiment and its noble leader, in the intimate, private and social relations of neighbors and friends, did not thrill at the recital of its splendid record. To those who have nobly fallen in the strife to sustain a nation's honor and a country's name, we have endeavored to do such homage as to show that we hold their names in grateful and reverent remembrance. Let us, also, have the satisfaction of testifying to the living heroes in this conflict, our deep appreciation of the self-sacrificing and devoted spirit which has conducted them through the path of duty to an undying fame.

We have entrusted to your custody and command a new draft from our best and freshest blood, and we feel that we could commit it to no safer or more conscientious care. Accept for yourself, and for the young men who go from us with you, our best wishes and our sincere hope for a safe and honorable return to our midst at the termination of your appointed service.

(Signed)
ALVAH CROCKER.
EBENEZER TORREY,
T. K. WARE,
L. H. BRADFORD,
And 39 others.

COLONEL KIMBALL'S REPLY.

"Hon. ALVAH CROCKER, Hon. EBENEZER TORREY, T. K. WARE, L. H. BRADFORD, Esquires, and others.

Gentlemen:—With feelings of the deepest gratitude I accept the gift of the noble horse and beautiful trappings so generously and kindly provided for me by your exertions and liberality. Accept my earnest and most sincere thanks for the same. I shall prize the gift more highly because it came unexpectedly, and from old and tried friends whom I have loved, honored and respected for many years. In accepting this testimonial, I do so, feeling that it is given not to reward me, but to show that my services in the field during the past few months are appreciated and recognized by you. If I have done aught that my friends at home feel is worthy of notice, I am well repaid for the dangers, privations and hardships to which I have been, with others, exposed. I claim nothing for myself. I have only done the duty which I owed to my country and to my fellow citizens.

If the noble old regiment, (the Fifteenth,) which I have had the honor of commanding for the past seven months, has earned and won for itself a name worthy of record, and a place in history, it is to them that the honor belongs, and not to me, for it was the united determination of officers and men to do their duty at all times and under all circumstances, that has earned for them honorably and justly, the name and the fame which they have acquired.

I need not remind you of the sufferings they have endured without a murmur, and the great sacrifice of life in behalf of their country, which has so fearfully thinned their ranks. It has been very great indeed; the dust of many a brave soldier of the Fifteenth hallows the hillsides and valleys of Virginia and Maryland, and that ground, though held by traitorous hands, is still sacred, and dear to us; and by the memories of the noble dead now sleeping their last sleep far away from their friends and homes, let us pursue this war more vigorously and earnestly to an early and successful termination; by the memories of the heroes who fell at Ball's Bluff, Fair Oaks and Antietam, as well as of those who have passed away none the less honorably because not in battle, we must, we will conquer.

In leaving you, to take my new command, it is fitting that I should say a word of the men who compose this new regiment. I found them to be men who have left their homes mostly from a patriotic sense of duty—men who are worthy of the Old Bay State. It will be my constant endeavor to watch over and care for them, and if my past experience is of any value, it is theirs freely and cheerfully.

I make no promises for the future, except that we shall at all times endeavor to do our duty to the best of our ability, keeping in view the noble cause in which we are engaged, and remembering that our friends at home are watching our course with great anxiety and deep solicitude, and praying for our success and safe return.

Thanking you again for this kind remembrance, and hoping to be able to show you that I highly appreciate this expression of your confidence and esteem, I have the honor to remain,

Most respectfully, your ob't servant,

JOHN W. KIMBALL, Col. Fifty-Third Reg't."

This Regiment was recruited mainly from the towns comprising the northerly portion of Worcester County, during the months of August and September, 1862, and was encamped at "Camp Stevens," Groton Junction. It was mustered into the service of the United States, October 17th. Colonel Kimball assumed command on the 29th of November, and on the same day the Regiment started for

New York to join Banks' expedition for the South. Upon its arrival at New York, it was ordered to "Camp Banks," L. I., where it remained less than one week, but suffered much from the inclemency of the weather, it being excessively cold, and having been furnished with shelter tents only for protection of the men. Upon a proper representation of facts being made at Head-quarters, the Regiment was transferred to Franklin Street Barracks, N. Y., where it remained six weeks. It may be proper to add that at the end of two weeks, the Regiment was ordered aboard the steamer Mississippi, to sail for its Southern destination, but from the fact of there being so much sickness among the men, it was not deemed advisable by the medical authorities to proceed to sea. The Regiment, in its exposure upon Long Island, had contracted much disease. The "scarletina" had become an epidemic among the men, and was increasing to an alarming extent. The Regiment was therefore ordered to disembark and return to the old quarters, where it remained until a comparatively healthy condition was again restored, and finally set sail on the steamer "Continental," January 17th, 1863, and after a very tempestuous and perilous voyage of twelve days, putting in for one day at Key West, reached the city of New Orleans January 30th, and at once went into camp at Carrolton, six miles from the city, and became a part of the Third Brigade, Third Division of the Nineteenth Corps. It remained at this point six weeks, the time being employed in bringing it to proficiency in drill and discipline. On the 6th of March the Fifty-Third embarked on board the steamer Crescent for Baton Rouge, arriving next day, and encamped three miles below the city in a beautiful Magnolia grove. On the 12th of March it was ordered on a reconnoissance up the river. It embarked upon two steamers, and under convoy of the gunboat "Albatross," moved up the river five miles, where a landing was effected. With an escort of eighteen cavalrymen, it proceeded cautiously across the country about one and a half miles to the Bayou Sara road, where it encountered and drove in the enemy's pickets. Returning, as per orders by the Bayou Sara road, it arrived at Baton Rouge the same afternoon, driving in a number of fine cattle.

On the evening of the 13th it marched with the Division in the expedition to Port Hudson; and on the afternoon of the 14th arrived at a point three miles from that place, where it was ordered to bivouac. This was the night of the bombardment and successful passage of a portion of the fleet past the formidable batteries of Port Hudson, a feat with but few parallels in naval history. The men slept upon their arms, expecting to be ordered at any moment to join in the attack by the land forces upon the enemy's works. Morning came, but no attack was made. A General Order from head-quarters of General Banks announced " that the object of the expedition had been accomplished," and the whole army was at once put in motion towards Baton Rouge.

The Third Division was halted and went into camp five miles out of the city, where it remained until March 20th. In the meantime the Regiment took part in a reconnoissance up the Clinton road some five or six miles, but with no important results. On the 20th the Division marched to Baton Rouge, and the Fifty-Third returned to its old camp and remained there until April 1st, when it was ordered with the rest of the Division to Algiers, opposite New Orleans, where it arrived the next day, and remained until April 9th, when it took passage in the cars for Brashear City, to join in the movement through the "Teche country." The Regiment marched April 11th, arriving at Pattersonville, eight miles distant, at seven o'clock P. M. On the next day at noon, moved forward about two miles, when the advance encountered the enemy's pickets. A brisk skirmish of some two hours followed, when (the enemy being pushed back) the line of march was again resumed, and continued for about two miles, when a sharp fire was opened from the batteries of the enemy, which were protected by a formidable line of earth works. A vigorous artillery battle ensued which lasted until dark. The Regiment, though under fire, suffered no casualties.

This was the first experience of the Regiment under fire. All the afternoon we had been making our way along with the sharp crack of the skirmishers' rifles in our immediate front, the heavier reports of the batteries which were "feeling the woods" in our advance, which with the lurid flames and heavy smoke from the burning buildings which the rebels had in their flight set on fire, or which our shells had ignited wherever they interfered with the range of our guns, rendered the march a very exciting one. This was all a new experience, not unexpected, but highly suggestive of what might be looked for on the morrow. The men laid down in line of battle, expecting that early dawn would summon them to the conflict. At day-light next morning firing was again opened upon us from the batteries of the enemy, and there was every appearance of hot work for us before the day closed. After remaining in support of a battery a short time, we were ordered to cross the Bayou to join in the attack upon the other side. The trying moment was at last upon us; we were to be involved in the "clash of arms" which was soon to take place, and the result, who could tell?

Our men seemed calm and determined. How would they bear themselves in their first battle?

We crossed the "Teche"—Oh, how fair and beautiful everything in nature looked that morning—How pleasant seemed this life, perhaps to be laid down ere the day should close! Never shone the sun brighter; never looked the running stream so pure and lovely; never seemed the verdure, wet with the dew of morning, so charming; never sung the birds more sweetly.

Can we give up all these scenes, and calmly yield up life here, in this strange land, far away from home and friends, perhaps to be buried and sleep forever in a nameless grave? Yes; even this for our country.

> "We must forget all feelings save the ONE—
> We must resign all passions save our purpose—
> We must behold no object save our Country,
> And only look on death as beautiful,
> So that the sacrifice ascend to heaven,
> And draw down freedom on her evermore."

With feelings akin to these, many noble men marched to the battle that day—some to their graves. We press rapidly towards the front, passing the dead and wounded as they are brought to the rear. But such scenes do not appal us now. We have chosen our lot and have no regrets. We have put on the "armor of battle" and with a firm trust in Providence, are ready for the conflict.

We soon reached the front, and were ordered to lie down in line of battle as a reserve. Several hours were spent here, with nothing to be done but listen to the screaming of the shells as they passed over our heads, and the rattle of musketry in front. At last, at 3 P. M., we were ordered forward to relieve the Thirty-Eighth Mass. Reg't, and to move in skirmish line "directly upon the works." We were thus engaged under a heavy fire of musketry and shells for five hours, until darkness prevented farther operations, gradually advancing to within one hundred and twenty-five yards of the enemy's works, which point we held through the night, being in advance of any other regiment. During the night there were unmistakable signs of evacuation by the enemy, and Colonel Kimball at once gave notice of the same at Division and Corps Headquarters, but no orders were sent him. In the morning, just at daylight, he caused Captain Stratton and ten men to move forward to draw the fire of the enemy, if still there, but no evidence of the same appearing, the whole Regiment was at once moved forward, and in a few moments had possession of the works, and notice of the same was sent to headquarters immediately. "Fort Bisland" was ours, and the flag of the Fifty-Third the first to be planted upon its ramparts.

The Regiment lost in this action one officer and thirteen privates killed and wounded. On this day fell the brave Lieutenant Nutting, in command of Company A, while gallantly leading on his men.

On the next day the Fifty-Third was ordered to reconnoitre the left bank of the Teche, to Franklin, distant ten miles, while the rest of the army moved up on the other side of the river in pursuit of the fleeing rebels. With an escort of a few cavalrymen, it proceeded cautiously along the country, across the fields and by plantation roads, and reached Franklin about dark, and joined the main body again, driving in about one hundred head of beef cattle, mules and horses. On the 15th the pursuit of the retreating foe was resumed, and vigorously prosecuted during the succeeding days, harassing his rear and capturing hundreds of "demoralized prisoners." Opelousas was reached on the evening of the 20th. The march had been a most fatiguing one, and the roads dry and dusty, but the men stood it like "veterans," and were in high spirits over the victory and the complete rout of the enemy.

The army rested at Opelousas for two weeks, the time being employed in drill and the ordinary picket duty.

On the 5th of May the march was resumed for Alexandria, one hundred miles distant, which was accomplished in four days, arriving on the evening of the 8th. The remnant of the rebel force, some fifteen hundred or two thousand of the five thousand we had fought at "Bisland," were driven far beyond Alexandria, when the pursuit was abandoned, and the army, by a very rapid movement was marched one hundred miles to Port Hudson, crossing the Mississippi at Bayou Sara. The Fifty-Third was left at Simesport on the "Atchafalaya," for guard duty for two days, when it embarked on the "Laurel Hill," sailed to Bayou Sara, and marched twelve miles to Port Hudson, arriving on the 22d of May, upon which day the investment of the place was made complete, our lines having joined those of another force, moved up from Baton Rouge.

May 24th the Third Division moved toward Port Hudson. The Fifty-Third was detailed by order of General Paine as guard for the engineer corps and led the column. After proceeding about two miles and entering the woods, the scouts reported a force of the enemy's skirmishers just in front. The Regiment was at once moved forward, and three companies, thrown out as skirmishers, soon became engaged with the enemy and succeeded in driving them back, which enabled the engineers to proceed in their labors. An examination of the ground induced them to abandon this route for another a little to the eastward, upon which the march was resumed. The Regiment took a position for the night in a piece of woods bordering a large open field.

Just before dark Generals Banks, Grover, Paine and Weitzel with their staffs rode forward to reconnoitre. As they emerged from the woods they received a volley from the rebels in the edge of the woods opposite, but fortunately all escaped injury. The Regiment was immediately got into position to repel an attack, but none was made. Five companies of the Regiment were posted on picket for the night, as it was considerable distance from any support. In the morning it was ordered to join the Brigade, and at one o'clock P. M., moved forward to the front, where the skirmishers were actively engaged. Arriving in their vicinity, the Fifty-Third formed in line of battle in support of the Ninety-First New York in the front line, which regiment it relieved at dark by order of General Paine, who accompanied his order with the complimentary remark that "he wanted *this* Regiment, because he knew he could depend upon it to hold the position through the night," though he knew the regiment had been on picket duty for the two preceding nights. Six companies were deployed in skirmish line and two held in reserve. Soon after taking position, an unfortunate accident occurred. The enemy having suddenly opened fire, it was quickly returned by two New York regiments in the rear, thus bringing the Fifty-Third between two fires. Fortunately, the firing soon ceased and the line remained unbroken, and but few casualties had occurred. It was here that Captain George H. Bailey of this town, lost his life. He was a brave officer and beloved by all. He had received his appointment as Captain of Co. A but one week before, and survived its previous commander (Nutting,) only six weeks. The position was held during the night, and after repulsing an attack of the enemy upon the left in the morning, the Regiment was relieved and passed to the rear.

May 27th was the day of the first general attack upon the works at Port Hudson. The Regiment was ordered to be in readiness to move forward at five o'clock A. M., at which time they stood in line and were briefly addressed by Colonel Kimball, who told them that hard work was before them but that he should expect every man would do his duty and obey strictly his orders. That if they were ordered to charge and take a battery, he expected them to do it, and asked if he could rely upon them in every emergency, when a hearty " yes" was shouted along the whole line. There is something very sublime in a scene like this; these heroic men standing there in the woods, on that beautiful May morning, perhaps the last they might ever see, listening to their Colonel's words, and waiting for the order to move forward into the fight. The writer well remembers that as he passed down the whole line and looked into the faces of the men, and saw nothing written there but dogged determination and calm resignation, that he received fresh inspiration for himself from the sight.

The Regiment was ordered forward at five and a half o'clock A. M., and moved in line of battle in rear of the Thirty-Eighth Massachusetts, and was soon under fire of shot and shell. The enemy was pressed steadily back and was soon driven inside his fortifications. The Regiment was moved to the front and supported the First Maine and Bainbridge's Batteries for two hours, when it was again ordered to the front line of skirmishers to relieve the Ninety-First New York, then holding a position at the brow of a hill within sixty yards of the rebel works, which point it held until the afternoon of the next day, engaging the sharpshooters of the enemy. The loss up to this time had been thirty killed and wounded.

June 1st the regiment relieved the Fourth Wisconsin, (occupying rifle pits at the front) which was accomplished without casualty at eight o'clock, P. M., which position it occupied until June 4th, losing five men killed and wounded. On the 5th it marched at half past four, A. M., as a part of the expedition to Clinton.

This march was an unusually severe one, on account of the intense heat. Several severe cases of sun-stroke occurred in the regiment on the first day. The expedition occupied four days, and resulted in driving the enemy from Clinton, without a fight.

Arriving back at Port Hudson on the evening of the 8th, it rested quiet until the 13th, on the evening of which day orders were given to join in the assault upon the fortifications of the enemy the next morning at three o'clock. The plan of the assault was promulgated to the troops who were to engage in it, in a general order detailing the position of each regiment, and the duties it was to perform.

As a matter of curiosity to some, the order of battle is subjoined:

General Orders   HEADQUARTERS THIRD DIVISION,
No. 64.   *Before Port Hudson,*
                          June 12*th*, 1863.

COLUMN OF ATTACK.

8th New Hampshire.   (Skirmishers.)   4th Wisconsin.

....

INTERVALS 2 PACES.

Five Companies 4th Mass., and 110th N. Y., with hand grenades.

....

38th Mass.   (Skirmishers.)   53d Mass.

....

INTERVALS 4 PACES.

Four Companies 3d Brigade, with 400 cotton bags.

....

3d Brigade.

....

2d Brigade.

....

1st Brigade.

....

50 Pioneers to level parapet for Artillery.

....

Artillery.

Nims' Battery.

1st. The hand grenade men carry their rifles on their backs, and carry each, one grenade. They march three paces in rear of the line of skirmishers. Having thrown their grenades, they go in as skirmishers.

2d. The cotton bag bearers march at the head of column, two hundred paces in rear of skirmishers. They fill the ditch to Company front. Having deposited their bags, they take arms and march at head of column.

3d. The whole movement will be in quick time. No double quick. But in case the skirmishers encounter batteries which they can take by a double quick advance, they will move in that step.

4th. The skirmishers will clamber upon the parapet, followed by the hand grenades, which will be thrown over into the works as soon as the skirmishers are on the outer edge of the parapet. The skirmishers will then rush in and gain ground forward, fighting, lying down, &c. &c., according to circumstances.

5th. As soon as the column is within the works, each Brigade will form their line of battle, and lie down until the Artillery is brought up, unless circumstances should necessitate different orders.

6th. ⎫
7th. ⎭ *(Have to do with the duties of officers.)*

8th. The men will carry two days' rations of hard bread in their haversacks, forty rounds of ammunition in their cartridge boxes, and twenty rounds in their pockets. Their knapsacks will be left in camp under guard of convalescents.

By order of Brig. Gen. Paine.

(Signed)

GEO. W. DURGIN, JR., A. A. A. G.

The plan looked very well upon paper, and seemed feasible. All saw that there was hard work to be done; that the struggle would be indeed desperate, but hoped it might be short, and that those who survived could rejoice in a complete victory. Thousands of men laid down to rest that Saturday night with the sad reflection that it might be their last on earth; yet they slept sweetly, as the tired soldier always will who puts his trust in God and the justice of his cause.

Sunday morning, the ever memorable June 14th, came, and just before daylight the Regiment was moved noiselessly forward to the point of assault and took its position in rear of the Thirty-Eighth Massachusetts, and in support of the Eighth New Hampshire and

Fourth Wisconsin deployed as skirmishers. The rebels soon discovered the movement and fiercely poured forth their fire. The line moved forward with great steadiness under a tremendous fire of shot, shell and musketry, the whole being led and directed by the gallant General Paine, and when within one hundred yards of the works a charge by the four regiments was ordered.

The line sprang forward with alacrity, advancing at double-quick close up to the works, with wild cheering and enthusiasm which promised well for veterans. But the supports did not come up and they were not strong enough to carry the works. A few entered and were captured, and the rest repulsed, were obliged to fall back to the foot of the ridge upon which the works were located, where by "hugging the ground," comparative safety was secured. Here, exposed to the fire of the sharpshooters, they were obliged to lie in the hot sun through that long midsummer day, unable to extricate themselves from the position, or to even get off the suffering wounded, until darkness came to their relief. No attempt was made during the day to rally for another charge, or to bring up troops for their support, and to them the day proved a failure, and a most disastrous one. The field was lost, but *all* was not lost. The record of the Fifty-Third and the three regiments which with them traversed that terrible field, stands out clear, and bright and glorious.

Of the causes of the failure of this assault we have our own views, but do not propose to criticise our superiors. Every one acquainted with modern warfare, knows the difficulties of successfully carrying a charge in the face of such strong fortifications as these were, subjected to a front and enfilading fire for a quarter of a mile across an open field, every rod of which was obstructed by fallen trees, blind ravines and ditches; and the failure in this case was not from any lack of effort, or enthusiasm, on the part of the brave General who led it, (and who lost a leg in the action,) or the officers and men who followed. The Fifty-Third was highly praised for its behavior upon this occasion, and Colonel Kimball, for special gallantry, was recommended for promotion.

This assault was a severe cost to the Regiment. About three hundred officers and men (eight companies,) went in, of which eighty-six were killed and wounded.

Here fell Captain Taft of this town, the third commanding officer of Company A lost in two months. Here also, fell the accomplished Lieut. Glover, and the genial, generous hearted Lieut. Vose. Also, severely wounded, Captains Stratton and the noble, chivalrous Washburn; the latter dying from the effects of his wound fifteen months afterwards. Colonel Kimball was slightly wounded on this occasion, for the first time in his many battles. The sacrifice did indeed seem great, where so little was accomplished.

We give below extracts from Colonel Kimball's Official Report:

"CAPTAIN E. H. FORDHAM, A. A. A. G.

Sir: I have the honor to report the doings of my command in the movement upon Port Hudson, from the 23d of May, to the 8th of July.

* * * * * * * * * * *

On the afternoon of 13th June I received orders to be ready to move the next morning at three o'clock, in an assault upon Port Hudson. At the time specified I was ordered by Colonel Gooding to move up the road in rear of the Thirty-Eighth Mass., to the point of attack, and then deploy as skirmishers, on the right of that regiment. During the march this order was countermanded by one from General Paine, directing me to deploy *in rear* of the Thirty-Eighth Mass., at a distance of ten or fifteen paces. This last order was executed by deploying five companies, holding three in reserve. We were at this time under fire, though partially protected by a hedge, behind which the deployment was made. At about fifteen minutes past four o'clock orders came to advance in quick time, upon the enemy's works, supporting the Thirty-Eighth, who were following a line of skirmishers and hand grenades. The men moved forward promptly, and, as they passed the hedge, received a terrific volley from the enemy who had been made aware of our approach by the loud cheering of the first line of skirmishers. They pressed steadily forward, keeping as good a line as the nature of the ground, ravines and fallen trees would admit, until the centre had reached to within twenty yards of the works, when we came upon the first line of skirmishers, who had been repulsed and were holding this position. I was here obliged to halt on account of the broken condition of my line, caused by the uneven state of the ground, and more particularly, the halting of the Thirty-Eighth Mass. at some distance in my rear, which detained the right and left of my line. The right soon came up, passing the Thirty-Eighth whose commander had declined to move forward until he received further orders, though requested so to do by my Adjutant, who had command of the right of my line. I immediately went to the left of my line to move it up, but found it utterly impossible so to do on account of the terrific fire from the enemy. At this juncture General Paine came up, and after examination of the line, gave the order "to charge forward and enter the works." I immediately repeated the order to my regiment, which sprang forward with an alacrity and determination worthy of veterans, some of the men reaching the works and falling at the ditch, while others entered and were captured. At this time General Paine fell severely wounded, as did also many of my best officers. The fire of the enemy was now so terrible that it was impossible to advance the men under it, and we maintained our position close up to the works during the day, keeping up a fire upon the enemy, receiving no orders until about ten o'clock, P. M., when I was ordered to withdraw and return to my position of the morning, being the last regiment to leave the field. I was able to get off all of my wounded, and most of the dead. The sufferings of the men through this day were severe in the extreme, lying in the hot sun, with no shelter; out of water and no chance of obtaining a supply, many of them lying in a position where any attempt on their part to move would subject them to the well-directed fire of the enemy's sharpshooters, rendered their condition very critical. They uttered no word of complaint, but all—the wounded and the well, bore their trials with the fortitude of martyrs. My loss this day was very severe, especially in officers, as the official list will show. We remained at our old camp in the woods until the 19th, at four o'clock P. M., when I was ordered by Colonel Gooding to go to the front and relieve the Thirteenth Connecticut, who were supporting Bainbridge battery, which position we held until the surrender of Port Hudson, on the 8th of July. In closing this report, I would take occasion to speak of the conduct of my Regiment during this protracted seige. Too much cannot be said in praise of both officers and men through all its trying scenes in the several engagements with which they were connected, and more especially on the occasion of the assault of the 14th, when, with unfaltering courage they pressed forward to the charge, having one-third of their number stricken down. My line officers, without exception, were prompt in the execution of of my orders, and exhibited an enthusiasm and determination which inspired and encouraged the men to brave and gallant conduct, and testimony to this fact is shown in the loss of Captain Taft, and Lieutenants Vose and Glover, and the severe wounds of Captains Washburn, Stratton and Mudge.

* * * * * * * * * *

Accompanying this, I hand you a list of casualties during the seige, in their proper order of dates.

And have the honor to remain,

Very truly your ob't servant,

(Signed) JOHN W. KIMBALL,

Col. Fifty-Third Reg't Mass. Vols."

Port Hudson surrendered on the 9th of July, 1863, and on the same day the Regiment was ordered on picket duty five miles in rear of the town, remaining until the 11th, when it marched to Baton Rouge. On the 15th it embarked for Donaldsonville, arriving the same evening. Here it remained in camp, engaged in drill and picket duty until August 2d, when it returned to Baton Rouge and remained until the 12th, when it embarked on board steamer Meteor, for Cairo, Ill., thence to be forwarded by rail to Camp Stevens, Massachusetts. It arrived at Cairo August 19th, and at Fitchburg August 24th, where a public reception was given the regiment, which was then furloughed one week, to report at Camp Stevens" August 31st, at which place it was mustered out of the service Sept. 2d, by Capt. J. R. Lawrence.

STATEMENT.

Original strength of Regiment,		950
Killed in battle, and died of wounds,	33	
Died of disease	132	
Discharged for disability,	53	
Deserted,	22	240
Mustered out,		710

It may be added that a very large number returned in a feeble condition, and some fifteen or twenty died in a few days after reaching home. The climate of Louisiana had told fearfully upon the men. No regiment has ever left the State which lost so many men by disease in the same length of time. Indeed, we think it may be stated as a fact that no regiment from this State has suffered more from *disease* during a three years term of service.

In closing the report of this Regiment, the writer would say that if it is more minute than the records of the others, it is for the reason that from his official connection with it, he is able to give a more particular account of its career than of others; and the fact that two entire companies of it were contributed by this town, would seem to justify a more extended history of its operations. All that he claims for it is, that although a Nine Months Regiment, t was fully equal to any regiment which ever left the State, and he only reiterates the oft-repeated remarks of the Generals whose command it was under, when he says: " it *ought* to have been a three years regiment."

The retrospection to him is a sad one, bringing up as it does the trying scenes through which we passed, and the recollections of the familiar forms and faces of dear friends now gone forever. Their memories are embalmed in all our hearts. " *Requiescent in pace.*"

HISTORY OF THE FIFTY-SEVENTH REGIMENT.

On the 17th of October, 1863, the President issued his call for three hundred thousand more men, to be furnished by draft upon the enrolled men, if volunteers were not furnished before a certain time. Our quota was found to be one hundred twenty men. Experience had shown that the best method of filling our quotas was to raise a company in town. Accordingly, the requisite authority was obtained, and Captain Levi Lawrence was designated to command it.

Recruits came very slowly, and it was not until the 1st of February, that enough men had been procured to muster a Company, and get ordered into camp.

Many public meetings were held. The first meeting we give an account of below, taken from the *Reveille*:

"RECRUITING AT FITCHBURG.—A preliminary meeting to make arrangements for filling the quota of this town was held last Saturday evening, November 28th. Captain D. H. Merriam was called to the chair. Earnest and patriotic speeches were made by Colonel John W. Kimball, Hon. Alvah Crocker, Hale W. Page, Esq., and others, after which the meeting adjourned to Monday evening of this week.

On Monday evening a full meeting of the citizens was called to order at the Town Hall, by Wm. H. Vose, Esq., and Hon. Alvah Crocker, on being elected to preside, addressed the assembly, urging the duty and importance of prompt and enthusiastic action in response to the President's call for men to aid our brothers in the field, and strike a final blow to the rebellion. He was followed by Colonel J. W. Kimball, Rev. George Trask, Rev. Mr. Hamilton, Lieut. W. A. Putnam, and others; all calling upon our citizens to do their utmost to respond to the liberal offers of the National and State governments for recruits.

A rallying committee of fifty-eight was chosen to canvass the several districts of the town."

This meeting appears to have had but little result, inasmuch as recruiting was quite as dull after it as before. A large number of our soldiers had just returned from one year's service, and the hardships they had suffered were patent to all, and we fear that the tales of their experience deterred many from enlisting. It was soon found that unusual efforts must be put forth. On the 26th of December another meeting was held, at which a bounty of one hundred dollars per man was offered to every one who would enlist. Subsequent to this, meetings were held *every evening for a fortnight*, and some accessions were made to the ranks nightly. These meetings were addressed by speakers from abroad, as well as by our own citizens; also, by the soldiers themselves, who had enlisted, and who made eloquent appeals to the young men of the town to follow their examples. Our people were thoroughly awake to the importance of furnishing the requisite number of volunteers, before the impending draft should be upon us.

As evidence of the feeling among some of our women, we subjoin the following letter published in the *Reveille* January 7th, 1864.

LETTER FROM "G. E. M."

"*Fitchburg, Jan.* 4, 1864."

Mr. Editor: I feel a strong desire to reach the ears of the people of F., and see no other way but through the press. Will you allow these thoughts a place in your paper? (that is if you deem them worthy.) Why is it that we are so slow in obtaining enlistments? Are there no patriots here? Shall we remain at ease while our government is ruined for want of assistance? Our brothers in the field are making fresh sacrifices upon their country's altar, while we—Oh! shame on us all! If there is *one spark* of patriotism felt in this town, let it kindle and spread, until there is sufficient to raise the desired number of men.

True patriotism is not bought with money; is not aroused by the firing of cannon, the ringing of bells, nor the making of bravado speeches, but by a cool, calm and deliberate consideration of our country's needs. Are not these needs forgotten or dimly seen through the offers of bounty or reward? This should not be. Let us examine what are the demands of our government, and then rise in our strength and meet them. Let us hear no more flimsy excuses for not enlisting. 'My wife isn't willing, or I'd go,' says one and another. I hope you never go *anywhere* she *isn't* willing.

Are we, then, my sisters, the holdbacks we are represented? Then let us rise and nobly do our part. Remember if we suffer in our country's cause, we also share in her glory. Brothers,

> 'See! our spangled banner waves
>   High above our brothers' graves!
> Will ye then be coward slaves,
>   Unworthy to be free?'
>
> Up! and arm you for the fight!
> Battle for your country's right!
> Put the traitor foe to flight!
>   God will speed his cause."

At last the Company was made up, and left for camp at Worcester, February 6th, 1864, and became a part of the Fifty-Seventh Regiment, of which the Colonel was the gallant William F. Bartlett, formerly of the Forty-Ninth, who had already lost a leg and received other severe wounds in Virginia and Lousiania.

We give below a list of names of the members of this Company, and the history of the Regiment from date of muster until discharge of same.

ROLL OF COMPANY F, FIFTY-SEVENTH REG'T.

COMMISSIONED OFFICERS.

Captain—LEVI LAWRENCE, Fitchburg.

1st *Lieut.*—CHARLES BARKER, Fitchburg.

2d *Lieut.*—ALFRED O. HITCHCOCK, Fitchburg.

NON-COMMISSIONED OFFICERS AND PRIVATES.

SERGEANTS.

Hastings John M., Fitchburg.
Barnard Charles E., Worcester.
Sabin George F., Fitchburg.
Bartlett James F., Fitchburg.
Southey John, Fitchburg.

Dunn William S., Fitchburg.
Wilkins Aaron, Fitchburg.
Davis Freeman, Lancaster.
Nickerson A. M., Sheffield.
Hannahan Edward, Milford.

CORPORALS.

Bigelow Calvin A., Fitchburg.
Southwick Francis, Worcester.

PRIVATES.

Bartlett G. A., Fitchburg.
Beckwith Herbert D., Fitchburg.
Babbett C. W., Fitchburg.

Baker John, Sutton.
Brigham O. A., Fitchburg.
Brown Robert, Fitchburg.
Brannon Patrick, Fitchburg.
Burke John, Fitchburg.
Barnes Charles W., Gardner.
Barnes W. F., Fitchburg.
Benson William G., Fitchburg.
Backant Joseph, Worcester.
Bishop A. J., Gill.
Clark Caleb, Fitchburg.
Classon Henry, Fitchburg.
Coughlin John, Fitchburg.
Costello Thomas F., Fitchburg.
Casey John, Fitchburg.
Changyou Joseph, Fitchburg.
Changyou William, Fitchburg.
Changyou Levi, Fitchburg.
Carey James, Fitchburg.
Crawford, John S., Sutton.
Carey Michael, Milford.
Dolan Timothy, Fitchburg.
Davis Oscar D., Fitchburg.
Delany John, Fitchburg.
Derby Edward M., Fitchburg.
Daily Charles, Fitchburg.
Edgecomb George R., Fitchburg.
Farnsworth Rufus S., Fitchburg.
Farnsworth Joseph W., Fitchburg.
Farrell Martin, Fitchburg.
Flagg Edwin A., Fitchburg.
Fuller Henry, Fitchburg.
Frost James M., Washington, Mass.
Gould Austin K., Fitchburg.
Gove Alfred E., Milford.
Goddard W. D., Royalston.
Gardner Horace O., Hancock.
Harris Michael, Longmeadow.
Hall Rodney, Fitchburg.
Henry George A., Fitchburg.

Hennessy John, Fitchburg.
Kielty Daniel, Fitchburg.
Lawless John, Fitchburg.
McDowell John, Fitchburg.
McIntire Albion C., Fitchburg.
McSherry John, Greenfield.
McMaster George C., Sturbridge.
Miles Michael, Fitchburg.
McCarty Patrick, Fitchburg.
Maynard John P., Dudley.
Nourse Stephen H., Fitchburg.
O'Donnell M., Fitchburg.
O'Brien Darby, Fitchburg.
Pine Edmund, Westfield.
Parks Fred W., Fitchburg.
Peabody William T., Fitchburg.
Ploof Louis, Northampton.
Partland Patrick, Fitchburg.
Ryan Charles, Adams.
Ryan Martin, Fitchburg.
Raymond Oren T., Fitchburg.
Richards James, Lee.
Roche Redmond, Dudley.
Sawyer Elgar F., Fitchburg.
Simmons W. T., Pittsfield.
Stiner Matthew, Northampton.
Sullivan John, Worcester.
Skye William, Fitchburg.
Sherman Edwin P., Adams.
Stevens A. W., Fitchburg.
Stock Henry, Hancock.
Suchay Abraham, Spencer.
Sweet Daniel J., Williamstown.
Sheahan R. J., Worcester.
Truss James P., Longmeadow.
Vickery Charles W., Hancock.
Wetherbee W. S., Fitchburg.
Wilkins Henry A., Fitchburg.
Watts George, Fitchburg.

The Regiment left the State April 18th, 1864, for Annapolis, Md., where it arrived April 20th, and joined the Ninth Army Corps, making a short stop only, and thence marched to Washington, where it arrived April 25th, and was immediately marched towards the front. It arrived at Rappahannock Station May 3d. On the 5th it crossed the Rapidan, and on the 6th was engaged in the battle of the "Wilderness." It entered the fight with twenty-four officers and five hundred twenty-one enlisted men, and was actively engaged one hour, losing in killed, wounded and missing, two hundred fifty-one officers and men. Their brave Col. Bartlett was again wounded in the head, and obliged to give up the command. On the 12th of May, at "Spottsylvania," the Fifty-Seventh was again in action and lost seventy-two officers and men. On the 18th in a reconnoissance, the Regiment lost seventeen more killed and wounded.

On the 19th the Regiment moved towards the North Anna River, arriving May 24th, and was ordered to cross the same and advance, for the purpose of testing the strength of the enemy. It was not a successful movement. The brigade having moved a half mile beyond the main line, was attacked on both flanks, and having no support, was obliged to fall back in some disorder, the Fifty-Seventh losing their Lieutenant Colonel and thirty-six enlisted men, wounded and taken prisoners.

From this point the Regiment marched to "Coal Harbor," and was engaged in the various operations in that vicinity, and thence marched to Petersburg, arriving there June 16th, 1864. The Regiment remained in this neighborhood for several months, and on the 30th of July, took part in the assault at the explosion of the mine. The following account of its part in this affair is from the Official Records.

"In the charge which immediately followed the springing of the mine, the regiment passed directly through the ruins of the fortifications into a covered way connecting with the fort, and running parallel with the front line of the enemy's works. Arriving at this point, and receiving a severe front, and right and left enfilading fire of musketry and artillery, and being much disordered by the uneven nature of the ground, the line halted and erected a slight work on the side of the way facing the enemy. Being ordered to maintain this position, the troops remained firm, and resisted every attempt of the enemy to dislodge them, until the charge and repulse of the Fourth Division (colored) Ninth Corps. This division fell back in the greatest confusion, the troops seeking shelter in the covered way, already densely filled by regiments of the First and Second Divisions. The repulse of the Fourth

Division was immediately followed by a charge from the enemy, who advanced his line to the brink of the covered way, delivering a heavy fire which added to the confusion of the troops, then so crowded as to be unable to make use of their fire-arms. At this period of the action the National standard of the Fifty-Seventh was captured; its guard and the greater portion of the left wing of the Regiment going with it.

All attempts to rally the troops proved fruitless, the men falling back as rapidly as the crowded condition of the passage would permit. The Regiment went in with officers, seven; men, ninety-one. *Six officers and forty-five enlisted men* were killed, wounded or missing, leaving the remnant of the Regiment in command of First Lieut. Doty."

From this time until the 29th of September, the Regiment remained in the vicinity of Petersburg, engaged in picket duty, &c. On the 30th it participated in the action of "Poplar Grove Church," numbering at the time but sixty men present for duty. In this action eight of these were lost.

On the 8th of October the Regiment moved with its Division in a reconnoissance in force, being deployed as skirmishers. The rebels were found in force, and orders were given to return to camp. The casualties were fourteen killed and wounded. On the 26th the Fifty-Seventh took part in the movement against the "South Side Railroad," and was engaged as skirmishers, losing but one man. On the 28th it returned to camp, remaining until Nov. 30th, when it went into the trenches in front of Petersburg.

On the 9th of December the Fifty-Seventh joined in another movement on the Weldon Railroad, marching some twenty miles out to Hawkinsville, which place it reached December 12th. Nothing of note occurred, and the return march was at once made. This march was a very severe one. At one time the Regiment was marched *eighteen miles without a single halt.*

The men suffered much from the severe cold, many of them being frost-bitten. Upon its return it was again ordered to the trenches where it remained through the year.

After the first of January, 1865, the Regiment laid in the lines before Petersburg, occupied with the usual outpost and camp duties, until the middle of February, when (with some other regiments,) it was ordered on a reconnoissance towards Weldon. The expedition was without any important result, but much suffering was experienced by the troops during the same, owing to the intense cold.

On the 24th of March the Fifty-Seventh relieved the Fifty-Ninth in the lines near Fort Steadman, and was engaged on the 25th, in the memorable repulse of Gordon's Corps, which inaugurated the closing scenes of the war. We extract an account of the same from the official record of the Regiment.

"At 3 1-2 A. M., the enemy in strong force carried the works held by the Fourteenth N. York Artillery, and flanked the line of the Fifty-Seventh, who fell back from the works, skirmishing as they went, and earning for themselves a proud record. Having at last reached a position which could be held, they there remained until supported by some troops of the Pennsylvania Division, when the Fifty-Seventh led the advance in the charge from that part of the field, and again entered their works in triumph, Sergeant Major, afterward Lieutenant Pinkham, capturing, by singular poetic justice, the flag of the Fifty-Seventh North Carolina."

From this time until the evacuation (April 3d,) constant demonstrations were made by both parties, but no general engagement was brought on. On the 2d of April, the Regiment, with the rest of the Brigade, was kept at work in a feigned attack upon that portion of the works, and succeeded in keeping the enemy from re-enforcing at other points on the line.

On the 3d of April, 1865, the Fifty-Seventh entered Petersburg, and was ordered to guard the roads to Richmond and Chesterfield, and on the 4th placed on similar duty upon the Boydtown and Cox's roads, and was finally established at "Wilson's Station."

Soon after the assassination of the President, the Regiment was ordered (with the Ninth Corps) to Washington, and placed on duty near Tennallytown. From this time until August, when the Regiment was mustered out, it remained in and about Washington, doing provost duty at various important points. It was mustered out July 30th, and at once proceeded to Readville, Mass., where it was paid off and discharged August 9th.

And this closes its record. It was organized, it will be remembered, as a "Veteran" Regiment, a title which occasioned some sneering at the time, for upon mustering the Regiment, it proved that but a small proportion of the men *were* Veterans. But if the title *was* miss-applied then, have they not earned it now? Most assuredly have they. All honor to the Veterans of the gallant Fifty-Seventh. Their term of service was a short, (about fifteen months) but it was indeed a bloody one.

As long as the "Wilderness," "Spottsylvania," "North Anna," "Coal Harbor," "Poplar Grove Church," "Hatcher's Run" and "Petersburg" areremembered, so long will be remembered the brilliant achievements of the Fifty-Seventh.

HISTORY OF COMPANY H, FOURTH HEAVY ARTILLERY.

The last company raised in Fitchburg during the war, was recruited under the call of the President of July 18th, 1864, for one year troops. Authority was given to raise a company of one year men for Heavy Artillery service. The large bounty offered, Two Hundred Dollars; the short term of service, and the prospect of a close of the war in a few months, were sufficient to speedily fill up the company with a splendid body of young men, a large proportion of whom had seen service in the nine months and three year regiments.

The Company was organized by the choice of E. T. Hayward, Captain; J. Henry Richardson, 1st Lieut., and Samuel A. Taylor as 2d Lieut. It left Fitchburg for Readville, August 15th, and left the State for Washington September 13th. There, with various other unattached companies, it was consolidated as the Fourth Heavy Artillery Regiment. The duty assigned to this Regiment was to garrison various forts on the Virginia side of the Potomac. This Company occupied for the greater portion of the time "Battery Garasche," where the men were drilled both in Artillery and Infantry practice.

The Company was most comfortably situated, living in commodious barracks, well fed, and nothing to complain of but "too much quiet." Of course the year's record so far as they were concerned was an uneventful one. Suffice it to say, that they did promptly and faithfully all they were ordered to do, and were much praised for their good drill and soldier-like conduct. The Regiment was mustered out of service June 17th, 1865, at Readville.

The following is a list of names of those composing Company H, of Fitchburg:

ROLL OF 24th UNATTACHED COMP'Y HEAVY ARTILLERY,
Afterwards Company H, Fourth Reg't H. A.

COMMISSIONED OFFICERS.

Captain—EBEN T. HAYWARD, Fitchburg.
1st *Lieut.*—J. HENRY RICHARDSON, Fitchburg.
2d *Lieut.*—SAMUEL A. TAYLOR, Ashburnham.

NON-COMMISSIONED OFFICERS AND PRIVATES.

SERGEANTS.

Rockwood George W., Fitchburg.
Wheeler Asahel, Ashburnham.
Clark James E., Fitchburg.
Page Seldon, Leominster.
Spencer Edward H., Fitchburg.

CORPORALS.

Brown Cyrus, Fitchburg.
Lawrence Ivers W., Fitchburg.
Waters Silas C., Fitchburg.
Gibson Artemas A., Fitchburg.
Lesure Thomas G., Fitchburg.
Chase Alvin B., Fitchburg.
Foster Waldo A., Leominster.
Polley Frank W., Leominster.

PRIVATES.

Ackley Edward W., Fitchburg.
Aldrich Frank S., Fitchburg.
Allen Charles W., Ashburnham.
Atherton Frank O., Leominster.
Baker Henry, Fitchburg.
Barrell Elmer C., Fitchburg.
Bemis Joseph C., Fitchburg.
Bolton Alonzo D., Westminster.
Babbitt Caleb H., Fitchburg.
Bigelow Charles D., Sterling.
Bigelow George E., Sterling.
Brown John A., Townsend.
Breed Isaac T., Ashburnham.
Barber Vernal, Townsend.
Butler Eli Henry, Hubbardston.
Chase George H., Leominster.
Chapman Samuel L., Sterling.
Cook Lucius M., Leominster.
Cook Joel S., Townsend.
Caswell Almon, Fitchburg.
Caswell Herbert C., Fitchburg.
Chase Andrew, Fitchburg.
Coolidge Louis W., Fitchburg.
Cushing Sewell G., Fitchburg.
Cushing Charles S., Fitchburg.
Davis George A., Fitchburg.
Davis Edwin J., Fitchburg.
Davis Charles H., Fitchburg.
Dodge Wooster F., Leominster.
Dudley Stephen W., Fitchburg.
Davis Martin V. B., Ashburnham.
Ellis George H., Townsend.
Elliot George P., Mason, N. H.
Earle Edward O., Fitchburg.
Eaton John, Ashburnham.
French Andrew J., Leominster.
Follansbee Frank F., Leominster.
Farrego James, Ashburnham.
Fessenden Albert H., Townsend.
Frost Sumner M., Leominster.
French George A., Fitchburg.
Fortin David, Fitchburg.
Freeman Charles N., Fitchburg.
Fuller Marshall R., Fitchburg.
Gale Darius M., Fitchburg.
Garfield Warren, Fitchburg.
Green Marshall D. E., Fitchburg.
Greenwood Theodore, Ashburnham.
Griswold Albert, Fitchburg.
Gunnison Horace A., Fitchburg.
Goodnow William F., Princeton.
Gibson Lemuel W., Fitchburg.
Gibson Daniel O., Fitchburg.
Gates Christopher, Townsend.
Hildreth Henry B., Townsend.
Hildreth John L., Townsend.
Hammond Frederick, Ashburnham.
Heywood Albert L., Lunenburg.
Hodgeman Freeman L., Mason.

Howe Leroy A., Ashburnham.
Harrington John N., Fitchburg.
Hayward Charles F., Fitchburg.
Herrick Noyes B., Fitchburg.
Hosmer Samuel, Fitchburg.
Hosmer Stephen C., Fitchburg.
Hughes Richard, Fitchburg.
Jewett George C., Lunenburg.
Johnson Charles H., Fitchburg.
Jordan John S., Fitchburg.
Jaquith Charles B., Ashburnham.
Jackman Noah G., Ashburnham.
Knapp John, Fitchburg.
Kendall George W., Leominster.
Lane Lowell S., Ashburnham.
Lovejoy Augustus, Townsend.
Lesure Henry A., Fitchburg.
Litch Charles C., Fitchburg.
Livermore Thomas, Fitchburg.
Lovewell Lyman S., Fitchburg.
Mack John, Fitchburg.
Marsh Palmer A., Fitchburg.
McCoy John, Fitchburg.
Melinday James A., Fitchburg.
Morrison James, Fitchburg.
Mills Hamilton A., Fitchburg.
Morse Harrison A., Leominster.
Morse William G., Fitchburg.
Neat William R., Lunenburg.
Parker Munroe R., Townsend.
Parker Alden W., Fitchburg.
Parkhurst James H., Fitchburg.
Payne George A. Fitchburg.
Polley George A., Leominster.
Priest Willard, Fitchburg.
Proctor Clarence D., Fitchburg.
Putnam Fred A., Fitchburg.
Ray Jason A., Westminster.
Reynolds Julius F., Fitchburg.
Rockwood Charles H., Fitchburg.
Rugg Jacob, Leominster.
Sanderson Martin, Leominster.
Sawin Daniel W., Leominster.
Sloan Samuel, Townsend.
Spaulding Benjamin B., Townsend.
Seaver Isaac 3d, Westminster.
Smith William H., Ashburnham.
Stafford Edward, Fitchburg.
Taylor Henry, Fitchburg.
Underwood George H., Fitchburg.
Webber Amos A., Fitchburg.
Wheeler Henry M., Fitchburg.
Whitcomb Gilman W., Fitchburg.
Whitman Waldo, Fitchburg.
Whitney George O., Ashburnham.
Whitney Joseph H., Ashburnham.
Willard Joseph M., Leominster.
Winch William J., Fitchburg.
Woolson Isaac M., Fitchburg.
Whitney William B., Leominster.
Wheeler E. O., Jr., Ashburnham.
Wilder Oliver D., Ashburnham.
Wright Elbridge A., Townsend.
Wilder Frederick A., Lunenburg.
Yott Charles, Fitchburg.

THE CALL FOR THREE MONTHS TROOPS.
1862.

In the latter part of May, 1862, occurred the famous retreat of General Banks down the Shenandoah Valley. The defeat of this army, and the advance of the rebels towards Washington occasioned great alarm for the safety of the Capital. The President issued a call to the Governors of the loyal States to send forward immediately to Washington, all the three months troops they could spare. At that time both the "Fusiliers" and "Guards" had efficient organizations, and were ready to respond in any sudden emergency. Governor Andrew's call upon the Militia was issued on Monday morning, May 26th, and reached our town about eight o'clock. All was excitement and activity. Captains Miles and Barker at once gave orders to their companies to assemble at their armories ready to proceed to Boston in obedience to the orders of the Commander-in-Chief. The men responded very promptly, and in course of the afternoon, both companies were ready to march; the Fusiliers with sixty-six guns, and the Guards with fifty-eight.

At five o'clock both companies took their departure for Boston amid the greatest enthusiasm of the crowds assembled to give them a parting word and a hearty cheer.

Among the incidents of this exciting day, may be mentioned the fact that when the order of Captain Miles reached the shop of Whitman & Miles (of which firm the Captain was a member,) fifteen men dropped their tools and stepped forth to join the ranks of the "Fusiliers," and the firm, not at all disturbed at this wholesale reduction of their "available force," at once gave another proof of their patriotism by presenting ten dollars to each of the fifteen. These troops arrived in Boston the same evening, and with the other companies from Worcester North, were quartered in Faneuil Hall. Here they remained two nights, expecting every moment to start for the "seat of war."

But the *scare* at Washington was soon over, and the Governor was telegraphed that the troops need not come forward, as the emergency had passed. The troops were therefore ordered to their homes, and our two companies came back in grand style during the afternoon of Wednesday. After parading the streets together, and going through a dress parade in battalion, under Captain Barker, they were treated to a collation by the citizens, and then dismissed, feeling that though their campaign had been a short one, it was not without result. It cannot be denied that both officers and men deserve much credit for the promptitude with which they rallied in obedience to orders, fully expecting that they would be wanted for three months, and with a fair prospect of being called into battle. All honor to them. To many it was their only march in the whole course of the war; but to a *majority* of them it was only preparatory to longer and sterner service.

The occasion and its results showed what we could do in a sudden emergency, and also, demonstrated the advantages of keeping our Militia thoroughly organized at all times.

We give the lists of these two companies, believing that it is due to the men who so promptly rallied to this sudden call, that their names should go upon record.

ROLL OF COMPANY B, OLD NINTH REGIMENT M. V. M.

COMMISSIONED OFFICERS.

Captain—EUGENE T. MILES.

1st *Lieut.*—GEORGE G. NUTTING.

2d *Lieut.*—D. W. TUTTLE.

ENLISTED MEN.

Atherton E. D.,
Atherton Geo. R.,
Bailey Geo. H.,
Brewer James H., Jr.,
Bickford Chas.
Brown Jos. W.,
Bowen Peer M.,
Bruce John F.,
Chaney Wm. B.,
Churchill Horace M.
Chase Jos. W.,
Chase Winslow O.,
Carleton Merrill,
Conner P. C.,
Dailey James,
Dinneen Patrick,
Eaton Wm H.,
Estabrook Jos. D.,
Emory Edward F.,
Farrar Eph. E.,
Farrar Frank F.,
Farnham Rensclear,
Farnsworth Marshall G.
Farwell Edward P.,
Glines Augustus M.,
Green Andrew J.,
Hayward H. Porter,
Heselan James,
Hartshorn Frank G.,
Hollingsworth Byron,
Harrington Cornelius,
Keyes Geo. E.,
Kendall Gilbert B,
Knowles Frank W.,
Kempton Alphonso,
Livermore Ozro J.,
McMaster Levi,
McMahan Edward,
McNear Louis D.,
Noonan Michael,
Palmer Frank L.,
Putnam John L.,
Putnam Chas. F.,
Putnam Marshall,
Putnam Cyrus,
Parkhurst Boardman,
Pierce George,
Powers Albert J.,
Pratt Charles E.,
Russell Charles F.,
Ruggles Gould G.,
Sweeney Chas. H.,
Stuart Chas. W.,
Spencer Edward H.,
Spaulding Josiah,
Spaulding George,
Sullivan John,
Tourtellott Albert D.,
Taft Jerome K.,
Tufts Joseph A.,
Upton T. C.,
Woodbury Oscar F,
Wheeler John A.,
Wheeler Horace E,
Wheeler Chas. H.,
Wyman Chas. H.,
Waters Silas C.,
Wetherbee Aaron F.,
Woolridge Wm.,

ROLL OF COMPANY E, OLD NINTH REGIMENT M. V. M.

COMMISSIONED OFFICERS.

Captain—JONAS COREY.

1st *Lieut.*—HENRY A. HATCH.

2d *Lieut.*—GEORGE L. CHIPMAN.

ENLISTED MEN.

Battles Nathan L.,
Battles Oscar A.,
Browning Silas W.,
Babbitt Willard N.,
Boutelle Warren P.,
Battles Fred. C.,
Bliss Garfield,
Barber Chas. S.,
Cochran N. L.,
Davis John E.,
Davis George W.,
Davis Oscar D.,
Davis Jona. D.,
Drake Jason W.,
Dunn John W.,
Dempsey John C.,
Farnsworth Lucius B.,
Flynn Jeremiah,
Goodrich Herbert D.,
Goodrich Harrison,
Hitchcock Joseph,

Harding John C.,
Harding Jabez I.,
Haskell H. N.,
Henshaw Edward,
Jaquith Levi L.,
Lamb Levi L.,
Lovewell Sewall K.,
Leonard Elbridge G.,
Litch Chas. C.,
Lailan Lewis,
Marble Stephen J.,
Mecorney John L.,
Minot Augustus,

Marshall George E.,
Morgan John L.,
Mack George W.,
Marshall Benj. F.,
McDuffie Stephen,
May Nathaniel,
Mansfield Geo. F..
Nutting John Q. A.,
Patch Ebenezer,
Phelps Chas.
Partridge Harlan P.,
Spooner Solon W.,
Stevens Samuel,

Smith Rufus H.,
Starkey Calvin,
Shiner Wm. H.,
Sawin Harrison P.,
Tucker Richard,
Underwood Wm. W.,
Virgil Daniel,
Vaughn Orlando S.,
Wiley Benj. K.,
Whitney Alonzo,
Wilson Carlos B.

14

HISTORY OF THE DRAFT.

The Spring and Summer of 1863 was a dull season for recruiting. The country had passed through two years of war; terrible battles had been fought; many precious lives sacrificed, and we had really made but little progress in conquering the rebellion. Congress had passed an act providing for a draft from the enrolled men of the country, for the purpose of filling up the depleted ranks of our armies. Meanwhile, the President had issued his call for another large levy of troops, to be filled by a draft on the 1st of July, if the volunteers were not forthcoming before that time. But little interest was manifested in filling quotas, as the provisions of the conscription act were such that any man drafted could be exempt from service by furnishing a substitute or paying three hundred dollars. As the time for drafting approached, there was much excitement on account of fear that there might be an outbreak in opposition to the same by those liable under the act, which did actually occur in New York and other cities, as many of our readers will sadly recollect. To guard against anything of this nature, in this town, a special police was appointed, and the town was regularly patroled for several nights. The day appointed for drafting from the enrolled list of Fitchburg, at last came, July 17th, 1863. Our quota was 241 men, and the following are the names of those drawn, giving a statement of those exempted, those who furnished substitutes, and paid commutation. But four who were drafted, were forced to serve. Their names are William Sawtell, Chas. H. Brown, 2d, Frank N. P. Jones, John Downes. The first two named died from disease contracted in the service. We know not what became of the others. The result of the draft here, as elsewhere, was a failure, so far as filling up the armies was concerned. The causes of exemption were so numerous that few men were accepted. The result in this town, as the list which follows will show, may be briefly stated :

Whole number drafted,	241
Furnished substitutes,	28
Paid commutation,	14
Gave personal service,	4
Failed to report,	14
Exempted for disability,	95
" " other causes,	86

THE DRAFT OF 1863.

ACCEPTED AND SERVED IN PERSON:

Frank N. P. Jones,
William Sawtell,
John Downes,
Charles H. Brown, 2d.

FURNISHED SUBSTITUTES.

Hiram A. Blood,
John Burney,
Henry P. Boutelle,
Silas Conant,
Josiah T. Colley,
Howard T. Clark,
L. Horace Dunnell,
Charles Derby, Jr.,
Sewell Foster,
Nathan L. Gee,
Eugene H. Hayward,
Joseph Haskell, Jr.,
Emerson W. Harris,
Samuel Hadley,
Charles H. Keyes,
Orrin Littlefield,
Frank L. Palmer,
Elbridge G. Stanley,
Daniel Sullivan,
John M. Stearns,
Joseph A. Tufts,
Henry Thrasher,
George H. Taylor,
Daniel B. Whittier.
George W. Weston,
Joseph W. Worcester,
Russell S. Waters,
John M. Whitney, 2d.

PAID COMMUTATION.

Lorenzo D. Warren,
Homer Thrasher,
Fred W. Smith,
Edwin H. Smith,
Frank H. Snow,
Francis S. Oxford,
Hiram S. Miller,
Jeremiah Greenwood, Jr,
Hiram D. Fletcher,
George W. Frost,
Charles L. Fairbanks,
Uriah E. Cleaveland,
David S. Barnes,
William Andrews.

EXEMPTIONS FOR VARIOUS CAUSES.

Charles W. Bellows, *Only son of a widow, liable to military duty.*
Daniel N. Bardeen, "
John May, "
William Moran, "
Willard I. Miller, "
John Shea, "
John Silk, "
Francis A. Smith, "
Melvin L. Crane, *Only son of aged or infirm parents.*
Calvin C. Gott, "
John O'Brien, "
Edward Turpin, "
Joseph F. White, "
Porter G. Barton, *Father of motherless children under twelve years of age.*
William L. Bullock, "
Charles F. Arnold, *In service 3d of March, 1863.*
Fred. H. Battles, "
Richard Hughes, "
William H. Hayden, "
Granville C. Hosmer, "
Joel K. Hosmer, "
Asa S. Jaquith, "
Horace E. Jennison, "
Azro B. Jaquith, "
George W. Kinsman, "
Michael McCarty, "
James Noonan, "
Frank Scott, "
George M. Smith. "
O. E. Skinner, "
Benjamin Watson,
Edward Balien, *Alien.*
Francis Braddish. "
John Conlin, "
Timothy Cahill, "
William Corliss, "
Martin Carey, "
James Callahan, "
Dennis Carey, "
John Dineen, "
Levi Dudley, *Alien.*
David Fitzgerald, "
Charles Flynn, "
James Gray, "
James Hurley, "
Owen Hurlpin, "
Henry Jackson, 2d, "
William Kenworthy, "
Timothy Leary, "
Michael Murphy, "
Owen M'Ardle, "
Thomas McQuinn, "
James Morean, "
William Mehan, "
John Moran, 2d, "
Daniel Noonan, "
Daniel Noonan, 2d, "
Daniel O'Connor, "
John O'Brien, 1st, "
Patrick O'Donnel, "
Michael O'Brien, "
Lemure Pierre, "
Thomas Quigley, "
Michael Quigley, "
William Robinson, "
Alexander Rieal, "
Arthur Roach, "
Patrick Shinen, "
John Steinback, "
James Shea, "
John Wilmot, "
Charles O. Andrews, *Non-resident.*
Edward P. Coleman, "
William F. Osgood, "
E. W. Perkins, "
Henry W. Stearns, "
Augustus W. Joslin, *Over 35, and married.*
Michael Honan, "
Edward Foley, "
Henry Classon, "
George Boyle, "
Edwin Blake, "
Michael Norton, *Dead.*
John Clark, *Enlisted before draft.*

EXEMPTIONS FOR DISABILITY.

Henry Allison,
Charles A. Bateman,
Charles W. Baldwin,
Otis Brigham,
Edwin S. Burnap,
Joseph Bigelow,
George F. Battles,
Benjamin F. Bailey,
Harvey C. Browning,
Jonathan H. Barbour,
Thomas Bailey,
Franklin W. Babcock,
Moses L. Clark,
John Choate,
Harvey A. Crehore,
Thomas Costello,
Edmond T. Carter,
George A. Cozzens,
John E. Davis,
Albert A. Deane,
Edward B. Dole,
Sherburne S. Dow,
William C. Emory,
Walter A. Eames,
Edwin A. Eaton,
Sidney P. Emory,
Daniel L. Fletcher,
Francis Fullum,
Ezra R. Farrar,
Henry Fuller,
George B. Fisk,
Daniel P. Gladding,
Josiah R. Goddard,
George S. Gibson,
James Goodrich,
J. Myron Goddard,
George L. Green,
Hosea Hadley,
Henry W. Houghton,
Eben T. Hayward,
Nathan B. Hadley,
Jared M. Heard,
David Hartwell,
George P. Hildreth,
Joseph Jones,
John S. Jordan,
Newell A. Jenne,
George P. King,
William Kelley,
George B. Knowlton,
George S. King,
Leonard L. Leland,
Albert Lee,
Sewell R. Lovewell,
O. J. Livermore,
Lowell N. Moulton,
Livy McMaster,
James A. Miller,
Daniel Morrill,
George F. Maynard, 2d,
D. H. Merriam,
Josephus C. Nourse,
John Ogden,
John O'Donnell,
Michael O'Donnell,
William O'Hara,
Abner W. Pollard,
James W. Pollock,
John L. Putnam,
Jerome D Place,
Levi W. Russell,
Silas Ruggles,
George W. Rice,
James H. Rogers,
Franklin L. Ruggles,
Orlando Remington,
Calvin L. Stockwell,
George F. Sylvester,
Henry A. Spooner,
Henry F. Smith,
Elijah G. Spaulding,
Irving W. Stockwell,
Elmer Southie,
Charles R. Sawyer,
O. P. Spurr,
Daniel Stearns,
C. C. Stratton,
John M. Tyler,
Charles H. Whittemore,
George Willard,
Lyman J. Wood,
Alonzo Withington,
Augustus N. Wiley,
Lewis N. Wilbur,
John A. Wheeler.

THE FOLLOWING FAILED TO REPORT:

John Foley,
Michael Clifford,
Henry P. Hill,
Wm. Boyden,
Patrick O'Brien,
Chas. W. Record,
John H. Goulding.

George H. Stark,
Victor Doll,
George Cowee,
John Clark,
George Searles,
Daniel Whalon,
Edward Boyle.

THE DRAFT OF 1864.

In the summer of 1864, another draft was ordered, to supply deficiencies in the quotas up to that date. Fitchburg was sixteen behind, and a draft was made for that number.

We give below a list of those drawn at that time, designating those accepted who were obliged to serve personally or furnish substitutes, as the provision for paying three hundred dollars in lieu of service had been repealed. To obtain these sixteen, four different drafts were made of twenty-two names at each drawing, there being eighty-eight names drawn in all, only sixteen of which proved to be acceptable recruits. These drafts took place at intervals of a fortnight, and although the number required was small, it was sufficient to keep the enrolled men on the "tip-toe of expectation," and served to swell the list of "Representative Substitutes," of which more hereafter.

LIST OF DRAFTED MEN.

Charles S. Farrar,	*Furnished sub.*	Chas. H. B. Snow,	*Furnished sub.*
Cyrus D. Blanchard,	"	Charles T. Crocker,	"
William A. Foster,	"	Otis T. Ruggles,	"
George P. Howland,	"	Charles A. Goodrich,	"
Leonard Hartwell,	"	George F. Hudson,	"
Lowell M. Miles,	"	Porter G. Barton,	"
John Mack,	"	John Delaney, 2d,	*Not accepted.*
Charles Arnold,	"	W. J. Hollingsworth,	"
Calvin Wallace,	"	Enoch P. Young,	"
Harrison Upton,	"	Eugene Flaherty,	"
Anson L. Marshall,	"	Michael Delaney,	"

John McCarty,	Not accepted.	Francis E. Williams,	Not accepted.
George Wilmott,	"	Charles W. Bellows,	"
Orrin A. Skinner,	"	Frank Safford,	"
Celestine Benettie,	"	Edward Connors,	"
Charles H. Reed,	"	Samuel Carter, 2d,	"
Thomas Fitzgerald,	"	E. H. Cate,	"
Henry F. Colburne,	"	F. L. Ruggles,	"
Jerry Murphy,	"	Lucius B. Farnsworth,	"
Martin Farrell,	"	George R. Edgecomb,	"
Henry P. Nichols,	"	Benjamin Cragin,	"
William John Dana,	"	George P. Bennett,	"
Augustine D. Waymoth,	"	Rufus G. Farnsworth,	"
William L. Eager,	"	Daniel Kiehy,	"
William Boyden,	"	Howard Marble,	"
J. J. Harnden,	"	Frank Sloan.	"
William K. Fletcher,	"	Jacob H. Fairbanks,	"
Joseph Farrar,	"	W. H. Jewett,	"
Thomas Conner,	"	Hosea W. Flagg,	"
Jonas Whitney,	"	John Flynn,	"
William M. Whitney,	"	Joseph Haselum,	"
J. Sumner Kinsman,	"	Peter Boutee.	"
Jerry Donovan,	"	Patrick Lahey,	"
Thomas Leary,	"	J. C. Moulton.	"
James M. Woodbury,	"	Michael Donovan,	"
Terrance Haverty,	"	E. S. Chipman,	"
German F. Ware,	"	C. W. Rockford,	"
Henry S. Sheldon,	"	Jared Whitman Jr.,	"
Eben F. Bailey,	"	John Drewery,	"
Lysander Andrews,	"	Thomas Kenacy,	"
Jerry O'Hearn,	"	William Hanna,	"
Jonas A. Cutting,	"	Charles F. Sylvester,	"
Aaron Wilkins,	"	Francis R. Billings,	"
Levi H. Richardson,	"	Edward A. Brown,	In service.

SUBSTITUTES FOR "ENROLLED MEN."

Pending the draft of 1864 an arrangement was made by which any person liable to military service could, in anticipation of the draft, put in for himself a *substitute*. Thirty-six of our citizens availed themselves of this privilege, at an expense of from five to seven hundred dollars each. They thus added men to the ranks, and by so doing, also reduced our quota to that extent, and it seems proper that they should have due credit for the same. We think that, as a matter closely connected with the history of the "draft," their names should be recorded. We therefore give them below, and also the names and reputed residences of their respective substitutes.

For this list, and other favors, we are indebted to Captain D. H. Merriam, late Provost Marshal of the Ninth District.

Names of Enrolled Men.	Names of Substitutes.	Residence.
Eugene T. Miles,	Charles S. Granger,	*Canada.*
Charles H. Wood,	George Jimmesson,	*Canada.*
George F. Vose,	John J. Ellis,	*Canada.*
Henry F. Coggshall,	George Wilson,	*Virginia.*
George F. Fay,	Edward Gill,	*Ireland.*
Samuel E. Crocker,	George Chapman	*Canada.*
Francis Sheldon,	George Duncan,	*Canada.*
J. F. D. Garfield,	John Kelley,	*Canada.*
Ezekiel Davis,	Chicken Big Fire,	*Canada.*
Samuel D. Sheldon,	William Big Fire,	*Canada.*
Henry Jackson,	James Upshur,	*Kentucky.*
Elliot N. Choate,	John O'Brien,	*Boston.*
George E. Towne,	John Burns,	*England.*
Joseph E. Manning,	Michael White,	*New Brunswick.*
Thornton K. Ware,	H. Michael Husband,	*New Brunswick.*
John Q. Wright,	Patrick Farmer,	*Ireland.*
Edwin A. Goodrich,	Charles Bauer,	*France.*
Isaac C. Wright,	Peter Masson,	*France.*
Edward O. Marston	Daniel McDonald,	*Canada.*
Aaron F. Whitney,	John Pearson,	*Canada.*
James F. Stiles,	Andrew Jones	*Virginia.*
Thomas F. Simonds,	Jacob Stone,	*Sweden.*
John J. Piper,	John H Lee,	*Virginia.*
George A. Torrey,	Francis Foster,	*New Brunswick.*
Charles J. Billings,	James Nottaway,	*Canada.*
Leander Sprague,	William Russell,	*Canada.*
Edwin D. Atherton,	Thomas McKenzie,	*Scotland.*
Joseph E Derby	George W. Waldren,	*Canada.*
Sullivan W. Huntley,	John F. Remington,	*England.*
Everett W. Bigelow	Joseph Thompson,	*Florida.*
Lyman Patch,	John Allen,	*Canada.*
David Hartwell,	Joseph Gill,	*Canada.*
Willard N. Ross,	Jale Mortel,	*Canada.*
Albert D. Tourtellot,	George H. Edgerlley,	*New Brunswick.*
Robert L. Goddard,	Andrew J. Rider,	*New Brunswick.*
Charles P. Connor,	Henry Moonshine,	*Germany.*

REPRESENTATIVE RECRUITS.

During the year 1864, Massachusetts, and some of the other loyal States, sent recruiting agents into the Southern States, at points occupied by our forces, for the purpose of enlisting negroes. The recruits thus obtained were apportioned among the various towns of the State, and thirteen were credited in our quota. Their names will be found in the roll at the end of this volume. An arrangement was also made by which any person who was not liable to draft by reason of age or otherwise, could deposit with the Treasurer of the Commonwealth $125, and have secured to him what was called a "Representative Recruit." But one individual in this town availed himself of this privilege. Hon. Moses Wood has the honor of being the man, and the name of his "sable volunteer" is Alfred Sawyer. We doubt not he did good service.

RELIEF TO SOLDIERS AND THEIR FAMILIES.

As the recent war was conducted upon a scale altogether unparalleled in the magnitude of its operations, so were the enterprises which were organized and carried on to mitigate its woes and alleviate its sufferings, commensurate with it. Government itself spared no pains or expense to provide for the comfort of the sick and wounded, and the histories of the magnificent contributions of the loyal people, and the operations of those beneficent organizations, the "Sanitary" and "Christian" Commissions, will be the wonder of succeeding generations. Besides these, every city and town had their local "Soldiers' Relief" Associations, which were active through the whole war, in rendering comfort to the soldiers and their families.

Fitchburg was in no wise behind her neighbors. While our brave boys were fighting the battles of their country upon distant fields, their welfare and comfort, as well as that of their families at home, became the object of the most tender solicitude of our citizens.

The record of their various benevolent enterprises forms a most interesting chapter in our history.

Of the numerous public movements in this direction, we propose to give as full an account as possible. Of the unnumbered and unnoted *private* offerings of the patriotic mothers and sisters and friends of the soldier, who can make an estimate? They are recorded, but not *here*.

We have seen that immediately upon the breaking out of the rebellion, the town voted a large sum for the equipment of our soldiers, and for the benefit of their families. At the first Annual Town Meeting thereafter, April, 1862, the following vote was passed:

Voted, That the Selectmen be authorized to pay for the support of the families of Volunteers such sums as they think their circumstances require.

This was repeated each year thereafter, and was in addition to the "State Aid" which was authorized by the Legislature to be paid by towns, and which was often found inadequate for the wants of some of the families of soldiers. So much for the town in its corporate capacity. We shall now speak of the various Relief Organizations, commencing with an account of the "Ladies' Soldiers' Aid Society." For the following account of the doings of this organization, we are indebted to the kindness of Mrs. Stephen Shepley, who cheerfully complied with a request to furnish the same, and for which she has our grateful acknowledgements.

HISTORY OF THE LADIES' SOLDIERS AID SOCIETY.

When the war had assumed such proportions that the magnitude of the struggle in which the country was engaged began to be realized, it was evident that it must enlist not only the sympathy but the active co-operation of all classes in community.

And while the land everywhere resounded to the tread of mustering regiments and the din of warlike preparation, and men turned self-sacrificingly from the unfinished work of farm, and shop, and store and office — women felt they could not idly look on; that there was work and place for them in the "uprising of a great people" against treason and oppression and for humanity and equal rights. Delicate women in thronged towns, and hard-worked women on lonely hill-sides, every pulse astir with love of country, moved by a common impulse, silently but earnestly banded themselves together in organizations, whose object was to soften as far as might be the untold hardship of soldier-life.

This was not all—women did more than this, and we approach with reverent feet, the thought of the uncounted households where mothers and wives, with unresting hands and hearts broken, but for the high, strong purpose that nerved them, made ready their loved ones, and saw them go out and away to war and all its terrible possibilities; and as we think of them sitting by desolate firesides, bearing through weary months a burden of sickening suspense, or the alternations of hope and fear over conflicting rumors, or the agony of certain bereavement, the most splendid heroism of the war seems not more heroic than the silent endurance of these. In every soldier-grave is buried not only the valor of man, but the devotion and self-sacrifice of woman. Those of our own town were no exception to others in their endeavor to inspire the soldier on the battle-field with the truest moral bravery—in the tedious monotony of camp-life with hope and patience, by their unwavering sympathy and appreciation; and when sick and in prison, causing their alleviating ministries to reach, and remedy in some wise, the suffering incident to the situation.

With the enlisting of the first Fitchburg men, the labors of the Fitchburg women began. They prepared and sent to the soldiers in camp such things as would best contribute to their comfort, and by frequent visits, made them feel they were not to be forgotten while away doing the strange work of war, but that home-care and affection would still and ever be exerted to the utmost for their well-being, wherever the chances of war might lead them.

That greater method and efficiency might be secured, the formation of a society was decided upon, and at a meeting held for that purpose, Sept. 16th, 1861, the organization known through the period of the war as the "Soldiers Aid Society," was formed.

The various religious societies were largely represented, and indeed the association included nearly all who were of an age to help on the needful work. The better to regulate their operations, a Constitution, framed by a committee consisting of Mrs. A. Emerson, Mrs. A. F. Adams and Mrs. C. Tolman, was adopted by a vote of the Society.

CONSTITUTION.

Art. 1. This association shall be called "*The Ladies' Soldiers Aid Society.*"

Art. 2. The object of the Society shall be to furnish to the Soldiers engaged in the present war of our country such aid as may be in our power.

Art. 3. The officers of the Society shall be a President, Vice-President, Secretary, Treasurer and twelve Directresses.

Art. 4. It shall be the duty of the President to preside at the meetings and to perform the duties that naturally fall to the office. In her absence these duties shall devolve upon the Vice-President. It shall be the duty of the Secretary to find a suitable place for the meetings of the Society, to notify the same, to keep a record of them, and if necessary, learn by correspondence the actual wants of the Soldiers. It shall be the duty of the Treasurer to receive the funds of the Society, and to keep an account of all the receipts and expenditures. It shall be the duty of the Directresses to make the purchases and prepare the work for the Society.

Art. 5. The meetings may be called at the discretion of the President, or at the request of six members of the Committee.

Art. 6. Any lady may become a member of the Society by the payment of twenty-five cents.

Agreeably to article third of the Constitution a board of officers was chosen for the ensuing year, consisting of

Mrs. E. TORREY, *President.* Mrs. A. NORCROSS, *Secretary.*
Mrs. N. A. TUFTS, *Vice-President.* Miss M. A. BROOKS, *Treasurer.*

DIRECTRESSES.

Mrs. L. H. BRADFORD, Mrs. B. LYON,
Mrs. E. UPTON, Mrs. B. SNOW, Jr.,
Mrs. J. UPTON, Mrs. H. M. LOUD,
Mrs. N. STONE, Mrs. F. BUTTRICK,
Mrs. W. KIMBALL, Mrs. J. B. PROCTOR,
Mrs. K. HARWOOD, Mrs. H. SIBLEY.

The money received for memberships and for the annual assessments thereon, was used in the purchase of material with which to work, and the funds of the Society were most opportunely replenished from time to time, by donations from private individuals, and from local organizations. The churches aided its support by their contributions, and generous sums were placed at its disposal by the Dramatic Club, the Musical Association, the Relief Committee; and the "Old Folks at home," too old to learn war themselves, sang their ancient melodies in concert, giving the proceeds in aid of the boys who were giving the strength of their youth to country.

It is not proposed in this sketch, necessarily brief, to enter into a detailed account of the Society. All that is aimed at, is to convey a general idea of its plans and their accomplishment. In no better way can this be done than by giving some of the letters of acknowledgement received from different regiments and associations; while at the same time, the letters will have a value themselves, as showing how susceptible the soldiers were to any care or thought that was taken for them.

Among the first results of the Society, as such, was the preparing a box of clothing and hospital necessaries for the Twenty-first Regiment, then at Annapolis; similar supplies for the Twenty-fifth at the same place, and a quantity of much needed blankets and suitable clothing for the approaching winter, for the Fifteenth Regiment at Poolesville.

No one could feel that in their efforts for the soldier they had assumed a needless, or a thankless task, when such expressions of gratitude from the recipients of their favor reached them as are contained in the subjoined letters.

"ANNAPOLIS, MD., *Naval Academy, Nov.* 27*th*, 1861.

MADAM : —

In behalf of my regiment, I return you my sincere thanks for the timely presents of nice warm socks and mittens, presented to them by the ladies of the "Soldiers Aid Society" of Fitchburg, and in the words of the men as they drew them on to their hands and feet, 'God bless the ladies of Fitchburg!' And it is cheering to us, who have left our homes, wives and children, and sacrificed all our cherished hopes on our country's altar, to see that those we have left behind are determined to do their part of the duties devolving upon all lovers of our glorious Union.

All honor is due the Association for this proof of the interest cherished by them for the government which was established by our fathers' blood, sustained by our mothers' prayers, and made sacred by the virtues of both, and with the help of God, shall be maintained by their children.

Once more I thank you for your kind gift, asking for your good wishes and prayers, and hoping that we shall never prove recreant to the cause, nor disgrace the flag which rebel hands and feet have too long trampled in the dust.

       T. S. FOSTER, Capt. Co. D, 21st Reg't M. V.
To Sec'y 'Soldiers Aid Society,' Fitchburg."

     "CAMP HICKS, ANNAPOLIS, MD, DEC. 13, 1861.
To the Sec'y of the Soldiers Aid Society,—

  DEAR MADAM: In behalf my command, I return you my sincere and heartfelt thanks for the very generous present of comfortables, socks, mittens, &c., presented them by the 'Soldiers Aid Society.' May the blessings of Heaven ever attend you, and every member of your Society.

       CHARLES H. FOSS,
        Com'g Co. F, 25th Reg. M. V."

     "POOLESVILLE, MD., DEC. 14th, 1861.
 Sec'y Soldiers Aid Society: I was surprised to learn through a friend that you had never received any acknowledgment of the receipt of those three boxes of blankets, &c., sent Co. B, Fitchburg Fusiliers. You are of course aware they were sent direct to Major Kimball, and I *think* I have heard him speak of having written you in regard to them. However, I will take this occasion to say they came safely to hand, and were *gladly* received. It is certainly a consolation to *know* that although we are absent, we are still kindly remembered by the generous ladies of your Society, and we have reason to feel that we shall not be allowed to suffer for the want of anything that will add to our comfort in camp during the present winter.

 You will please accept the sincere thanks of every member of our Company, and extend the same to the Ladies of the Soldiers Aid Society, for the very generous supply of blankets, socks and mittens, and

    I am, Very Respectfully,
      CHAS. H. EAGER, Lieut. Com'g Co. B.

 Who could be other than faithful to the men who were faithful themselves, not only to government in its hour of peril, but to the best instincts of our nature as well; not forgetting amid the hardening tendencies and exhausting toil of campaign-life—a life that supposes constant privation and danger and death itself; not forgetting to thank in fervent words friends at home for every exertion put forth in their behalf?

Articles of convenience and comfort were sent to the Thirty-sixth Regiment at Worcester, and the Fifty-third Regiment at Groton, and elicited the accompanying letter from the former, and a set of resolutions, enthusiastic in their gratitude, from the latter.

"CAMP WOOL, WORCESTER, AUG. 9, 1862.

To the Pres't of the Ladies Aid Society, Fitchburg:

I am directed by Capt. Barker to acknowledge the receipt of fifty-five towels and needle-books, so kindly furnished his company by the ladies of your Society. Such a remembrance can not but be appreciated by men, who, having known what home is, sadly miss its many little conveniences in the camp.

'Please send in your orders,' was written on the bundle.

Can you furnish the company with *flannel shirts?* The shirts furnished by the Government are of the coarsest kind of cotton. They are not suitable for this kind of life at all. The health of the men requires that they should be cast aside. Moreover, the men would make a better appearance about the camp, as the cotton shirts become very easily soiled. We would like to have the shirts of the same color—gray.

With many thanks for favors already received,

I remain, Yours very truly,

HENRY S. BURRAGE."

"*The Fusiliers to the Ladies of Fitchburg.*

CAMP STEVENS, GROTON JUNCTION, Nov. 28th, 1862.

WHEREAS, The Ladies of Fitchburg have done very much for the benefit of the soldiers here encamped, and by so doing have nobly made manifest more fully to our view that noble trait of character which enters so much into the composition of every true and noble woman, namely, true benevolence, and whereas, believing it is our duty as men and soldiers, to in some way tender an acknowledgment of these many favors to the donors,—therefore,

Resolved, That we, the members of the Fitchburg Fusiliers (Capt. Miles) sincerely believe that the assertion is true that "the liberal soul shall be made fat," and that if you "scatter your bread upon the waters, after many days that ye shall receive it again many fold."

Resolved, That we tender our sincere thanks to the ladies of Fitchburg, who have at home and in our camp, done what they could to make our lives pleasant and happy.

Resolved, That it gives us courage to go forth to battle for the right, when we view that nobleness of character, and holiness of love of country, manifested by fair woman in the many ways she has of showing it to the world.

Resolved, That we ask God, the Almighty Ruler of all, to bless the noble women of Fitchburg.

Resolved, That these resolves be tendered to the ladies of Fitchburg, asking them to accept them with our hearty God bless them, through the columns of the papers of Fitchburg.

These resolves were unanimously adopted, November 29th, 1862.

GEORGE H. BAILEY, 1st Serg't."

If there were those who had made some sacrifice of time or ease for the soldier's sake, they were more than compensated by this tribute of generous praise, and by the consciousness of having done good and served the right. The heart deserved pity that was not lifted up by a great unselfish resolve to do something worthy so rare an opportunity as such times and events offered.

The last named regiment, (Fifty-third,) after starting for the seat of war was detained long in New York city amid circumstances of peculiar discomfort, and wishing to cheer them with some token of home condolence, the Society despatched to them the first day of January, 1863, a "happy new year," not of words only, though they were not wanting, but whose most tasteful manifestation was an *inviting* dinner. "Wishes" took form and shape in fat turkeys rightly roasted, and such plum puddings and pies as every son of the regiment knew could not be made anywhere outside of the dear old New England home he was leaving. The dinner performed its mission to the hearts, as well as appetites of those for whom it was intended, judging from the acknowledgments.

"NEW YORK, JAN. 10, 1863.

Sec'y Ladies' Soldiers Aid Society,

MADAM: I beg to acknowledge the receipt of your kind and patriotic note of the 2d inst., also, the generous New Year's dinner furnished us under the auspices of your most noble and benevolent Society. In behalf of the company under my command, I most sincerely thank you.

It is unnecessary, as well as impossible, for me to express to you by the multiplicity of words, the feelings which the soldier experiences on such occasions as our last New Year's dinner, and I can only wish that your Society might have been present to witness the joyous effects of their kindly deeds. Allow me in this connection, to express to you my deep obligations and thanks for the very many favors bestowed upon the company under my command, by your Society during the past three months. May God bless and crown all your efforts to relieve the necessities, and to lighten the burden of the soldiers, with the utmost success.

I am, madam, most respectfully,
Your ob't servant,
EUGENE T. MILES,
Commanding Co. A, 53d Reg't M. V. M."

"FRANKLIN STREET BARRACKS, NEW YORK, JAN. 4, 1863

Sec'y Ladies' Soldiers Aid Society of Fitchburg,

Yours of the 3d inst. was received yesterday, also, the boxes of provisions so kindly contributed by your Society, which were received by the company with loud applause and many cheers for those of our friends who have so often remembered us in our absence since we left our own dear homes, families and friends.

We feel assured that although we are absent, we are not forgotten by our many friends at home. We hope our absence from our friends to the call of our country, may, and will be beneficial to all who remain at home, as well as to those of us who have volunteered our services to help put down this terrible rebellion.

In behalf of the officers and members of Company B, I most cheerfully return you our warmest thanks for the bounteous supply of provisions you have so generously contributed at this time, also, you will please accept our heartfelt thanks for the many articles we have before received at your hands.

Yours very respectfully,
JONAS COREY,
Captain of Co. B, 53d Reg't M. V. M."

It was the design of the Society to make its own townsmen its first care, and after meeting their needs, extend its aid to the loyal army in general, being limited only by its capacity to do. The main channels through which its labors were given to the cause were the Sanitary and Christian Commissions, two great streams of blessing flowing all over the theater of conflict, penetrating the wards of every hospital, and reaching every red field of combat, where their tender, sacred offices could avail aught for the wounded, the dying, or the dead.

Another very efficient branch of the service through which this Society acted, was the " Mass. Relief Association," located at Washington, which, as its name would indicate, made the suffering sons of Massachusetts its more especial charge.

Added to these, numerous contributions were sent to various other points. To the " New England Soldiers Relief Association" in New York City, to the " Worcester Relief Society," and to individuals laboring in hospitals, who were known to the Society and who applied to it for assistance. From these wide-spread sources, frequent letters were received, testifying to the readiness of the Society in answering calls made upon it, and to the value of its donations. A few of the letters it may be interesting to preserve.

"WASHINGTON, D. C., OCTOBER 20, 1864,
Sec'y Soldiers Aid Society, Fitchburg, Mass.,

MY DEAR MADAME: I acknowledge with pleasure the receipt of two boxes of hospital supplies from the ladies of Fitchburg, forwarded through Surgeon General Dale. I am deeply grateful for this mark of your confidence in our Agency, and for your appreciation of the needs of our suffering soldiers. Many of the articles sent to us are forwarded directly to City Point, where we have had an Agency since that became the base of operations.

It is our aim that no Massachusetts soldier shall want for anything; and, while all our monied expenses are met by the State, we rely on the noble women of the Commonwealth to supply the comforts and luxuries.

Will you please convey to the ladies of Fitchburg my thanks for their generous contribution. I am, Madame, Your obedient servant,

GARDINER TUFTS, *Mass. Military Agent,*
By J. S. VASSALL, Ass't."

"N. E. WOMEN'S AUXILIARY ASSOCIATION, BOSTON.

To the Soldiers Aid Society of Fitchburg,

LADIES: The work that for so long a time has occupied the hearts of the women of the land, is a bond of common interest among us all, that seems to draw us into closest sympathy, and to ask for some direct expression. It is with the feeling of long companionship that we now address you.

For three years many of us have been at work, with one purpose—of relieving, so far as might be, the necessary hardships of the loyal army. We began uncertainly, sending our gifts somewhere where soldiers were, but with no system, with no assurance that they would accomplish our intention. Then came the Sanitary Commission, with its wonderful plan of wise economy, of tender pity, of careful justice, appealing straight to the heart of the people and the soldiers. How joyfully we seized its promise! and now we see how well it has been redeemed.

It is two years and a half since the New England Branch began its work, and its record shows how true the homes have been to the camp. We who have the privilege of receiving the gifts of New England, read many a letter whose words make our tears rise, and our hearts stir. They come with the clothes of the dead son, or husband, sent with tender yearnings for all those who suffer and "may die like him for their dear country," or with gifts that are thank-offerings for the lives yet spared, or from little children who want to take their share in helping the brave soldiers. The many fears and sorrows of the people, find soothing in the work that nothing else can give.

We all see, I think, how our own personal efforts and sacrifices influence the welfare of the army and the country. Each one's share is little towards such an end, but in the mass, its power is beyond our estimate. Not only does our duty lie in giving, but in believing.

We owe our country our unwavering faith. We should never forget to keep the truth and justice for which we fight, clear in our own and others' minds. We owe our deepest sympathy and encouragement to the men who must fight these battles, so marvellous for their courage, so fearful in their misery. In such times as these, a woman's courage is as precious as a man's; it is the spring from which the army gets much of its patience. And so in our woman's way we help to fight the battles. If we do our duty, the future will bring many blessed memories. What bitterness would be in the thought that we had been dead to the opportunities of such times!

There never has been so much call for relief, as now; the army is larger than ever before. We have every stimulant to hope; the end seems to draw near! Let us take new heart in our work!

With hearty interest, truly yours,

MARY G. LORING, *Sec'y Exec. Com.*

"U. S. Gen'l Hospital, Annapolis, Md., March 19, 1863.
Secretary Ladies' Aid Society, Fitchburg, Mass.:

DEAR MADAM: I take pleasure in acknowledging the receipt of three valuable and precious boxes, one cask, and one keg of pickles, all of which were most acceptable, came to us in good order, and in a good time, just as we are receiving so many of our poor starved prisoners.

Please accept our most hearty thanks for them; rest assured that it made our hearts glad to see so many *nice* things before us for our poor 'boys.' Boats are coming in daily, loaded with these *starved prisoners*. Since last Sabbath (week) we have had 143 (one hundred and forty-three) deaths in this hospital. We are losing so many of our brave and *noble* men—is it not sad? One poor, dying boy said to me this morning: 'Sister, shall I never see mother again? I had hoped to go home and die with her—I cannot, but I die among friends.' Daily do we hear similar expressions, which are very trying. Though our experiences are sad, there is *real* pleasure in doing the *little* we can to alleviate so much suffering as we see among the returned prisoners. Again thanking you for your very liberal donations to this hospital, and bidding you who are engaged in this noble work, God speed,

I am yours, Very Respectfully,

R. S. ELLIS."

"NEW YORK, SEPTEMBER 20, 1862.
Secretary Soldiers Aid Society:

MADAM: In behalf of the Ladies of this Association, I beg to acknowledge the receipt of your two large boxes—as well timed as they were complete.

Yours respectfully,

FRANK E. HOWE,

Fitchburg, Mass. *Supt. N. E. Soldiers Relief Ass'n.*

"WORCESTER, MASS., MORNING OF THE 27TH FEB., 1862.
Sec'y Soldiers Aid Society,

DEAR MADAM: The Worcester Soldiers' Relief Committee acknowledge the receipt of a box and a bundle of supplies for St. Louis, from the "Ladies' Soldiers Aid Society" of Fitchburg.

It was a very opportune, as well as generous donation, and we thank you, and the ladies of your Society for forwarding them at this time, when there is so great demand for supplies in the Western Department. United as we are in a common cause, and stimulated by a common sympathy for the sick or wounded soldier, much, I doubt not, will be done to relieve the suffering which can not be prevented.

We have heard of your active labors in this National interest, and it is pleasant to feel that we are laboring together, in a noble cause.

Yours very truly,

S. P. MILLER, *Sec'y of Com.*"

The amount in money received and expended while the organization lasted, was something above fifteen hundred dollars. No estimate could be made of the value of what was given beside money, but that liberal things were devised, closely-packed boxes of clothing, bedding, and delicacies for the sick, could frequently and fully attest.

There were special seasons in the history of the Society that stand out prominently against a back-ground, of stated meetings and regular on-going work. Seasons of aborbing interest, when the members were aroused by some imperative call, that flew from lip to lip, and from house to house, reminding one of an old rallying cry of the Highland Clans—

> "The muster-place be Lanric mead—
> Instant the time—speed, clansmen, speed!
> Herald of battle, fate, and fear."

And home cares were put by, while all hurried to the meeting-place, to help in the painful exigency that had so hastily summoned them together. One such occasion was when tidings came that the National Capitol was in danger, and men were needed in its defence, and two companies from this town were ordered to report in Boston, ready for duty, at a few hours' notice. The record of the Society says: "Forthwith, the ladies, Monday morning though it was, snatched sewing implements, and in rapid haste gathered at the Town Hall, to fit out our men with flannel shirts and other appropriate garments, and sewing-machines and busy fingers vied with each other to achieve the work." Again, when listening ears caught the echo of such pitiless strife as at Gettysburg, the Wilderness, and other places alike memorable for their wild work of death, there was hurrying to action. The cry that swept up from those war-strewn plains, for help, for thousands of brave men ready to perish, was thrilling in its effect. Every household was laid under contribution for their relief, and such motive power as the heart only can supply, was added to hands already used to work, at thought of wounds needing that moment, perchance, the soft compress, or lint, or bandage, and the sinking forms needing the cordial and restorative, all being so rapidly got in readiness. May Heaven avert a recurrence of such scenes.

The close of the war brought back to many members of the Society, fathers, husbands, and sons, unharmed. In the homes of others, the vacant chairs to-day are eloquent of what a costly thing to them has been the preservation of our Republic.

With the disbanding of the army, the necessity of a Soldiers Aid Society ceased; and it held its last meeting June 22d, 1865, no member regretting she had been identified with its labors, but rather that it could not more truthfully be said of her, "she hath done what she could."

THE SOLDIERS' RELIEF COMMITTEE.

This Committee was a large one, appointed from all sections of the town, and had its origin at a meeting of the citizens, held at the Town Hall, on the 26th of September, 1861, "to organize for the more effectual aid and comfort of the soldiers in the field from this town, and their families."

The following were chosen "a committee to raise funds to aid enlistments, to procure comforts for our soldiers and their families, and take such other action in the matter as may be deemed expedient."

T. R. BOUTELLE,	CHAS. BURLEIGH,	C. W. CARTER,
ALVAH CROCKER,	T. S. WILSON,	EDWIN JACKSON,
L. H. BRADFORD,	A. P. KIMBALL,	DANIEL WORKS,
J. B. LANE,	N. S. BOUTELLE,	JOEL PAGE,
H. A. WILLIS,	WM. WOODBURY, JR.,	J. P. PUTNAM,
H. L. REED,	JOSEPH UPTON,	M. L. HOLDEN.

The Committee proceeded at once to their labors, and collected a large amount of money and farm produce, as well as clothing; and chose the following as an Executive Committee to distribute the same wherever needed:

T. R. BOUTELLE, ALVAH CROCKER, L. H. BRADFORD, H. L. REED.
H. A. WILLIS.

This sub-committee immediately issued the following circular:

TO THE PUBLIC.

"The undersigned, members of the Executive Committee raised from the 'Soldiers Relief Committee,' chosen at a meeting of citizens, September 26th, 1861, and charged with the duty of receiving and disbursing subscriptions (whether clothing, provisions, fuel or otherwise) made for the relief of the families of Soldiers absent at the seat of war, would announce, that the charitable offerings of our fellow citizens have been such as to enable them to meet in these particulars the present wants of such needy families. Being prepared, therefore, and desirous of relieving the genuine necessities of all those whose relief appropriately belongs to them, they would request that any and all cases of destitution in the families of Volunteers may be reported to either of the gentlemen of the Committee without delay, that they may receive the aid which humanity and patrotism alike bid us to bestow."

[Signed by the Committee.]

This Committee had just got fairly at work when the disastrous battle at Balls Bluff occurred. It will be remembered that our Company in the Fifteenth Regiment suffered terribly in that engagement, and Captain Simonds, with eighteen of his men, were taken prisoners. Of their fate we knew nothing until November 20th, 1861, when letters were received from Captain Simonds, informing us that they were in prison at Richmond, and making an earnest appeal for help for his men, who were suffering for want of clothing and money. A public meeting was called and held the same evening, at which letters were read from Captain Simonds containing most affecting appeals in behalf of his men, who, he said, had done all that men could do under the circumstances in which they were placed, and were now suffering in prison, without sufficient clothing, and barely food enough to sustain them, and asked if something might not be done for them. The brave, large hearted Captain, indifferent as to his own fate, could not bear to see his men suffering. "God bless them, he says; they are all good men and true, and deserve to be cared for."

A subscription list was opened upon the spot; and during the evening and the next day, $700 in cash was raised; and about one hundred dollars' worth of clothing contributed by the different traders. The money and other supplies were put into the hands of the "Soldiers Relief Committee," who proceeded, in connection with the Ladies Aid Society, at once to make up a large package of clothing, blankets &c., to forward to Richmond. It being doubtful whether the goods and money proposed to be sent would go through if merely forwarded by Express, it was decided to send a special messenger with them to Fortress Monroe, to make arrangements with the General commanding for getting them through the lines. Accordingly, on Monday, November 26th, Mr. Willis of the Committee, started with the same for Fortress Monroe, and also for a visit to the camps of the Fifteenth, Twenty-First and Twenty-Fifth Regiments. His success is chronicled in the following extract from a letter which appeared in the *Reveille* of December 6th, and the letter following it from Captain Simonds, received in about three weeks after the goods were forwarded from Fitchburg.

MR. EDITOR: Having been delegated by the Soldiers' Relief Committee of this town to proceed to Fortress Monroe for the purpose of forwarding money and articles of clothing to our unfortunate soldiers at Richmond, and thinking some report from me might not be unacceptable to the many friends who so promptly came forward with their generous subscriptions, I beg the privilege of the columns of your paper for that purpose.

On Monday, Nov. 25th, I left Fitchburg, accompanied by a friend, for Fortress Monroe, with an ample supply of clothing and money for the prisoners of Co. B. We arrived safely at our place of destination on Wednesday morning, the 27th. We at once sought an interview with Gen. Wool, who commands that post, for the purpose of advising with him in relation to sending the articles forward to Richmond. We found him in the midst of official business, but he was not too busy to give to us his attention and advice in so humane an object as that which we brought to his notice. He appeared to take the greatest interest in the object of our visit, and told us at once that he thought there could be no difficulty in getting the articles through to Richmond, and into the hands of those for whom they were intended, inasmuch as he had just received a letter from Gen. Huger who commands at Norfolk, giving permission to him to send any articles of comfort he might think best to the prisoners at Richmond. At a second interview on the next day, arrangements were perfected for sending the goods, money, and letters, by 'flag of truce,' to Norfolk, thence to be forwarded by express. On the next day, Friday, the 29th, they were sent up, together with some packages from other sources, and I doubt not that ere this they have reached their destination, and gladdened the hearts of our brave but unfortunate soldiers. It is hoped that before many days official acknowledgment of their receipt will be received.

Having completed our business at this point, we left Fortress Monroe on the evening of the 29th, for Annapolis, where are stationed the Twenty-first and Twenty-fifth Mass. Regiments. The former is quartered in the Naval School building, as most of your readers are aware, where they have remained for many weeks, and we learn that their presence and conduct have been very acceptable to the people of this ancient city. They will probably remain at this post for the present. The Twenty-fifth Regiment, Col. Upton, is encamped on a very pleasant spot, about 1 1-2 miles from the city. They appear to be in excellent health, and under the best of discipline, as who could doubt they would be, under such officers as Upton and Sprague. It is expected that this regiment will leave, during the present month, in Burnside's Division, and is to form a part of the First Brigade under Brig. Gen. J. G. Foster, of Conn , he already having assigned it the post of honor —the right of the Brigade. This Regiment had been pronounced by Gov. Andrew and others to be the finest which had left the State. Quartermaster Brown dispenses the substantials from his office in the Navy yard. We are under obligations to him for his generous hospitality. Leaving Annapolis, we started for a visit to the gallant Fifteenth Regiment at Poolesville, via Washington. We reached their camp on Monday evening, after nine hours ride from Washington, in an old-fashioned stage coach, and over a road which pen would fail me to describe. But the hearty greetings which we received on our arrival, from officers and men, at once dispelled any recollection of hardships endured in reaching their camp.

We found the regiment in comparatively good health, and the best of spirits. The disaster of October 21st, though it must have had a depressing influence for the time being, has not had the effect to dishearten or demoralize the regiment at all, so far as I can judge. It is very gratifying to observe the spirit of content and of determination which prevails among the men. In my two days visit to their camp I did not hear the first word of complaint or discouragement."

"RICHMOND, DEC. 15TH, 1861.

MR. WILLIS—

Dear Sir: Your letter bearing date Fortress Monroe, November 25th, came to hand on the 13th inst. I had previously received the clothing, on December 3d, and a letter from A. P. Kimball, informing me of what had been done by the generous people of Fitchburg, of which I have acknowledged the receipt. The cause of the delay of the money I am unable to account for, and began to feel somewhat anxious about it, being informed that it was sent at the same time with the clothing; but now it is all right. I feel under great obligations to yourself and others, who have been so prompt and generous in this matter. Believe me, dear sir, you and they have the heartfelt thanks of myself and those of my companions who are unfortunately here in Richmond. It is a fact of which I shall ever speak with pride, that *Fitchburg was the first* and *only town as yet to aid her prisoners*, and Massachusetts the only State. Since the clothing came from Fitchburg, clothing of all kinds, enough for three hundred and fifty men, has arrived, sent by the State authorities of Massachusetts, for the relief of her men now here in captivity, placing them in comfort in this respect for the winter.

The members of Company B, for whom you inquire, I am sorry to say I have every reason to believe are no more. C. D. Monroe died in the hospital at Leesburg. He was shot through both legs, and died under the operation of amputation—so I am informed. Privates Scott and Benjamin I cannot give any account of, but they are missing from camp, and I think they must have been killed on the field of battle. They were all worthy and true men. "Peace to their ashes."

Five members of the Fifteenth have died here. Two of Company B are sick with measles, but I hope for their recovery.

With many wishes for your prosperity and happiness, I am, sir,

Yours most truly,
C. S. SIMONDS,
Capt. Co. B, 15th Reg't.

H. A. WILLIS, ESQ.

Thus it will be seen, and it is a fact of which we may well be proud, that Fitchburg *was the first in the whole North to extend succor to her suffering prisoners* in the hands of the rebels, an example which was promptly followed by many other communities, and continued from time to time until the barbarity of the rebel authorities put a stop to it, and the horrors of Andersonville, Salisbury and other foul prisons, followed.

During the winter of 1861 and 1862 the Relief Committee were fully organized and at work, relieving the needy families of soldiers.

Our citizens nobly responded to all their calls for money and provisions, and we believe that all were well provided for. At Town Meeting, December 14th, 1861, one thousand dollars was appropriated and placed subject to the order of the Committee as per vote as follows:

"*Voted*, That the town appropriate $1000, which sum shall be put into the hands of a committee of five citizens with full discretion and power to appropriate the same for the soldiers of this town now in, or who may be in, the army, in such manner as they may deem expedient; and that T. R. Boutelle, Alvah Crocker, L. H. Bradford, H. L. Read and H A. Willis be that committee."

The operations of this committee extended over a period of two years, when its labors ceased.

The whole amount of cash contributed to its Treasury by subscription, donations of individuals, from the "Amateur Dramatic Club," and town appropriation, was about two thousand dollars, all of which was judiciously expended for the benefit of the soldiers and their families. The amount of clothing and farm produce received and disbursed was also large, but no accurate account of the same has been preserved.

Although this Committee ceased to exist after October, 1863, the following pages will show that the welfare and comfort of our soldiers continued to be, as it had been, an object of the highest regard and constant, watchful care of our citizens.

After nearly all of the great battles, committees were sent to the front with large quantities of supplies—and to care for and bring home the wounded.

AFTER "BALL'S BLUFF."
1861.

The disastrous battle of Ball's Bluff was fought October 21st, 1861. News was received a few days later of the terrible suffering our men had undergone in the unequal contest. This was the first battle in which Fitchburg men had been engaged, and it produced much excitement, for details of the affair came forward slowly.

We think, however, that a public meeting was not called, but that the Selectmen, after conferring with some of the leading citizens, decided to send a committee to the camp of the Fusiliers immediately, and Dr. Alfred Hitchcock, A. P. Kimball, C. Marshall and Stephen Shepley were selected to go. They left at once for Poolesville, Md., taking with them supplies of clothing and delicacies for the sick and wounded. They spent several days with the soldiers, and returned, bringing with them George T. Daniels and G. Bowman Simonds, both badly wounded.

They reported the remnant of the regiment in good health, and as full of fight as ever. The sight of faces from home seemed to cheer them much, and there is no doubt that the policy thus inaugurated of sending committees of citizens to the front, after severe battles, and which was continued through the war, was highly beneficial as well as gratifying to the soldiers. It gave them assurance of the regard in which they were held by their fellow citizens at home, and did much to sustain them in the hour of trial.

AFTER "ROANOKE ISLAND."

Immediately upon receipt of news of the battle of Roanoke Island, the Soldiers' Relief Committee, in connection with the Ladies' Aid Society, sent Hale W. Page, Esq., and L. H. Bradford, Esq., to the scene of action to look after the dead and wounded of the Twenty-first and Twenty-fifth Regiments. Dr. A. Hitchcock of this town, was also sent by the Governor in behalf of the State. They were very successful in their mission, and after spending a few days with the regiments, administering to the comfort of the sick and wounded, they started on the return, with about a dozen wounded soldiers belonging in this town, arriving about the 10th of March. We subjoin their report.

REPORT OF THE ROANOKE COMMISSIONERS.

"*To the Selectmen of Fitchburg, and the Chairman of the Soldiers' Relief Committee:*

GENTLEMEN :—We submit a joint report of our mission to Roanoke Island, to look after our sick and wounded soldiers of the battle of February 8th. Immediately after being designated for the object, we made hurried preparations for our journey, and arriving on Monday, February 17th, at Philadelphia, we were furnished with free tickets to Baltimore and back, by H. F. Kenney, Esq., our former townsman, who afforded us other facilities for our comfort and transportation. Arriving at Fortress Monroe with letters from our Selectmen and Hon. Alvah Crocker, we at once obtained an interview with General Wool, who endorsed our papers "to any master of a vessel going South, as a patriotic and merciful mission." We left Hampton Roads on the steamer Jersey Blue, Captain Jackaway, the same afternoon, with two hundred and fifty soldiers from the hospital at Annapolis, going to join their regiments in General Burnside's expedition.

After sailing down the coast to within a short distance of Cape Hatteras, the wind from the northeast, with heavy squalls and a rough sea, the storm all the time increasing, the captain deemed it imprudent to proceed, gave orders to about ship, and we returned the next day to the place of our departure. On Thursday we left again in the same steamer, but a northeast storm coming on when outside of Cape Henry, we returned inside of the lighthouse, and came to anchor under the guns of the blockading steamer Cambridge, and laid there through the storm until the 23d, when a boat coming alongside from her, we concluded to leave our crowded vessel and seek another conveyance. The officers of the steamer were mostly Massachusetts citizens, and offered us the hospitalities of the ship and conveyance to Fortress Monroe, which we gladly accepted. On Tuesday, the 25th, we took passage on the steamer Eastern State, Captain Teel, and had a pleasant voyage except once in the night we got into the breakers on the rebel coast, arriving at stormy Hatteras Inlet after our third attempt, in safety. We at once addressed ourselves to the task of getting conveyance to Roanoke Island, and after spending four days, bandied about from steamer to steamer, were offered a passage on the old ferry boat Chancellor Livingston, which was loaded with men and material, including one hundred and fifty horses of Captain Belcher's Fourth Rhode Island Battery. After sailing, we learned that his acting physician, James S. Greene of Fitchburg, was sick at the hospital at the Inlet, and we determined if possible, to take him home with us on our return. We arrived at Roanoke Island March 2d, being the fifteenth day of our journey, and after a weary walk up the beach three miles in a dripping rain, we reached Colonel Upton's Headquarters. Like a true soldier as he is, he at once welcomed us to Camp Foster and to his hospitalities. We here met the other staff officers of the Twenty-fifth Regiment Mass. Volunteers., who gave us a hearty welcome.

Col. Upton and Quartermaster Brown when informed of the object of our visit, thanked us with tears of gratitude again and again, assuring us how highly they esteemed the kindness and sympathy of friends at home in sending us down after their sick and wounded, and said if we had brought thousands of dollars from our citizens it would not have begun to do them as much good—it plainly showed they were cared for while breasting the possibilities of war.

After spending nearly four days on the island, renewing old friendships and forming new, visiting the sick and wounded, seeing and taking by the hand all of our townsmen, and in looking out the graves of the dead, we began to make preparation to return home, and suggested that packages or letters entrusted to our care, would be safely delivered. At our embarkation we had upwards of forty boxes of trophies, nearly the whole for Massachusetts, and a large number of letters.

We went on board the steamer Ellen S. Terry, the 5th inst., with about two hundred souls; one hundred and twenty-five were sick and wounded, the victims of the battle of February 8th, in charge of Dr. Alfred Hitchcock of this town, sent home by General Burnside. The Dr. had kindly obtained transportation, and invited us to assist in alleviating the sufferings of the brave fellows. On the 6th inst. we arrived at Hatteras Inlet, but too late to pass over the "Swash" that night in the steamer. About 8 o'clock we obtained a boat's crew from a distant vessel, and late at night we landed at Fort Hatteras, and started over the beach for Fort Clark, and found our sick townsman, Mr. Greene, in the hospital. The commander of the post, Col. Nagle, of the Forty-eighth Regiment of Penn. Vols., having his camp some four miles up on the island, one of our number made an early visit to his quarters, through a perfect hurricane of wind and sand, and obtained the necessary furlough for Mr. Greene. That day we had the hardest blow of the season, and our steamer, in attempting to come down, went on to the "swash," where she stuck fast, with her flag hung in distress, until near sunset, when she steamed off the quicksands. The next morning, being the

8th inst., we engaged a platoon of contrabands, and took our sick friend and his luggage on board of the steamer, and, being all on board, we left the inlet, and went over the bar in safety.

We reached Baltimore the next night, at half-past eleven o'clock, and landed some forty of our passengers, and as we desired to land our sick and wounded at Philadelphia, one of us traveled the streets of Baltimore until half-past two o'clock in the morning, in pursuit of a pilot to take us through the Cheaspeake and Delaware Canal. One having been obtained, the steamer left at three o'clock for Philadelphia, where we arrived at sunset, landing at the depot of the Camden & Amboy Railroad Co. Suitable cars having been provided, we found it no easy task to remove our sick and wounded, fifteen of whom were obliged to be carried from the steamer on litters. We left at night, arriving the next morning by day-light at Jersey City. Soon afterwards, Col. Frank E. Howe came over, and proposed that we proceed over the ferry with teams to the Park Barracks in New York, where breakfast was provided for us. At two o'clock P. M., we left for the depot of the New York & New Haven Railroad Co., on 27th street; but our men, sick and wounded as they were, and their luggage, were refused admittance, until the arrival of Colonel Howe, at about three o'clock, who gave his personal security for our transportation, and we left the city, arriving that evening at Springfield at nine o'clock, where a bountiful supply of refreshments was served in the cars by Mayor Bemis. Just before midnight, we reached Worcester, and the Mayor, Hon. P. Emory Aldrich, met us at the depot, and carefully brought us to the Bay State House, where all our wants were generously provided for by the city. At about noon the next day, being the 12th inst., we arrived at Fitchburg, having been absent twenty-five days.

In this account our townsmen will see that ours was no pleasure trip, except the pleasure of finding our hearts and hands filled with constant labor for the sick and wounded; not of our own town only, but all of the sick and suffering whom a common cause had made brothers.

L. H. BRADFORD,
H. W. PAGE.

Fitchburg, March 13th, 1862."

AFTER ANTIETAM.

1862.

The battle of Antietam was fought Sept. 17th, 1862, and immediately upon receipt of the news of the same, a meeting of the citizens was called to take measures for the relief of our suffering soldiers at the front.

A large amount of money and supplies were contributed, and a committee chosen to visit the late battle-field and administer to the comfort of the sick and wounded. The committee consisted of Dr. Alfred Hitchcock, Alvah Crocker, A. P. Kimball, Benj. Prentiss, Norman Stone, and Alonzo Davis.

They visited Sharpsburg, Frederick, Middletown, Harper's Ferry, and Washington, and found much to be done for our poor soldier boys. Through them, every sick and wounded soldier of the Fifteenth and Twenty-first Regiments received five dollars in cash, of which they were sadly in need, not having been paid off for five months.

They obtained the consent of the authorities to take the wounded home, but were unable to procure transportation from the government, and returned without them. But Mr. Crocker immediately returned to Washington, and through the combined efforts of Dr. Hitchcock and himself, arrangements were soon perfected, and a large number of the men brought safely to their homes.

These gentlemen deserve much credit for their indefatigable efforts for the soldiers' comfort. Dr. Hitchcock's skill as a surgeon was in ample request during his stay in the neighborhood of the battle field where thousands were languishing and suffering from wounds of every description. They have the gratitude of many a soldier, as well as that of their fellow citizens.

AFTER FREDERICKSBURG.
1862.

No committee was sent to the battle field of Fredericksburg immediately after the battle, but supplies were promptly sent forward as usual. Our army went into winter quarters soon after at Falmouth, and during the winter two prominent members of the Ladies' Soldiers Aid Society (Mrs. E. Torrey and Mrs. L. H. Bradford) visited the camps of the Fifteenth and Twenty-first Regiments, taking some little comforts for the boys, and what was more, taking to them by their own presence, the assurance that the wives and sisters and daughters of Fitchburg were working as earnestly in their behalf as ever, and would continue to do their share as long as they should need their sympathy and care. We doubt not that their visit did something to cheer the drooping spirits of our brave ones during this, the darkest winter of the whole war.

AFTER "GETTYSBURG."
1863.

The following account of measures taken for the relief of our soldiers immediately after the battle of Gettysburg, is from the *Reveille* of July 16th, 1863:

"In view of the wants of our sick and wounded now lying in Baltimore, Philadelphia, and in the vicinity of Gettysburg, and the probability of another battle, notice was given from the several pulpits of Fitchburg, on Sunday, July 12th, 1863, of a meeting of citizens in the evening to take measures to raise and forward supplies. The meeting was fully attended, and was opened with prayer by Rev. Mr. Heard. Hon. Alvah Crocker presided, and T. K. Ware, Esq. was chosen secretary. A general committee was chosen, and one lady and one gentleman from each school district, to solicit supplies and subscriptions. Messrs. Crocker, Heard, and Hitchcock addressed the meeting, setting forth in earnest and eloquent terms the wants and sufferings of our brave soldiers, and Rev. Mr. Brooks made the closing prayer. The results of this appeal to our citizens were the following contributions, which were forwarded Monday evening in charge of H. F. Coggshall, to Mr. Stuart at Philadelphia, disbursing agent of the Christian Commission, to be distributed in the hospitals and otherwise, for the benefit of such of the sick and wounded soldiers as may be in the most urgent need, Mr. Coggshall being instructed to offer his services in the distribution, should they be needed.

One thousand sixty-nine dollars and sixty cents in money, three hundred eighty-nine cotton and woolen shirts, seventy-eight sheets, fifty-one pairs socks, forty handkerchiefs, sixty-eight pillow cases, six vests, fifteen pairs pantaloons, three dressing gowns, three pairs slippers, fourteen pairs drawers, twenty-eight towels, eight pillows, thirty-four linen and cotton coats, three boxes and fifty-three cakes soap, two bags sago, one bag hops, one bag rose leaves, eighty-one cases jellies and preserves, three bags of apple, thirty-seven dozen cases condensed milk, one hundred and one bottles wine, eight of rum, one of brandy, one of whiskey, and a large quantity of compresses and bandages, the whole being carefully packed in nine barrels and five large boxes, each barrel and box containing in the top a schedule of its contents. It is but just to state that this noble contribution is but an addition to the constant and regular supplies which have been forwarded through the " Ladies' Aid Society" and other channels, by the citizens of Fitchburg from the commencement of the war, amounting to many thousands of dollars."

Subsequent to sending the above, Dr. Alfred Miller and George Robbins were sent to the front to personally care for our wounded. They spent several days in the hospitals at Gettysburg and vicinity, and rendered good service to the suffering soldiers. We regret that we have no report from them to give insertion here.

WHAT WAS DONE WITH THE SUPPLIES.

REPORT OF CHAIRMAN OF CITIZENS' COMMITTEE.

" The committee chosen by the citizens of Fitchburg at a meeting held on Sunday evening, July 12th, for the purpose of raising money and articles of clothing, wines, etc., wish to have the citizens know what use was made of the supplies so generously, and so promptly contributed.

On Monday, July 13th, money had been contributed by our citizens to the amount of one thousand seventy-nine dollars and sixty cents ($1079.60,) also, nine barrels and five boxes of articles of clothing, bandages, liquors, etc., for the sick and wounded at Gettysburg and other hospitals, which was disposed of as follows:

```
Paid W. & E. Lewis for thirty-one dozen cans condensed milk, ......$77.50
     Ira Carleton & Co. for meal to pack glass in,..........................7.80
     George H. Stuart, Chairman U. S. Christian Commission,......900.00
     Expenses of H. F. Coggshall to Gettysburg,........................32.00
     Balance of money to Ladies' Soldiers Aid Society, ................62.30
                                                                        $1079.60
```

H. F. Coggshall, Esq., as agent, left Fitchburg on Monday, July 14th, at 5½ P. M., with the packages and money, and arrived in Philadelphia and delivered them to Geo. H. Stuart, Esq., chairman of the U. S. Christian Commission, on Tuesday, at 12 o'clock. Mr. Coggshall went forward to Gettysburg, arriving there Thursday morning, under the direction of Mr. Stuart, and took charge of the delivery of the packages at the hospitals at Gettysburg. Much credit is due to Mr. Coggshall for the prompt and efficient manner in which the contributions were forwarded to the points where needed. ALPHEUS P. KIMBALL,

Chairman of Town Committee.

AFTER THE "WILDERNESS."
1864.

The news of the battle of the Wilderness reached us on Sunday, May 8th, 1864. A meeting of the citizens was called for the evening of that day, at the Town Hall, and was fully attended.

An Executive Committee, consisting of A. P. Kimball, T. K. Ware, L. H. Bradford, Rodney Wallace, H. F. Coggshall, H. A. Blood, J. E. Manning, A. R. Ordway and E. T. Miles, was chosen, to receive and disburse contributions. The result of the meeting and the efforts of the next forenoon, amounted to $1700 in cash and sixteen barrels and bundles of carefully selected stores for the sick and wounded, with which Messrs. A. Hitchcock, H. A. Goodrich and E. B. Hayward started for the front, on Monday evening. How they discharged their trust is well shown by the following able and interesting letter:

LETTER OF ALFRED HITCHCOCK AND OTHERS.

"*To A. P. Kimball, Esq., Chairman of Citizens' Committee, &c:*

DEAR SIR:—The undersigned, under instruction from your Committee, left Fitchburg, May 9th, 1864, having in charge the funds and supplies entrusted to us for the relief of the wounded soldiers in the recent battles in Virginia. We reached Washington Tuesday evening, May 10, and immediately reported to the Surgeon General, who detailed us for duty at Fredericksburg, and ordered transportation for ourselves and stores. We reached Belle Plain Wednesday, and reported to Dr. Cuyler, Medical Director of the post, and at his request spent a day there among the wounded, who were arriving in great numbers, en route for Washington. We placed our supplies at this place in charge of the Sanitary Commission, and through their courtesy had them transported direct to Fredericksburg, where they arrived safely in advance of us. We reached Fredericksburg Friday morning, being obliged to camp on the road Thursday night to escape surprise and capture by the guerrillas. Our train consisted of fifty returning ambulance wagons, guarded by cavalry, and our transportation in that train, though against the rule, was due to the courtesy and humanity of the Medical Director at Belle Plain. On reaching Fredericksburg, we immediately reported to Dr. Dalton, the Medical Director at that place, who assigned us to duty with the 9th Corps hospitals, Dr. George W. Snow being the surgeon in charge. The surgeons, weary and exhausted with the week's incessant labor, seemed eagerly grateful for professional assistance, as well as for the no less important aid of good nurses. We entered upon our duties at once, and with little intermission found ourselves constantly and laboriously employed until the morning of our departure, May 21st. Our own townsmen were found as soon as possible, and we can assure you they were studiously cared for, and made very happy by the reception of some of the substantial tokens of your charity. The names of the men and the character of their casualties are already in your possession.

But not to those alone did we restrict our labors, or the disbursement of your charities. The authority given by the Surgeon General enabled us to make requisition on the Government, or the Sanitary or Christian Commissions for any needed supplies they had on hand, so that virtually the supplies you sent by us were actually distributed to the sufferers themselves, so far as we had occasion to do so. The balance was distributed on the order of ourselves or other surgeons, to the most needy, without regard to locality or rank.

The supplies you forwarded by Messrs. Benton and Browning reached Belle Plain in safety, and there remained a day or two, until we wrote to Dr. Cuyler, Medical Director, stating the great destitution at Fredericksburg, when he kindly forwarded them (in violation of red tape) in the Medical Purveyor's train. These supplies we had placed in the care of Dr. Snow, surgeon in charge 9th Corps hospitals, to be drawn upon by our orders, and when we left, by the orders of Messrs. Benton and Browning, who still remain on duty, so that this second instalment of supplies reached its destination in the care of, and will be disbursed by your own agents. The third instalment of supplies, which you sent to Gardner Tufts, Esq., at Washington, we directed to be forwarded at once to Miss Clara Barton, at Fredericksburg, to be disbursed at her discretion, and her discretion, wisdom and fidelity are well known in this State, as well as through the army of the Potomac.

It ought, perhaps, here to be stated that the government officials, and the managers of both the Sanitary and Christian Commissions, up to the 15th or 16th instant, entirely under-estimated the magnitude of the exigency. They all said that enough, and even a surplus of stores had gone forward. In this respect they were all mistaken. Representations of the facts, and complaints of the great destitution soon reached Washington, and about the 17th or 18th inst. new vigor was evinced, and vastly more ample supplies arrived at Belle Plain, with the needed wagons and horses for transit to Fredericksburg, both from the Government proper and from the two Commissions. When we left, on the 21st inst., there was no longer a destitution, with the exception of cot beds, and these in large numbers were met on Saturday being transported to Fredericksburg. Since the battles, there have been about eight thousand treated in the hospitals at Fredericksburg, many of whom have already been forwarded to Washington, and there now remain about six thousand under treatment. We were highly pleased with the perfect harmony and fraternity which exists, particularly among the working men of the two commissions. They cordially honor each other's requisitions, and seem only ambitious to see which can easiest and quickest furnish the needed cordial to the wounded by the wayside. In all these terrible scenes of suffering we saw no Priests or Levites, but all seemed prompt and kind in using the bandage, or the oil and wine, Samaritan like, for binding up the wounds, without questioning their sectarian origin or mode of contribution. All seemed eager for present duty, content to wait the Divine benediction, "Inasmuch as ye have done it unto one of the least of these, ye have done it unto me."

We received from your treasurer, on our departure, $500 in money, and from that we have disbursed and paid out for travelling and other expenses, the sum of $142.69, and have on hand, which we herewith return, the sum of $357.31, as per schedule annexed.

From our observations in the field and in the hospitals, we are satisfied that your contributions had better be chiefly sent in hospital supplies, more especially such articles as the Ladies' Soldiers Aid Society can make, such as shirts, (of cheap fabric) drawers, socks, bandages, old linen or cotton cloth, cast off shirts or pants, if mended and fit for a few days wear; cordials, and every article for the sick diet, including canned fruits, jellies, pickles, etc.

The privation and hardship incident to the energetic and quick discharge of our duties as almoners of your bounties to the wounded soldiers of the army of the Potomac, is more than compensated by the joy and gratitude we witnessed from those suffering men. We close our report, invoking for all givers and recipients of these well timed charities, the blessing of Him who, though the God of battles, is mindful of the fallen sparrow, and fails not to temper the wind to the shorn lamb.

ALFRED HITCHCOCK,
E. B HAYWARD,
H. A. GOODRICH.

Fitchburg, May 24, 1864.

This prompt and generous action of our people was extensively noticed by the public journals of the State, and Fitchburg, for her repeated efforts in this direction, became noted for the very liberal care she bestowed upon her soldiers.

During the same week, several hundred dollars were raised and forwarded to the Sanitary and Christian Commissions, and additional supplies and nurses were sent out at the instance of the Committee who remained in the hospitals in and around Fredericksburg.

AFTER BATTLES BEFORE PETERSBURG.
1864.

In the latter part of May and first of June, our Twenty-fifth and Thirty-sixth Regiments were engaged in the battles before Petersburg, and at "Coal Harbor," and suffered severely. The Citizens' Committee delegated Mr. H. A. Hatch to visit the Regiments with supplies, and care for the wounded. He was not able to reach the front, but visited all of our men in the hospitals near Fortress Monroe, and administered to their necessities. He discharged his trust we believe in a manner satisfactory to the Soldiers and to the Committee.

Of course we cannot begin to put upon record here an account of all that was done for the soldiers in the field by the "Volunteers" at home. New enterprises in their behalf were constantly being set on foot, and money flowed like water whenever an emergency came. Nearly all gave liberally according to their means. There were many noted instances of marked liberality in contributions as well as the most self-sacrificing labors of those who were ever foremost in the good work, and we would be glad to record their names, but where all did so well, it would seem invidious to make special mention of any particular cases.

We have no accurate record of the whole amount contributed for the relief of the soldiers during the war. From the best estimates we can make, we find that the amount received and disbursed by the various organizations and committees is from ten to twelve thousand dollars. And this was principally for the benefit of the soldiers themselves. Much was also done for their families in the way of supplies, of which no estimate is made, and the town authorities were called upon to assist, to some extent, the families of soldiers, which we have not taken into the account.

Our citizens were fully awake to the condition and wants of the men who went to fight our battles. Few, if any, communities can show a better record in this regard. We may well look back upon it with pride, but not in a spirit of boasting; for did we do anything more than duty demanded? To have fallen far short of that, would indeed be mortifying now. All who worked or contributed, have their reward in the consciousness of good deeds, well done.

LETTER FROM AN AGENT OF THE CHRISTIAN COMMISSION.

The following letter was written by Mr. Frank H. Snow of this town, who, in the spring of 1865, gave a few weeks of service to the noble work of the Christian Commission.

As a description of the scenes at the rear of a battle field, we have thought it worthy of insertion here.

"HEADQUARTERS CHRISTIAN COMMISSION,
5th Army Corps, Nottoway C. H., Va.,
April 29th, 1865.

To THE SENTINEL:—Since the Army of the Potomac broke camp one month ago to-day, it has achieved victories which at that time would have been regarded as the wild dreams of an enthusiast, but which now constitute the most glorious chapter in the military history of our nation. The 'hundred days' of Napoleon, productive of nought but bloodshed, lose all their lustre in comparison with these thirty days of Grant, within which, with a loss of life and limb comparatively slight, we have witnessed the death struggle of the most gigantic rebellion the world ever saw.

The surrender of Johnston's army, announced to our troops yesterday morning by a dispatch from General Grant, has served partially to remove the deep cloud of grief which has covered our army since the assassination of its beloved Commander-in-chief, and all are filled with joy once more at the thought of a speedy return to home and friends.

Perhaps a few notes of the campaign may not be uninteresting to the readers of the Sentinel.

Wednesday, March 29th.—At three o'clock this morning, the Fifth Corps silently and cautiously left its position on the extreme left of the lines near Petersburg, and swung round as rapidly as possible in order to outflank the rebel right, and strike the South Side R. R. This road runs from Petersburg to Lynchburg, and is of inestimable value to the rebels as a source of supply. In order to conceal our movement, if possible, from the enemy, the drummers were all left behind, to sound the morning reveille at six o'clock, as usual.

Eight delegates of the Christian Commission accompany the columns of the Fifth Corps. We have one large wagon heavily laden with supplies of cordials and delicacies for the sick and wounded, and our smaller wagon, which we call "coffee machine," but to which the soldiers have to-day applied a great variety of names, such as "Flying Artillery," and the "Wandering Jew." It is *sui generis*, being the only one in existence, and somewhat peculiar in appearance. It is in two parts, like a piece of artillery. The forward part, or limber, contains an abundance of ammunition, in the form of tea, coffee, corn-starch, farina, sugar, and condensed milk. Attached to the limber is the artillery itself, consisting of three large boilers for the making of tea and coffee by the wholesale. The arrangement for fuel much resembles that of a steam fire engine, so that a fire may be kindled at a moment's notice. Underneath all, is a wood-box, and above all, three smoke-pipes penetrate the air. This invention is intended for use upon the battle-field, and has often been of great service. By it twenty-five gallons of tea and coffee can be made in fifteen minutes, and the supply kept up as long as needed.

After marching, with as much rapidity as was consistent with caution, until four o'clock, P. M., our advance guard met the enemy, and a sharp encounter ensued,—the first engagement of the campaign—short, but bloody. As soon as the rapidity of the firing indicated the fact that our services were needed, five of our number started on the double quick for the front, with the "coffee machine." We reached the scene of conflict just at the right time. The wounded were being brought in ambulances and on stretchers, to the "Spain House," situated about a half mile from the woods, where the fight was fiercely raging. The house is soon filled with bleeding, mangled, tortured heroes, who wait patiently, and many of them until morning, for their turn upon the amputating tables. The ground about the house, for rods, is soon covered with the poor fellows, who now lie so thick that care must be taken not to step upon them. In less than half an hour after our arrival, we have an abundance of hot coffee, beef tea, and milk punch in readiness, which we distribute among the sufferers, thus mitigating their almost maddening thirst, and furnishing nourishment and stimulus to their exhausted physical energies. Many a "God bless you" do we receive for the Christian Commission, and not a few, unable to speak, give expression to the depth of their gratitude by an appreciative look, or grasp of the hand.

Late at night, having hastily pitched our tent, we roll ourselves in our blankets and take turns in sleeping for an hour or two. Strange to say, our sleep is most sound, though surrounded by groaning and dying men."

Friday, March 31st.—The 5th Corps, having held the battle-field of Wednesday, advances again this morning. Having proceeded several miles with slight opposition from the enemy, Lee precipitates against it a heavy force of infantry in the hope of breaking our lines by an overwhelming attack. The attempt was at first successful, and our boys were driven back for two or three miles, leaving their killed and wounded in the hands of the foe. In the afternoon however, the lost ground was re-taken, our lines were advanced nearly to the South Side Railroad, and a junction was formed with Sheridan and his cavalry.

While the rest of our number remained with the wounded at the Spain House, two of us were detailed to go forward to the battle-field with canteens filled with water and stimulants. We approached the scene of active conflict during the time of the temporary repulse of our forces. As we entered a large open field some half a mile from the advance line, whence proceeded the incessant booming of artillery and heavy roar of musketry, great numbers of men came running toward us upon the double quick on their way to a place of safety. Some of them were non-combatants, but by far the greater number were soldiers skulking from duty—men upon whom the faithful have bestowed the most opprobrious epithets. A provost guard was soon sent back to check the farther progress of this cowardly panic. The wounded were being brought out from the woods beyond the field and sent back in ambulances to the hospital. Among them was General Dennison of the Maryland Brigade. We passed into the woods and soon came in sight of the front line of our forces and could see the flash of the guns as they dashed against the rebel lines. Now and then a Minnie ball would come flying by us with its peculiar, sharp, whistling sound. We passed along the second line of battle, and administered doses of Jamaica Ginger to our wearied boys who had been on their feet in mud and rain for thirty-six hours. About this time the tide of battle turned, and possession was gained of the battle ground of the morning, upon which the killed and wounded of both sides were still lying just where they fell. In the midst of the woods was a cleared spot about one acre in extent, where occurred the bloodiest conflict of the day. Men lay thickly strewn upon the ground, many of them cold in death, their unclosed eyes turned upward in vacant stare, and their stiffened hands and arms raised toward Heaven as if in supplication to God for vengeance upon their murderers. In one part of the field lay four Union boys side by side, all killed in the most shocking manner by the same relentless cannon ball.

And, O, what agony was depicted upon the features of many of the wounded men. Here lay little John Rogers of the Eleventh Pennsylvania Regiment, mortally wounded in the abdomen, and suffering the most excruciating tortures. There lay a man with a terrible gash in his head through which the brains protruded in ghastly profusion. It was an inestimable privilege to be allowed to moisten the parched lips of these patient sufferers with a little cold water from the spring near by, or to note down a few farewell words of some dying boy to his much loved mother. Surely this nation is paying a terrible price for indulgence in the enormity of chattel slavery.

While the fight was raging most fearfully this morning, an incident occurred which excited the wonder of all who beheld it. In the centre of the clearing above referred to, stood a little hut occupied by a colored woman with her two children, one of whom was nine years old, and the other but just old enough to walk. The mother, by reason of sickness, was unable to make her escape from the danger, but remained within her dwelling all through that fearful day. A kind Providence watched over her and shielded her from harm. While the storm of lead was at its height, she sent forth her little ones hand in hand, to make their way if possible, to a place of refuge. By an unseen hand they were almost miraculously guided across that terrible field, and through three lines of battle, until they reached the rear of the Union army. Here they were cared for by one of our delegates, who next morning restored them to their anxious mother after the battle storm had rolled onward so far as to make their own abode a place of safety. Even thus through four years of deadly conflict that same unseen hand of God has guided four millions of that sable race from bondage to freedom.

OUR PATRIOT DEAD.

> "They never fail who die
> In a great cause; the block may soak their gore;
> Their heads may sodden in the sun; their limbs
> Be strung to city gates and castle walls—
> But still their spirit walks abroad. Though years
> Elapse, and others share as dark a doom,
> They but augment the deep and sweeping thoughts
> Which overpower all others, and conduct
> The world at last to freedom."

We approach with reverence the subject of "our dead." We know full well that *no* pen can do them full justice. We would be glad to speak individually of all the brave ones whose names appear in the list below, but for want of space, can only give obituary notices of a few of those best known to us, as representatives of the rest, of whom we must speak in general terms. Of the eight hundred (more or less,) of Fitchburg men who have served in the army at different times during the war, one hundred forty-two, or upwards of one in six, have fallen by the bullet or by disease contracted in the service.

Most of the great battles have found victims of our citizens. They fell at Ball's Bluff, Bull Run, in the battles of the Peninsula, at Antietam, Fredericksburg, Port Hudson, Gettysburg, the Wilderness, Petersburg, Richmond, and on scores of fields of minor importance, and their remains make sacred to us the soil of nearly every Rebel State. Thirteen commissioned officers and one hundred twenty-nine enlisted men make up Fitchburg's "offering" upon the altar of our country.

Here is our "Roll of Honor." We have endeavored to make it as correct as possible, and think it nearly perfect. This list simply gives the names, company and regiment of the fallen, without specifying the manner or cause of death, &c., but by reference to the alphabetical roll at the end of this volume, particulars will be found.

THE "UNRETURNING BRAVE."

OFFICERS.

Lt. Col. Geo. E. Marshall, 40th Rgt.
Capt. Clark S. Simonds, 15th "
" John Murkland, 15th "
" Geo. H. Bailey, 53d "
" Jerome K. Taft, 53d "
" Joseph W. Gird, 57th "
Lieut. George G. Nutting, 53d Rgt.
" Chas. E. Upton, 25th "
" James Graham, Jr., 25th "
" Geo. B. Simonds, 15th "
" Henry A. Beckwith, 21st "
" Fred. H. Sibley, 36th "

John M. Whittemore, 3d Assistant Engineer, Gunboat Mohican.

ENLISTED MEN.

George Adams, Co. B 15th.
Harrison W. Battles, D 21st.
Henry D. Brigham, B 53d.
Wm. S. Bardeen, A 53d.
Alvaranzo Bigelow, D 21st.
Horace R. Barker, D 21st.
Wm. S. Boynton, D 21st.
Thomas Bartlett, A. 53d.
Chas. P. Battles, A 53d.
George L. Boss, B 15th.
Herbert D. Beckwith, F 57th.
Ozro A. Brigham, F 57th.
Chas. H. Brown, 2d, 22d.
James Brownson, D 21st.
Andrew M. Brock, D 21st.
John Campbell, B 15th.
Daniel Carpenter, B 15th.
Horace M. Churchill, A 53d.
Edward L. P. Cochran, B 53.
Israel Cummings, D 21st.
Geo. P. Cotting, F 25th.
Henry J. Cutting, A 36th.
Wm. M. Caldwell, F 57th.
Gilbert Cheney, D 2d.
Joseph W. Chase, A 36th.
Chas. W. Crehore, A 30th.
Rufus H. Carter, D 21st.
Samuel F. Dadmun, F 25th.
Edward M. Derby, F 57th.

Edwin A. Derby, F 1st.
Geo. A. Davis, H 4th H. A.
Romanzo Downe, Navy.
John W. Eager, C 25th.
Artemas W. Ellenwood, F 25th.
Amos S. Eastman, D 21st.
Edward P. Farwell, A 53d.
John Flynn, A 36th.
Henry A. Friar, E 33d.
George G. Farwell, A 32d.
Artemas S. Farwell, F 25th.
Chas. E. Goodrich, D 21st.
Edwin Hartwell, D 26th.
Geo. H. Howe, H 21st.
David A. Harrington, A 53d.
Francis D. Hill, A 53d.
Wm. Hodgman, D 21st.
Frank A. Hildreth, B 15th.
Chas. Hall, F 25th.
Rodney Hall, F 57th.
Edwin Holman, H 23d.
Wm. Howard, I 6th N. H.
John M. Hastings, F 57th.
Henry K. Hill, G 2d H. A.
Wm. H. Hayden, Navy.
Jere. Harrigan, A 36th.
Joseph Hunes, A 36th.
A. J. Hartwell, A 36th.
Henry L. Joslin, B 15th.

Michael Kavanaugh, C 28th.
J. Henry Kendall, A 53d.
Geo. E. Knight, A 36th.
Daniel Kiely, F 57th.
Geo. E. Keyes, A 36th.
Lewis M. Kimpton, D 20th.
Geo. Lowe, F 25th.
Philip Lane, A 14th.
Amos W. Lawrence, B 15th.
Jefferson C. Lakin, D 2d.
John L. Lamson, I 25th.
Alvin W. Lamb, A 32d.
Chas. D. Monroe, B 15th.
Simon F. Marshall, 3d Cavalry.
Chas. F. Montjoy, D 21st.
Michael Miles, F 57th.
John Marsh, B 15th.
Simon May, D 21st.
Michael McMahon, E 25th.
Patrick McCarty, F 57th.
Thomas Mahan, A 36th.
John Markham, I 70th N. Y.
James McIntire, G 21st.
Ai D. Osborne, B 15th.
Thomas Oaks, A 36th.
Jerry O'Brien, F 57th.
Geo. W. Philips, B 15th.
John H. Prichard, G 2d H. A.
Wm. T. Peabody, F 57th.
Horace T. Pope, B 15th.
Fred W. Parks, F 57th.
Wm. H. Partridge, F 25th.
Cyrus Putnam, F 25th.
Henry O. Pierce, D 2d.
Eldridge L. Robinson, F 53d.
Martin Ryan, F 57th.
Wm. Roach, F 25th.
Owen T. Raymond, F 57th.
Robert W. Sampson, F 12th U. S. I.
Orwell L. Stockwell, A 36th.
Patrick C. Sullivan, K 28th.
Michael Spencer, C 28th.
Wm. H. Shattuck, A. 53d.
Chas. W. Stuart, A 53d.
Wm. H. Simonds, A 53d.
Solon W. Spooner, B 53d.
Samuel Stearns, B 15th.
William Skye, F 57th.
William Sawtelle, G 32d.
Timothy Sheahan, A 5th.
Thomas Scollay, B 15th.
Albert A. Smith, K 36th.
George C. Taylor, B 15th.
James Townsend, A 32d.
Thomas Tolman, D 22d.
Calvin E. Tolman, D 21st.
James M. Underwood, M 2d Cal. Cav.
N. Bradlee Upham, A 53d.
Edwin F. Vose, D 2d.
Henry S. Woodbury, A 53d.
Chas. M. Whitney, D 21st.
Geo. G. Winchester, A 53d.
Fred. L. Works, A 53d.
Benj. K. Wiley, B 53d.
Albert C. Wisley, B 53d.
Robert F. Webb, A 36th.
Milan B. Waite, F 25th.
Oliver H. Whittemore, F 25th.
William Wooldridge, A 53d.
George Watts, F 57th.
Ambrose Wilkins, 7th Batt.

CORPORAL F. A. HILDRETH, CO. B, FIFTEENTH REGIMENT.

Corporal Hildreth was the first victim of the war from this town. He died of disease at Poolesville, Md., Oct. 7th, 1861.

He was but nineteen years old, and came, originally, from Lunenburg, though he had lived among us for some time previous to the war. He had been a member of the "Washington Guards," but as the "Fusiliers" were the first to organize for the war, and as he was anxious to enter the service, he at once enlisted in that Company. He was a good soldier, and his many excellent traits of character had endeared him to all his comrades.

His was the first death in their ranks, and they felt it deeply. It brought home to them and to us, the fact that some must perish for the cause, and that their exposed lives must necessarily become the prey for disease in every form, as well as for the bullet of the enemy. He was buried with military honors at Poolesville, Md. It was proposed to have his remains brought home and buried with due honors, and arrangements were made by the "Guards" to receive them; but for some reason it was decided to leave them where they were buried for the time being, and we think they still rest there. There let him rest—near to that fatal field of Ball's Bluff, where his comrades a few days after his death were called to suffer so much. His grave may yet be an object of pilgrimage to his fellow soldiers in years to come, when they shall seek to visit the spot which was their home for so many months, and where they met their first great trial.

CAPTAIN C. S. SIMONDS, FIFTEENTH REGIMENT.
(COMMUNICATED.)

Captain Clark S. Simonds was born at Groton, Mass., on the 24th of February, 1834, and was killed on the 17th of September, 1862, at the battle of "Antietam," in Maryland, being twenty-eight years old at his death.

His parents moved to Fitchburg when he was quite young, and he resided there most of the time until his death. He was a man greatly beloved and highly esteemed by all who knew him. His character was above reproach. He early took a deep and lively interest in the Volunteer Militia of the State, and particularly in the "Fitchburg Fusiliers," of which company he became a member, and by strict attention to the duties incumbent upon him, and his firm adherence to discipline, coupled with that geniality of disposition so peculiarly his, he won for himself the honorable position which he held at his death, by the unanimous wish and vote of his company.

At the breaking out of the war, he was one of the first to lay aside the civic dress and don the uniform of the patriot, which he wore with marked distinction to himself and great credit to the town. His company ever stood at the head in point of drill and discipline, in the glorious old Fifteenth Regiment. Upon the 21st of October, 1861, he crossed the Potomac river at Ball's Bluff, at the head of his company, (against the earnest protestations of his friends, for he was exceedingly weak from loss of blood from a wound received the evening before while marching to the river from Poolesville,) to meet the enemies of his country for the first time. Never did men march with firmer step and stronger determination to conquer or die, than did his command led by him they all loved, and in whom they placed the utmost confidence. His company being thrown to the front as skirmishers, he accompanied them in command, and while there engaged with the rebel skirmishers, the rebel cavalry, by a sudden dash around their left flank, succeeded in capturing several of the company, and among them, Captain Simonds. He was taken to Richmond and immured in Libby Prison until February 19th, 1862, when he was exchanged. He immediately rejoined the Regiment at Harper's Ferry on the day that it started for Richmond, via the Peninsula. He was in all the battles of the Peninsula in which the Fifteenth Regiment took a part; went with them to the Second Bull Run; thence up through Maryland to the fatal field of Antietam. On that memorable morning, when the trumpet sounded the advance, well do we remember the coolness and quiet manner in which Captain Simonds moved his men to the front, and with what courage and determination he fought during that terrible engagement in which, in the short space of less than twenty-five minutes, over one-half of that gallant regiment lay dead or wounded upon the field; with what reluctance he gave the order to his men to fall back, in obedience to superior officers. He passed safely through that awful storm of shot and shell, to fall by a random shot thrown into the little grove where the regiment was re-forming after having fallen back from their first position, standing in his place just behind his company, cheering them by his noble words of encouragement and hope, and regretting the loss of those who had fallen, while the tears rolled down his manly cheek as he looked for those he loved, and found their places vacant, a rebel shell came whirling and shrieking through the wood, striking the ground about thirty yards in advance of the line, ploughing up the earth, yet speeding on its mission of death. It struck Captain Simonds directly over the heart, killing him instantly. He fell without a groan, and the last word he uttered was "Colonel," addressed to him who by the misfortune of another, was in command of the regiment. His men gathered around him, and with tears coursing down their bronzed cheeks, they tenderly bore him to the rear, hoping that he might yet speak to them once more, but no, he was dead. Leaving him with friends, they returned to their duty, pledging anew their lives, if need be, upon the altar of Liberty. Oh! what a sacrifice! Why should this noble man be selected for the altar on that fatal day? And yet, could the question have been put to him that morning, are you willing to sacrifice your life to-day in defence of our noble flag and the principles it represents? he would have responded unhesitatingly, yes, a thousand times, if need be, for what is my life compared with the safety and happiness of my country?

His was a noble life and a glorious death; he died as he had lived, a true man and a pure patriot, worthy to have his name written in the Temple of Fame, high up among those noble men of the Revolution who sacrificed their lives to gain their country's independence, and thus bequeath to their children the blessings of liberty. They died to secure, he to maintain, preserve and perpetuate those blessings.

He sleeps the sleep of the brave, near his own beloved home, and

> "When Spring, with dewy fingers cold,
> Returns to deck his hallowed mould,
> She then shall dress a sweeter sod
> Than Fancy's feet have ever trod."

J. W. K.

CAPTAIN JOHN MURKLAND, FIFTEENTH REGIMENT.

Capt. Murkland will be pleasantly remembered by many of our citizens. Though not a native of Fitchburg, he was for several years a resident of this town. When the war broke out, he was among the first to enlist in Co. B, Fifteenth Regiment, and was immediately appointed a sergeant, which office he held until after the battle of Antietam, when he was promoted to a Captaincy for special gallantry on that occasion. He had merited, and was fairly entitled to promotion long before this, but was unfairly dealt with in the matter through the influence of persons *not then* officially connected with the Fifteenth Regiment. He was raised to Captain from the rank of Sergeant, on recommendation of Gen. Gorman and Col. Kimball, and we give below the letter of Gen. Gorman to Gov. Andrew, which will be read with interest.

HEADQUARTERS 2D DIV., 2D ARMY CORPS,
Bolivar, Va., Oct. 19, 1862.

Brig. Gen. Schouler, Adjutant General:

SIR :—Since the death of the gallant captain of Co. B, (Capt. Simonds,) there is a vacancy. I now beg leave to present the name of first Sergeant John Murkland. He is eminently fit and qualified, and is now in command of his company. He has nobly won this merited promotion by his gallantry on the battlefield of "Antietam." When Capt. Simonds fell, Lieut. Col. Kimball took the dying man's sword off and said, " I want you to take this sword and lead this company; *will you do it?* He answered gallantly, " I will do so—any where you may order!" This noble answer, made in the face of death and danger, ought to win for him from his country a medal, and *two* captain's commissions, if need be. I trust his Excellency will reward this special gallantry at once.

I am, General, truly yours,
W. A. GORMAN, Brig. Gen.
Commanding Division.

The Governor immediately forwarded a commission, also wrote a letter to the regiment highly complimentary of Murkland, and giving his reasons for his departure from usual custom in thus elevating him at once to a Captaincy. The appointment gave great satisfaction to the regiment, and to his many friends. He was killed at Gettysburg, while bravely leading his men into action.

As a man, he was genial and kind hearted, and beloved by all who knew him. As a soldier, he was prompt and efficient, and a thorough disciplinarian, while none braver than he ever trod the field of battle. His death was deeply lamented by his fellow soldiers and a large circle of friends.

SERG'T GEO. C. TAYLOR, FIFTEENTH REGIMENT.

Young Taylor was one of the early victims of the war. He was among the first to enlist for "three years or the war" in Company B, Fifteenth Regiment. He was at once appointed Sergeant, and filled the office with great ability. He was a thorough soldier. In him were the attractions of youth, a generous-hearted nature, unflinching courage, and a conscientious regard for duty, which secured the affection and regard of all his comrades. After he had enlisted, he was asked by a friend if he expected ever to return. He quickly answered "I shall *go* to the war, and I shall *return*, if God is willing."

He fell upon the terrible field of Ball's Bluff, where so many lives were uselessly sacrificed. His career as a soldier was indeed a short one, but his record is a proud one.

Never soldier entered the service from a purer sense of duty than he. Had he lived longer, we cannot doubt he would have taken a high position in his regiment, for he had already shown the more noble qualities of a man and a soldier.

> "Brave youth! by few is glory's wreath attained,
> But death, or late, or soon, awaiteth all;
> To fight in Freedom's cause is something gained,
> And nothing lost to fall."

AI D. OSBORNE, CO. B, FIFTEENTH REGIMENT.

Ai D. Osborne was born at Ashburnham, in 1833, and the most of his life was spent in our midst. We all remember him as a school-mate,—a modest, unassuming boy, but one who was a general favorite, because of his very amiable character—one who was always ready to share the burden of another, or to espouse the cause of the weaker party in the difficulties incident to school-boy life.

In 1857, he enlisted into the "Fusiliers," to serve for five years. When, in 1861, the war broke out, and soldiers were wanted, and his company decided to volunteer, he cheerfully went with them, saying that "he had belonged to the company for pleasure, and he should not leave it when he was most needed." To his mother he said: "Mother, somebody *must* go, and it is no worse for me to go, than others; all who go leave friends behind." He left with his regiment, and shared its experiences for four months, when at the battle of Ball's Bluff, October 21st, 1861, he received the wound which cost him his life.

We have seen numerous extracts from his letters and diary that indicate great conscientiousness and a keen sense of his duty as a man and a soldier. In one he says: "we expect an onward movement — we are in good spirits, and trust in God and our officers."

In another, speaking of the vices of the army, and especially that of profanity, he says: "but when I return, as I trust I shall, I hope no one will ever have occasion to blush with shame for any habits or vices which I have contracted in the U. S. service."

On the day before the battle, he speaks of the impending conflict, and says: "I am well, and ready for any duty that may devolve upon me." He was shot through the knee during the next day, taken prisoner and carried to Leesburg in an ambulance, together with Thomas P. Taylor, of his company, where they arrived at about four o'clock, P. M. As the attendants were about to take him from the ambulance, he said: "take Taylor out first; he is wounded worse than I am;" thus exhibiting the noble, chivalrous nature of another Philip Sidney.

His leg was amputated the following Thursday, and was so cruelly and clumsily done, that he died from the effects of it and subsequent ill treatment. Immediately after the amputation, he was carried into the room with his friend Taylor, who said to him, "I am very sorry for you," to which he replied "yes, I know you are very sorry, Tom, but what will my poor mother say?" In a few minutes he added, "Let us be men, and call it a misfortune." After this, he grew very cheerful, and had soon formed his plans for the future, after he should be released and fully recover from his wounds. But alas! he was only released by death, which took place Dec. 1st, 1861. His remains were buried at Leesburg, Va.

LIEUT. G. BOWMAN SIMONDS, FIFTEENTH REGIMENT.

The following article appeared in the *Reveille* of June 21st, 1864, and was written by one of our citizens, who knew the subject of it and his family.

"THE WIDOW'S SACRIFICE."—Private letters have brought to us the sad news of the death of three noble brothers who have fallen in the great struggle for the Nation's life. Lieutenant G. Bowman Simonds, of Company B, Fifteenth Mass. Regiment, was killed in one of the late series of battles, while fighting bravely with his company. He volunteered with his brother Clark Simonds, in the first company that went from Fitchburg. He was wounded at Ball's Bluff in the first battle in which the regiment was engaged, and came home on a furlough, but as soon as he had recovered sufficiently from the effects of his wound, he returned to his company, and remained with it until the time of his death.

His gentle and quiet deportment, and almost boyish appearance gave little token to those who did not know him intimately, of the stern devotion to duty, and manly courage which inspired him.

One who, with others, accompanied him, then a mere boy, from the battle-field of Ball's Bluff, speaks in feeling terms of admiration of the quiet and uncomplaining fortitude with which he endured his suffering, and of the gratitude with which he accepted the care they felt themselves only too privileged to be able to give. He has sealed his devotion with his blood, and his widowed mother is now bereft of her last son.

Three boys, all who were given her, has she freely given to her country. Captain Clark S. Simonds fell on the field of Antietam. Aaron Simonds died in camp, after an honorable service at Port Royal, and now the third and youngest has left her. The warm sympathy of every heart which can be made to throb by noble and generous sacrifices, she will receive; but who will venture to regard with *compassion* the mother of three such sons?

Rather may we envy the lot of her who at the end of a long and blameless life may look forward to find such treasures in Heaven. W.

JOHN M. WHITTEMORE—NAVY.
(COMMUNICATED.)

John M. Whittemore was born in Cambridgeport, Massachusetts, September 11th, 1835, and was the third son of Rev. Thomas Whittemore, D. D.

After leaving school, he was for sometime clerk for his honored father in his office in Boston, but possessing an ardent love for mechanics, especially that of steam-enginery, he could not content himself at any other business, and on leaving his father's office, he spent some time in preparing to become a scientific mechanic. He studied engineering thoroughly, was well versed in the popular works on the subject of mechanism, and for several years was employed in the engineering department of the Vermont and Massachusetts Rail Road. He was also a fine draughtsman.

He was married February 27th, 1861, to Miss Josephine, daughter of Rev. Joseph P. Atkinson, of Orange, formerly of Laconia, N. H., who survives him.

When the government of the United States appointed a competent and learned committee to examine applicants for engineers in the naval service, Mr. Whittemore appeared before them, and after a thorough examination, he was accepted, and informed by them that from sixty-four who had applied, four only would be commissioned, and he was one of that number.

On the 4th day of October, 1861, he was ordered to join the U. S. sloop-of-war Mohican, at the Charlestown navy yard; and on the 12th of the same month, he sailed for Fortress Monroe.

Many interesting incidents of the voyage, and of the severe storm between Fortress Monroe and Port Royal, are found in a journal which he kept. The last record in it reads as follows: "Thursday, Oct. 7th.—This morning is lovely. No air stirring. Hauled short on the anchor at 9 o'clock." This was within an hour or two of his death. The post assigned to him in action, was at the signal bell-pull on deck, to convey the orders of the captain in regard to moving the ship, to the engineers below. Here he fell, alongside the mid-ship gun. He was killed instantly, and while cheering on the men at the gun, by a piece of shell which passed through the head.

In the afternoon of the next day he was buried with funeral honors, in the rear of Hilton Head Battery. The vessels of the navy each wore colors at half mast. A mocking-bird whistled mournfully from a neighboring tree, while the burial service was being read by Chaplain Dorrance, of the Wabash.

It would seem that Mr. Whittemore had a strong presentiment of death, and his associates say that on the night before the battle, after giving directions as to the disposition of his body and effects in case he should fall, he spent an unusual length of time by himself, in reading his Bible. He is dead, but his relatives and friends have the satisfaction of knowing that he died nobly and in a glorious cause. The first martyr upon South Carolina's soil, in maintaining the honor and integrity of the nation against a most wicked rebellion, his memory will be embalmed in Massachusetts breasts with the heroes of the 19th of April and the 21st of October. His remains arrived in Cambridgeport on the 3d of December, and were buried at Mount Auburn with military honors.

Mr. Whittemore was always fond of books, had a retentive memory, and a mind well stored with knowledge. He was well versed in the histories of the leading minds of the day, who are known as artists, poets and historians. He also possessed great conversational powers, and could converse with ease and fluency upon the topics of the day. He was noted for his generosity; his feelings were easily moved for the suffering and needy, and the hand of charity was never offered in vain. Many poor ones, whose suffering he had relieved, were constrained to drop a tear of regret when their young friend and benefactor passed from earth.

LIEUT. HENRY A. BECKWITH, TWENTY-FIRST REGIMENT.

The following sketch of Lieutenant Beckwith is from the sermon preached at his funeral, by Rev. Elnathan Davis:

"Henry A. Beckwith, whose death has called us together to-day, was born in Gilsum, N. H., July 12th, 1836. About the year 1850, he became a resident of Fitchburg, which has ever since been his home—made doubly homelike by his marriage some three years ago, with Miss Sarah J. Steele, of this place. In July of last year, he left us as a member of Company D, Twenty-First Regiment, commanded by Captain T. S. Foster. He was in the battles of Roanoke Island, Newbern, Camden, Second Bull Run and Chantilly, Va., in the last of which he was mortally wounded Sept. 1st, 1862. Four days afterwards, in the hut of an old slave woman, on the border of that disastrous field, he died. He had risen to the position of First Lieutenant of his company, was cordial and manly in his deportment, brave and skilful as an officer, much beloved by his companions, and died universally respected and deeply regretted by his regiment—the war-scathed Twenty-first. What he was as a son and brother, as a husband and friend, I need not say. Few men have left a dearer home, or more loved and loving friends, to plunge into this terrible strife; and in few homes will the memory of the lost soldier be more tenderly cherished. To those who so truly loved him, and especially to the wife of his youth, these old words shall thrill with a new and deeper meaning—

> 'Green be the turf above thee,
> Friend of my better days!
> None knew thee but to love thee,
> None named thee but to praise.'"

CALVIN E. TOLMAN, TWENTY-FIRST REGIMENT.
(FROM THE "REVEILLE" OF SEPT. 11, 1862.)

HONOR TO THE BRAVE.—We are called upon to record the death of more of our brave Fitchburg men who have fallen on the field of battle. Calvin E. Tolman was a printer in the Reveille office, and enlisted in the 21st regiment, which left about a year since. He was in all the battles in which this noble regiment has had a part, at Roanoke, Newberne, Manassas and Chantilly. In this last bloody engagement of Sept. 1st, he was shot through the head, and died almost immediately. Young Tolman was much esteemed by all who knew him; faithful, earnest and patriotic, he enrolled his name and went out with the volunteers of Fitchburg, from a pure sense of duty. There is the consolation for his bereaved parents and friends, that he never failed in his duty, and that he died as a soldier should, fighting bravely in the van in defence of his country."

LIEUT. CHARLES E. UPTON, TWENTY-FIFTH REGIMENT.

Lieut. Upton was one of our most youthful officers. We think he was the youngest in commission from this town, being but twenty years old at his death. He was one of those who seem to have been born with the elements of a true soldier in his nature. He was one of the first to enlist in the 25th regiment, and was immediately appointed a sergeant in Co. F. Though so young, he showed marked ability in the duties of his office, and secured the respect and love of the men with whom he was connected. His efficiency and gallantry soon won for him a second lieutenant's commission, which was followed in a few months by a promotion to a first lieutenancy. He was placed in command of company I, and led it in the battle of Arrowfield Church where he lost his life. We cannot close this notice any better than by giving a copy of a letter from one of his comrades soon after the battle, and which we take from the correspondence of the "Worcester Spy."

"In the list of killed on the 9th inst., you will find the name of Lieut. Charles E. Upton. In Lieut. Upton's death we have met a severe loss. He had just been promoted to a first lieutenancy, and had his life been spared would have won higher honors during the bitter struggles of this campaign. But an all-wise Providence has otherwise decreed, and though we shall miss the kind and genial comrade, the brave and gallant soldier, and the true and affectionate friend, yet we bow in humble submission to His holy will. I send you the following extract relating to his death, from Colonel Pickett's official report of the battle of Petersburg:

"First Lieutenant Upton, in command of company I, was killed. In the loss of this officer the regiment and service have lost one whose place it will be difficult to fill. Young, brave and patriotic, he was among the first to offer his services to his country, entering into all the trials and hardships of a soldier's life with a cheerfulness of disposition and a buoyancy of spirits, which won for him the respect and confidence of his superior officers; prompt in the performance of, and attentive to all his duties, kind and affectionate to all under his command, he gained the respect and love of all who knew him. He met a soldier's death, dying at the head of his command as victory crowned our efforts."

LIEUTENANT FRED. H. SIBLEY, THIRTY-SIXTH REGIMENT.

Lieutenant Sibley originally enlisted in the Fifteenth Regiment and served in it for the first year of its term of service, as a Corporal and Sergeant of Company B. Here he showed marked abilities as a soldier, and in the summer of 1862, he was recommended to the Governor for a Commission in the Thirty-sixth Regiment, then forming, and received a commission of Second Lieutenant August 22d, 1862. He served with his regiment one year, being present in all its engagements and marches until July, 1863, when (his regiment being then in Mississippi on the arduous Vicksburg campaign,) he was taken ill with chronic diarrhœa, and on the return of his regiment through Kentucky, he was sent to the hospital at Louisville, where he survived but thirty-six hours. His death occurred August 17th, 1863. His remains were brought home by his father, and repose in our peaceful cemetery. He left a young wife to mourn his loss, to whom he had been married but a short time.

The following extract from the pen of a brother officer, will show in what estimation he was held in his regiment:

"Although a stranger to you, Lieutenant Sibley deserves more than a passing notice. I was intimately acquainted with him, and *knew* him well. He was formerly connected with the Fifteenth Mass. Regiment and had been, I think, in ten general engagements and skirmishes. He was one of the finest men I ever knew—an accomplished soldier, a true patriot, an honorable, upright man. His gentlemanly deportment had won for him the esteem of all who had the pleasure of his acquaintance."

We are told by those who knew him better than we did, that he was a general favorite wherever he was. We know that he was brave and chivalrous, for we have on record in another part of this volume, the part he took in saving his Colonel not only from the hands of the enemy, but from a watery grave in the Potomac. All such noble spirits we should delight to honor, and their memories should be peculiarly precious.

LIEUT. COL. GEORGE E. MARSHALL, FORTIETH REGIMENT.

The following extract from "Reed's Hospital Life in the army of the Potomac," contains a fitting tribute to Lieut. Col. Marshall, and will be read with interest.

"While we were waiting the arrival of the wounded, we went in search of the Fortieth Massachusetts Regiment. The headquarters were under a thick bower of magnolia leaves, and we received a cordial welcome from Lieut. Col. Marshall. The men were resting on their arms, their knapsacks being merely unstrapped, and their guns lying within reach, ready for marching orders The men were full of spirits and enthusiasm, although in the midst of a severe campaign. They were to enter upon their work again to-morrow, few of them probably realizing that the setting sun of that day was to be the last that many of them would ever look upon. As we sat in this cool, shady spot, a staff officer rode up with orders to have the regiment prepared to move at a moment's notice, and we left the column ready for its march. The skirmishing previous to the battle of Cold Harbor had begun. The heavy guns were distinctly heard that morning—that desultory firing, ominous of the coming engagement. The regiment joined its brigade, marched to Cold Harbor, and, before another sun had set, the Colonel and one hundred of his brave men were dead and buried on the battle field. The fire of a genuine patriotism burned in the heart of Colonel Marshall. Bold as a lion, he was as sensitive as a girl. With utter fearlessness in danger, nothing could touch so quickly those finer sensibilities of honor as the slightest intimation of reproach, that from any cause he was neglectful of his duty. The life of a skilful officer, of a devoted, earnest and faithful man, was thrown away in rashly vindicating himself from an aspersion as unjust as it was inconsiderate; and when the noble fellow fell, the tears of his men watered his grave. The brown, haggard soldiers, with powder-stained hands, placed him reverently under the sod, with his comrades who fell at his side.

The sight of a field of carnage must not be described. But in the rear of it we can see groups of men sitting under trees, or lying in agony, having crawled to some shady spot, to brook-side or ravine, where they may bathe their fevered wounds or quench their thirst while waiting their turn to be removed in ambulances to the hospital."

LIEUT. GEORGE G. NUTTING, FIFTY-THIRD REGIMENT.

Lieutenant Nutting was killed in battle at Fort Bisland, La., April 13th, 1863.

He was an old soldier of the Militia, and held a commission in the Fusiliers previous to going into the service. The call for nine months men found him among the first to volunteer to go, and he entered the service as First Lieutenant of Company A, Fifty-third Regiment.

He proved an efficient officer and a thorough disciplinarian. He was a great favorite with the men under his command, for whose comfort he was ever careful and solicitous. He had the command of his company in the battle in which he lost his life, and was observed through the thickest of the contest leading his men with a calmness and fearlessness truly his own. He was shot through the head and died in half an hour. Col. Kimball, in a letter announcing his death, thus speaks of him:

"Our much loved Lieutenant Nutting is no more. He fell nobly while gallantly leading his men close up to the enemy's works. He was cool and determined, and exhibited while in battle the same noble and manly traits of character which always governed him in civil life—that is, to do his duty, *his whole duty* without hesitation or fear. His company acquitted themselves handsomely, moving forward under a severe fire from a concealed foe, with promptness and great courage, at every order to advance. They were in the most trying position of any company in the line. The last time I saw Lieutenant Nutting alive, I gave him orders to move his men forward ten paces, and extend intervals to the right twenty-five paces, to prevent the enemy turning our right, which I much feared they would attempt to do. He sprang forward and gave his orders as coolly as if on dress parade, encouraging his men by his personal bravery, as well as by words. My attention was immediately called to another part of the line, and I left him, knowing that my orders to him would be carried out if it were in the power of man to do it. I saw him no more till I saw him the next morning, calmly sleeping his last sleep, having fought his last battle, and looking as natural and happy as in life. May we ever cherish his memory, and remember that he died as he had lived, true to the Old Flag, and bravely fighting for the country he loved so well. Peace to his ashes! May he receive a crown of glory in a better world, as a reward for duty nobly done."

His loss was severely felt by both officers and men of the regiment, for his many good qualities had endeared him alike to all, while his great ability as an officer was felt and appreciated by his brother officers and superiors.

FRED L. WORKS, CO. A, FIFTY-THIRD REGIMENT.

He died of disease at Opelousas, La., April 23d, 1863, aged twenty-one years. He was the son of Daniel Works, of this town, born and bred here, and had seldom left the quiet of his father's farm, until his country called for his services. He was not slow to respond, but with his brother, and some of his near neighbors and comrades, enlisted in the 53d regiment. He was a thoroughly conscientious young man, and ever followed the path of rectitude. He was of a mild, amiable disposition, and drew to himself the love of his comrades and friends. As a soldier, he was true and faithful to every duty. He shared the fortunes of his regiment until after its first battle, in which he bore himself most bravely. After the battle of Fort Bisland, the regiment marched very rapidly in pursuit of the enemy, towards Alexandria. Fred had been unwell for some days, but would not give up until obliged to. On the fourth day of the march he was obliged to succumb, being already in a burning fever. He was placed on a horse and carried to Opelousas, where he died in less than a week. His brother was with him, and took care of him until his death. His funeral took place the next day from the hospital, and was attended by his company and the field and staff officers. We well remember the sad occasion. The services at the house were held just before night, and it was almost dark before the mournful procession, with muffled drums and "arms reversed," started for the little cemetery where his remains were to be deposited. Arriving there, we assembled about the grave, and by the pale light of the moon, the services proceeded. A most impressive prayer was made by the chaplain, after which the body was lowered into the ground. Then three sharp volleys over his grave, told the villagers that another Union soldier had gone to his long home. He sleeps among a most rebellious people, but they will respect his grave. It is not impossible that the time *may* come, when they or their descendants can pay it due reverence.

HENRY S. WOODBURY, CO. A, FIFTY-THIRD REGIMENT.
(COMMUNICATED.)

A private in Co. A, 53d Regiment Massachusetts Volunteers, was a native of Fitchburg, the youngest son of William Woodbury, Esq., of unblemished character, of marked amiability, the hope and stay of his aged parents, he went to the war, from the purest motives of patriotism, leaving to the care of others, dependent loved ones. He shared in the privations of the early history of his regiment, always full of hope for the future, his letters breathed the ardor of one who had the interest of his country always near his heart, but soon after reaching Baton Rouge, La., he was attacked with chronic diarrhœa, and before his entire recovery, his regiment was ordered to Port Hudson, and he would not consent to be left behind, took his place in the ranks, went, and returned again to Baton Rouge. But the effort was too much for him, weakened as he was by disease, and again he returned to the hospital, where everything was done for him by his comrades, but on the 30th of March, 1863, he died peacefully and hopeful that he should meet loved ones in a better land. His body was tenderly and carefully taken to New Orleans, by Chaplain Whittemore, encased in a beautiful metallic casket, and sent to Fitchburg, and it rests in the new cemetery of his native village. But long will his memory be cherished by a fond wife and only child, and those who knew and loved him so well. A few more years and they shall reach that better land,

> "Where hand to hand firm linked at last,
> And heart to heart enfolded all—
> We'll smile upon the troubled past,
> And wonder why we wept at all."   L. H. B.

CAPTAIN GEORGE H. BAILEY, FIFTY-THIRD REGIMENT.

The following letter from the Chaplain of the Fifty-third Regiment to the friends of Captain George H. Bailey, is a just tribute to the memory of a brave man.

"IN THE FIELD NEAR PORT HUDSON,
June 2d, 1863.

MR. JOHN L. BAILEY,

Dear Sir :—You have doubtless before this, received the sad intelligence of the death of your beloved son. I would not add new pain to your heart by a recital of the wounds he bore, the sufferings he passed through, were it not that a sense of duty urges me to bear testimony to the worth of a gallant officer, a noble soldier.

George had just been elected Captain of a company with which he had long been identified. They knew him,—he had been a tried servant, a true companion in arms; by him they chose to be led; their hopes were high— his were exalted. New dangers were to be encountered, and we commenced our attack upon Port Hudson. None were more earnest in the contest than Company A, and George was the equal of the most brave. On the night of the 25th of May, while leading his command forward as skirmishers, the rebels opened a wild and rapid fire upon them; he fell, having been shot through the side and arm. He was carried from the field back two miles to a sugar house, which was converted into a hospital. Here he received good attention from Mr. Spaulding, who was sent to take care of him. He began however, to fail, and died on the 28th. I saw him once after he was carried to the hospital; he was cheerful in his mind, and expressed a hope of getting able to do duty again. He was very sorry to have been wounded so early in the struggle. When he found he must die, he was frequently seen engaged in silent prayer. To questions asked by Mr. Spaulding, he gave answers such as warranted him to believe that George was not only prepared for the great issue of life, but the Christian's hope was his. The last words he uttered were, "It is all right."

In view of this assurance, may we not feel that though a good man has fallen, though the loss among the dear ones is great, yet has he gained in exchange, eternal life, immortal happiness! May the consolation of the just be yours. May you be able, even in tribulation, to rejoice and say, "all things shall work together for good to them that love God."

It was our intention to have sent the remains of your son home, but circumstances would not permit, therefore, we were compelled to give him a burial near the battle ground. It is a spot easily found, quiet and retired, not liable to be disturbed. We had quite a service, for we buried at the same time, Lieutenant Colonel Rodman, of the Thirty-eighth Mass.

Deeply do I sympathize with the afflicted widow, and pray God that He may temper her mind to a resignation to His will, and pour into her heart the oil of consolation.

Truly yours,
B. FRANK WHITTEMORE,
Chaplain 53d Reg't M. V. M.

PRIVATES EDWARD P. FARWELL, AND J. HENRY KENDALL, OF CO. A, FIFTY-THIRD REGIMENT.

These two young men, both of whom lost their lives at Port Hudson, the one by disease, and the other on the field of battle, deserve more than a passing notice.

They are representatives of one class of our soldiers, and that is the noble, enthusiastic, conscientious " boy soldier." Both were of the very youngest that went out from us. Young Farwell was but eighteen at the time of his enlistment, of rather slender constitution, but quite well matured. Full of courageous patriotism, when in the summer of 1862, the call came for nine months troops, he was filled with an earnest desire to go forth and do battle for his country. His friends remonstrated with him on account of his youth and slender health, but his only answer was " some must defend the country, and I feel it my duty to go." Of course, his friends yielded. He went, but returned no more. He followed the fortunes of his regiment to Port Hudson, where he was laid low with a fatal disease, and lived only to see the surrender of that stronghold, and to die within its fortifications, on the 19th of July, 1863. He was a brave soldier, a genial companion, a kind-hearted, affectionate boy.

We close this notice with an extract from a letter from the chaplain of the regiment, to his parents. He says:

" When the regiment moved from Port Hudson, July 11th, he was too sick to go with them, and he, with his cousin, Wm. H. Simonds, were left behind, both in a critical condition. Side by side, they lay for several days, till Saturday, P. M., when Edward rapidly failed. At dark, he knew no one but his cousin, and soon was senseless, apparently free from all pain, and dropped asleep calmly, and without a struggle, Sabbath morning at two and one-half o'clock. Mr. Simonds says that Edward was constantly talking of "going home," that he never gave up the idea but that he should go when the regiment did, and the night he died, when insensible to objects around him, thought he was at home, and spoke of friends there. Ambitious almost to the last, he could not bear to lay down his energies for usefulness; but poor Edward was compelled to succumb. Disease had nestled long in his vitals, and he was willing to be administered unto. I cannot, however, conceive a more appropriate place to fall, if the soldier boy must die, than in the stronghold of that power which he with the rest of the brave and the noble, had so long striven to overcome."

J. Henry Kendall, our other "boy soldier," was wounded at Port Hudson, June 14th, 1863, and died June 24th, following.

He was but a delicate boy, not quite seventeen when he enlisted, and really never should have been accepted in the ranks. But though small and delicate of frame, his courage was the most undaunted. Twice before had he offered himself and been rejected on account of his youth. Conscientiously believing that it was his duty to give up a good situation, to leave a widowed mother, to go forth to endure all the hardships and privations of a soldier's life, it was futile to attempt to convince him to the contrary. Men were not volunteering very fast; the call was urgent, the danger seemed imminent. He (brave young soul) felt it, and when his mother plead with him, that he should not think of going into such service, on account of his extreme youth, his reply was: "Mother, if the *men* will not go to the war, the *boys* must." He enlisted in the 53d. Delicate as he was, he endured the rough life, the long marches, the hot climate, exceedingly well, though his naturally slender form grew but more thin. But his courage held out to the last. The writer remembers a conversation with him the night before the battle in which he received his fatal wound. He said to him "Henry, do you not find this a much harder service than you expected when you left home?" He said, "It is hard, much rougher than I thought we should get it, but I am in for it, and I intend to make the best of it, and do my whole duty to the end." Dear child! nobly had he done every duty required of him, nobly did he perform his part on the next day, charging with the very front line up to the works, and receiving there the wound that cost him his life. He was sent to the hospital at New Orleans the day after the battle, suffered amputation, and died among strangers. Of his last hours we have been unable to get an account, but we doubt not that if he was conscious, that he passed to the world beyond perfectly composed and satisfied that he had done what he could for the sake of his country and the dear old flag. His remains were brought home, and he sleeps on the hill-side, "over the river."

> "Blest youth, regardful of thy doom,
> Aerial hands shall build thy tomb
> With shadowy trophies crowned;
> Whilst Honor bathed in tears shall rove,
> To sigh thy name through every grove,
> And call her heroes round,"

CAPTAIN JOSEPH W. GIRD, FIFTY-SEVENTH REGIMENT.

Captain Gird was killed in the battle of the Wilderness, May 6th, 1864.

Of his early life we know but little. He came among us, a young man, some two years before the war, and was connected with the "*Reveille*" as an assistant editor. He was intelligent and studious, and gave promise of a useful life. He was manly and generous hearted, and gained for himself many warm friends. He was earnestly patriotic, and was early in the field to do his share in sustaining the Government in its war against traitors. He enlisted in the Twenty-fifth Regiment, and served in the ranks for one year, when he was promoted to First Lieutenant in the Thirty-sixth Regiment, where he served about the same time, and was promoted to Captain in the Fifty-seventh Regiment in the autumn of 1863, while the regiment was being raised. He at once commenced recruiting a company, and, in pursuit of that object, addressed "war meetings" in Worcester, Fitchburg, and other places. Many of us remember his earnest appeal to the young men of this community, urging upon them their duties to their country. His company was at last filled, and left for the front, April 18th, 1864, and, in less than three weeks, was engaged at the Wilderness, where Captain Gird fell. No truer, or braver officer ever drew a sword, while none have entered the service from purer motives, or from a more conscientious sense of duty.

He left a wife, to whom he was married a few months before.

SIMON S. MARSHALL, THIRD CAVALRY.

(FROM THE SENTINEL OF SEPT. 5, 1862.)

"Sergeant Simon S. Marshall, son of Abel Marshall of this town, died at St. James Hospital, New Orleans, from the effects of a wound in the leg, received while in a skirmish with the enemy at Baton Rouge, in July last. Young Marshall entered the service of his country early, enlisted as a private in the third battalion of Massachusetts Mounted Rifle Rangers, Captain Magee, where he was soon promoted to the office of Sergeant, which position he held at the time of his death. The battalion with which he was connected, composed a portion of General Butler's force, which after a short tarry at Ship Island, found its way to New Orleans, after its capture by Farragut. Sometime in June his company was sent to Baton Rouge, to act against the numerous guerrilla parties that infested that region. It was in a skirmish with a party of guerrillas that young Marshall received the wound which caused his death. He lost his life in endeavoring to rescue a comrade who was surrounded by the foe. He gallantly rushed to the rescue, and thus gave his life in the sacred cause."

We publish below a letter from Dr. Paine, who attended him during his sickness, and cheered him in his last hours:

St. James Hospital,
New Orleans, La., Aug. 17th, 1862.

Miss Lottie Marshall :—I have sad news to tell you, and I might as well speak out at once. Your brother Simon was wounded in the battle of Baton Rouge, on the 5th of August. A bullet passed through his right thigh, midway between the hip and knee. From the wound he has had several hemorrhages, all more or less severe. In a weak state he was brought from Baton Rouge to this hospital, where he came under my charge. When I first saw him he was very weak from loss of blood. I at once set about giving him such tonics and stimulants as I thought would mend his condition. He did well up to this morning, when a discharge of pus and clotted blood took place from the wound, immediately followed by a serious, and, I fear, fatal hemorrhage. Evidently an artery had been wounded by the ball, and the only question was—should I cut down and tie the artery? I thought him too weak to stand the operation; but I called in two brigade surgeons, who were of the opinion that he would die during the operation. He seemed quite calm this afternoon, and I thought it right to acquaint him with the idea that I thought that his recovery would be extremely doubtful. He said he was ready to go; he embraced the Christian belief sometime ago, and believed that he should soon be with Jesus. I took the chaplain of my regiment, Rev. Mr. Chubbuck, to your brother's bedside, and each prayed in turn. It was a solemn scene, and touched me deeply. I thought of the near ones and the dear ones at home, as I bathed his pallid brow, and performed those tender offices that a mother or a sister can do so well. "Tell my mother," said he, "that I die a true Christian." "Tell my sisters to seek the Lord while he can be found, for they may be taken away in a moment. Oh! tell them I am not dead, but only gone before them to prepare a place for them. I shall ever be near them and watch over them." At another time he said, "tell my sisters that I died a *soldier!*"

This is sad news to send, but you must try and bear up under it, and remember the words of your dying brother—that only in Jesus can you find rest and freedom from all earthly cares and sorrows. You have my heartfelt sympathy in this, your hour of trial, and believe me,

Yours very truly,
J. T. PAINE,
Ass't Surg. 31st Mass. Reg't.

P. S.—Your brother died this evening, at twenty minutes to seven. I was with him to the last. The last time he spoke was when I asked him if he knew me. He said, "Yes, you are the doctor." He took my hand in his, and soon after died very quietly. He had a friend, Mr. J. A. Page, of the 4th Massachusetts Battery, who attended him day and night almost, and is deserving of your thanks.

I enclose a lock of your brother's hair.   J. T. P.

JOSEPH LOWE, JOSIAH C. TRASK, FREDERICK KIMBALL,
OF LAWRENCE, KANSAS.

These three men, our former townsmen, though not citizens of Fitchburg at the breaking out of the rebellion, yet seem to have claims upon our notice in these "memorials." They all fell in the "Quantrell raid" upon Lawrence, Kansas, Aug. 21st 1863. Many will well recollect Lowe and Kimball as worthy and respected men, while with us, and young Trask will be remembered as a bright and promising boy. They all emigrated to Kansas while that State was fighting out her battles against the slave power, and stood up manfully and boldly for freedom. In that terrible night of the massacre, so full of horrors, Lowe lost his life by being suffocated in a well, whither he had gone to rescue the mayor of the city, who had sought refuge there from the infuriated gang of desperadoes. Kimball, in attempting to escape to a ravine, was discovered by the demons, halted and shot in cold blood, and young Trask was called out from his own house, and cruelly murdered in the presence of his wife. The remains of Lowe and Trask were brought to Fitchburg and buried. The funeral of Mr. Trask took place September 3d, and that of Mr. Lowe, September 4th. The latter was conducted by the "Masons." The former was held at the Trinitarian Church, and from Rev. Mr. Davis' sermon, preached on the occasion, we are permitted to make the following extracts, believing them to be a just tribute to a "noble young hero."

"Fourteen years ago I first knew Josiah C. Trask. He was a frank, glad, impetuous youth—the elements of a great life within him, and vital force enough to make that life, should these elements be perverted, a memorable wreck, or if consecrated, lift it into preëminent usefulness and imperishable honor. For years I watched with unwonted interest the development of that life. But with native nobleness of mind, he had also upon him the constant pressure of that wide, warm, earnest, liberty-loving, pilgrim faith, which, thank God, has never wholly died out from the homes and churches of New England. Before he left Fitchburg, many a friend beside myself rejoiced to see these elements worthily rounding into form — a form of character which after years were making compact and beautiful.

Look at a few traits, which will be at once recognized by those who knew him:

INDUSTRY.— Who ever knew him otherwise than busy? He was preëminently so; and, as the years went on, and he entered more fully into the battle of life, he seemed to act on Cecil's motto — "Do something — *do it — DO IT.*"

SELF-RELIANCE.— When, at the age of sixteen, he left home, to find employment in his chosen profession, his father said to him, "Shall I not give you letters of introduction and recommendation to gentlemen in the city, my son?" His reply was characteristically full of this manly trait: "I think not, sir; I can introduce myself, and intend to be my own recommendation."

REGARD FOR FREEDOM.— It was this that led him to Kansas seven years ago. It was this that kept him there — that he might help *permanently* to secure in that young and thriving State the inheritance whose purchase had cost so much blood and treasure. He was asked, some time previous to his fall, "What will you do if the guerrillas invade your State?" His reply was brave and characteristic: "I'll die for Kansas!"*

UNSELFISHNESS.— "Was my son a Christian?" asked his father of the business man in Kansas, who of all others knew him best. "No, sir, not by profession," was the reply; "but he was unselfish. He loved God, and he loved his fellow-men." In short, he seems to me to have heard King David's charge to his kingly son: "Show thyself a man!" and to have consecrated the energies of his nature to fulfil it.

And must this life, so earnest and so full of promise, go out in darkness?

* "O, fateful prophecy! O, fresh young lips,
   That uttered it half smiling! Did no drear
Forecast of evil, like a dark eclipse,
   Blanch their bright bloom the while, as with a mortal fear?

'I'll die for Kansas!' Ay, and he *has* died!
   Died in the freshness of his young renown.
O, reverently, my country, yet with pride,
   Give him his well-earned due, a martyr's name and crown!

And 'bleeding Kansas,' as she counts her slain,
   And Freedom, numbering up her martyred dead,
Shall make brave mention of his sacred name,
   And weeping say, 'For us, for us his blood was shed.'"

No—it cannot be. He has neither lived nor died in vain. I recognize in this young man—strong, beautiful, intelligent, unselfish—and the fiend, who, nigh his own threshold, in the gray of that terrible morning, drew the murderous rifle upon him, the fitting representatives of the two civilizations, the Pilgrim Rock and the Slave Oligarchy, now in deadly conflict on this continent. As the accursed assassin smote down this young man, so the relentless slave power is striving to trample down into utter ruin all that is precious in

"The land which our fathers loved—
The freedom which they died to win."

Let this bloody deed be a warning to the land, and, with its kindred atrocities, impress the people with this fact, that, if the nation shall live, slavery must die!

We have thus given appropriate notices of our own, and such as we have been able to gather up of some of our "fallen heroes." Few among those whose names appear in the long list we have given, who might not truly be spoken of in terms as high as those who have been more particularly noticed. To the credit of Massachusetts, it may be said, that a large majority of her soldiers were young men of character and standing in society; men who went to fight, not for hire, nor for the excitement of the service, but from true love for their country, and with a full appreciation of the justice of the cause in which they were engaged. They fought in the most holy cause that ever freemen fought, or freemen fell; and in their deaths have they most nobly illustrated the old Roman maxim, "*Dulce et decorum est pro patria mori.*" Not all fell upon the field of battle, but not less honorable the deaths of those who yielded up their lives in the hospitals, or those more unfortunate still, who endured the untold miseries of a rebel prison, and who perished by slow starvation.

Our common grief is poured out for them all—our common gratitude is due them all. While we are conscious of the debt we owe to the brave survivors of many a hard fought field, more tender are the ties that bind us to the memory of our dead heroes. To their honor there should be built in our midst, an enduring monument; whether a granite shaft, "memorial hall," or otherwise, it matters not, so that these names shall be cherished to remote posterity; so that it shall be a memento to the children, (as they grow up and learn the lessons of the past,) of the valor, the patriotism, and self sacrifice of those who laid down their lives that they might enjoy the blessings of free-government, and that the country might be forever rid of that which has well nigh crushed its being—human slavery. But not alone by monumental piles shall their memories be preserved. As has been nobly said by our worthy Governor—

"All generations shall commemorate their valor and their patriotism. No ties of kindred can impose limitations upon the grief and gratitude in which they shall be held and treasured. *The country shall be their monument.*"

SOLDIERS' FUNERALS.

During the war, seven public military funerals have been held in this town.

The first, of Captain C. S. Simonds of the Fifteenth Regiment; second, Lieutenant Henry A. Beckwith of the Twenty-first; third, Lieutenant Nutting of the Fifty-third; fourth, Lieutenant Sibley of the Thirty-sixth; fifth, Captains Bailey and Taft of the Fifty-third; sixth, Privates Farwell, Stuart and Kendall of the Fifty-third, with Sergeant Marshall of the Third Cavalry, and seventh, that of Lieutenant Colonel Marshall of the Fortieth.

Our space will not allow us to give in detail, an account of each, and we therefore give, in full, only the account of the first, second, and last, with a brief reference to each of the others.

Captain Clark S. Simonds fell at Antietam, September 17th, 1862, and his funeral occurred September 23d.

The following account is taken from the *Reveille* of Sept. 25th:

FUNERAL OF CAPTAIN CLARK S. SIMONDS.

The funeral of Clark S. Simonds, captain of the Fitchburg company in the 15th regiment, took place at Fitchburg, on Tuesday afternoon. The banks, stores, and other places of business were closed, flags were draped in black, and the citizens generally gathered together, to manifest their respect and affection for this brave officer, whose noble death on the battle-field, in defence of his country, was in harmony with the manly virtues which adorned his character as a son, husband, father and citizen.

The remains lay in the lower hall, the coffin covered with the national flag, for the honor of which the deceased had sacrificed his life. A photograph of life-like appearance, was resting upon the coffin, and with sword, belt and sash, brought vividly to mind our late friend and citizen, who has passed away from earth in the defence of his country. The tokens of friendship which adorned the coffin in the way of flowers, wreaths, &c., were most excellent and appropriate, and were kindly contributed by Mrs. A. P. Kimball, together with others, among whom may be mentioned, Mrs. L. H. Bradford, Mrs. Sylvanus Wood, and many others whose names we could not ascertain. We also noticed a beautiful bouquet placed upon the speaker's stand in the upper hall.

The funeral services took place at the town hall, consisting of a sermon by Rev. A. J. Weaver, prayers by Rev. Kendall Brooks and Rev. A. O. Hamilton, a requiem by Mrs. C. M. Lowe, an original hymn by Mrs. C. A. Mason, and music by the choirs of the several churches. Appropriate addresses were also made by Rev. William G. Scandlin, late Chaplain of the Fifteenth, and Rev. E. Davis, of Fitchburg.

The funeral procession, escorted by the band of the Twenty-fifth Regiment, from Worcester, was composed of the relatives of the deceased, the Fusiliers and Guards, the ex-members of the Fusiliers, the several Fire companies of the town, and other citizens, under the command of Capt. Eugene T. Miles.

There were present, Col. Ward, Rev. Mr. Scandlin, Lieut. Goddard, and Surgeon Bates of the Fifteenth, Capt. Howe, of Gen. Sedgwick's staff, Lieut. Col. Sprague of the Twenty-fifth, and Major Foster of the Twenty-first.

The pall-bearers were Capt. Foss of the Twenty-fifth, Capt. Page of the Eleventh, Capt. Davis of the Twenty-first M. V., Capt. Walker of the Twenty-first, Lieut. Lawrence of the Twenty-fifth, and Lieut. Barrett of the M. V. M.

The ceremonies were impressive and earnest, and bore emphatic but melancholy testimony to the honor in which the memory of the deceased will ever be held by his fellow townsmen.

Capt. Simonds fell on Wednesday of last week, in the fierce battle led by Hooker and Sumner, in the moment of victory, struck by the fragment of a shell, dying almost instantly. He was twenty-eight years of age, and leaves a wife and two children to mourn his loss and revere his memory.

FUNERAL OF LIEUTENANT HENRY A. BECKWITH.

(FROM THE SENTINEL.)

"The body of Lieutenant Beckwith, of Co. D, Twenty-first Mass. Regiment, who was killed at the battle of Chantilly, September 1st, arrived home on Saturday last, in charge of his wife and Henry A. Willis, Esq., and the funeral took place in the Town Hall on Sunday. The exercises were of a solemn and interesting character. The Hall was densely packed with our citizens, who assembled to witness the last funeral rites to the dead soldier.

The exercises commenced by the singing of a hymn by the choir, under the direction of Prof. E. H. Frost; followed by Reading of the Scriptures by Rev. A. J. Weaver; Prayer by Rev. A. Emerson. Rev. E. Davis preached the Sermon, giving a sketch of his life and character, and drawing an appropriate lesson from the sad occasion. The services in the Hall closed with prayer by Rev. Kendall Brooks, singing by the choir, and benediction by Rev. A. O. Hamilton.

The hall was draped in mourning, and decorated with national flags. Beautiful bouquets were placed upon the speaker's table, and on the wall were hung splendid portraits of Gens. Washington and Burnside, encircled with wreaths of evergreen and flowers intermingled, and below, made of evergreen and flowers, were the words "Twenty-first Regiment"—presenting a beautiful display, and exceedingly appropriate. The decorations were put up under the supervision of Mr. Samuel Bowman, assisted by Mr. E. C. Spooner, a member of the Washington Guards. The wreaths and bouquets were arranged and contributed by Miss Nancy Hodgman, Mrs. Davis, Mrs. William Wood, Mrs. T. S. Foster, Misses Carrie and Lizzie Stone, Mrs. Pratt, Mrs. L. H. Bradford, and others.

The procession was formed in front of the town house, in the following order: The Ashburnham Cornet Band, Washington Guards, under the command of Capt. Jonas Corey, ex-members of the Guards, the workmen of the Putnam Machine Company, the hearse, mourners in carriages, and citizens.

The solemn procession marched with slow and mournful tread, to the grave, where the remains of the dead soldier were deposited in their last resting place.

FUNERAL OF LIEUTENANT GEORGE G. NUTTING,
OF THE FIFTY-THIRD REGIMENT.

First Lieut. Nutting was killed at Fort Bisland, La., April 13th, 1863, while bravely leading his company in an assault upon the "works" of the enemy. His remains were immediately sent home and given a public burial, May 1st, 1863. The occasion was a sad and interesting one. Business generally was suspended, the flags floated mournfully at half mast, many emblems of mourning were displayed, and everything gave token of a genuine, public grief. The services were held in the Town Hall, which was beautifully decorated for the occasion, after which the procession was formed and proceeded to the cemetery, escorted by our two militia companies, and followed by the whole fire department, and a large concourse of citizens. The customary salute was fired, and the soldier was at rest. The whole proceedings under the supervision of Capt. E. T. Miles and A. P. Kimball, Esq., were very successful, and highly imposing.

LIEUTENANT FREDERICK H. SIBLEY.

The funeral of Lieutenant Sibley took place from the Universalist Church, August 27th, 1863, his remains having arrived two days before, in charge of his father, who went to Kentucky to bring them home. A large concourse of his friends and acquaintances assembled to pay the last tribute of respect to the "fallen soldier." The services were very impressive, the sermon being preached by Rev. Mr. Weaver.

The escort on the occasion was the Fitchburg Fusiliers, of which corps he was formerly a member.

The occasion was a sad one, and in marked contrast to the demonstration of three days previous, when the Fifty-third Regiment was so joyfully welcomed home.

So conflicting are the vicissitudes of war.

FUNERAL OF CAPTAINS BAILEY AND TAFT,
OF THE FIFTY-THIRD REGIMENT.

Captains George H. Bailey, and Jerome K. Taft were both killed at Port Hudson, La. The former fell May 25th, 1863, and the latter June 14th, 1863. Both commanded Company A, of this town, Bailey having been commissioned as Captain ten days before his death, and Taft but four days before he fell.

Their remains were brought home soon after the return of the regiment, and their funeral occurred October 5th, 1863. As on former similar occasions, no pains were spared to make the ceremonies worthy of those in whose honor they were held. The fact that both had commanded the same company, and fell within so short a time of each other, added interest and sadness to the scene, now that, side by side, they rested on one bier. Both Fitchburg companies of the regiment, were out for escort duty, and many of their brother officers were present to do honor to their fallen comrades. The obsequies were a credit to those who had them in charge, and a noble tribute to the brave men they commemorated.

FUNERAL OF SERG'T SIMON MARSHALL, OF THE THIRD CAVALRY, AND PRIVATES FARWELL, STUART, AND KENDALL, OF THE FIFTY-THIRD REGIMENT.

This was a peculiarly touching occasion. Here were the bodies of four enlisted men, who had fallen on distant fields in Louisiana, all to be borne upon the same bier. Their remains were brought home in the spring of 1864, by Mr. Josiah Spaulding, who made a journey to Louisiana, to procure them, and the funeral was held April 6th, 1864. The services were conducted by the several clergymen, and Rev. A. Emerson preached a discourse in which he paid feeling tributes to their memories, and gave some very interesting personal reminiscences of them. With martial solemnity they were borne to the cemetery and buried, to sleep in their soldier graves, till the last grand "reveille" shall wake them to eternity.

The following hymn, written by Mrs. Caroline A. Mason, was sung on this sad occasion:

> Wrap the dear old flag around them!
> Done at length with earthly strife,
> Let the symbols still surround them,
> Guarding which, they perilled life.
>
> They, the young, the good, the gifted!
> Fallen in their early prime—
> O'er them let no dirge be lifted,
> But sweet pæans, strong, sublime!
>
> Oh! dead heroes! dead no longer,
> Battle scarred and sick no more!
> Were our faith and hope but stronger,
> Should we thus your loss deplore?
>
> Sighing in our human weakness,
> "Give, oh give them back we pray?"
> Rather, should we not in meekness
> Lift our streaming eyes, and say,
>
> "Fold them, Father, kind and loving!
> Fold them on Thy gracious breast;
> There, Thy care forever proving,
> They shall see Thee, and be blest."

FUNERAL OF LIEUT. COLONEL GEORGE E. MARSHALL,
OF THE FORTIETH REGIMENT.

Lieut. Col. Marshall was killed at the battle of Coal Harbor, June 1st, 1864. He was buried on the field, and his remains were not recovered until the spring of 1866. At the annual Town Meeting, April 9th, 1866, the town voted to give his remains a public burial, and the "Committee on a Monument to our fallen heroes," was instructed to make all necessary arrangements, and take charge of the same.

Thursday, the ever memorable 19th of April, was selected as the day for the services. It was providentially one of the most beautiful of the season, and everything seemed to favor the sad occasion. Business was entirely suspended during the afternoon. The funeral was a very imposing one, and was attended by his Excellency Gov. Bullock and his staff, Ex-Gov. Andrew, members of the city government of Chelsea, and of the Legislature, who arrived in a special train from Boston, at one o'clock, P. M., and were received by the committee of arrangements, and escorted to dinner at the American House, and thence to the Town Hall.

The Hall was decorated with remarkable taste and skill. The casket containing the remains was placed on a catafalque in the centre of the Hall, and covered with an American flag, upon which was placed the sword of the deceased officer. A large and beautiful wreath of japonicas and laurel, adorned the head of the casket, and a single large white lily formed a most appropriate ornament at its foot. Suspended above the catafalque was a tasteful design intended to represent a star, with a large rosette depending from its centre, formed of the National colors, contrasting gracefully with the deep black and pure white of which the rays of the star were composed. A large golden eagle was represented as hovering above the casket, being heavily festooned with crape. The arrangement of flags and drapery over the platform, was in the form of a large shield, and was in harmony with the decorations in the centre, and around the sides of the

Hall. On each, and between every ray of the star above the casket, was inscribed the name of some battle in which the deceased had taken part. Four large photographs of the young officer were placed around the casket on the catafalque, surrounded with laurel wreaths, and at intervals were vases of flowers.

The seats had been removed from the sides of the Hall, in order to admit the Military Escort, and the Fire Department. The seats in front, and to the right of the passageway, were occupied by the immediate relatives of the deceased, and those to the left by parents who had been bereft by the casualties of war. The Governor and Staff, with Ex-Governor Andrew, and several members of the Legislature, occupied seats on the platform. The Army and Navy Unions of Fitchburg and Leominster, attended in a body, and were ranged at the right of the Hall, with the Fitchburg Fusiliers, numbering sixty men, Captain Kimball commanding. On the opposite side of the Hall stood the Fire Department, with the chief engineer and board of assistants, in all about three hundred men. The gallery and floor were filled to their utmost capacity, and deep interest was apparent in every countenance.

The exercises were opened by singing, by a select choir, of the following hymn, composed for the occasion, by Mrs. C. A. Mason:

BROUGHT HOME.

Home,—to the spot where first
  He drew his happy breath;
Home,—with the stillness on his brow,
  The hush and calm of death!

Oh, reverent be your grief
  Above the sleeping one;—
Not as he went, returns again
  The Soldier and the son!

So prompt at duty's call,
  So dauntless and so brave;—
To shield his bleeding Country's life,
  His blood, his life he gave.

Rest, Soldier, Patriot, Friend!
  In your young manhood rest;—
Your Country's blessing o'er your bier,
  Her flag about your breast.

> With Winthrop, fair and young,
>   And Lyon, brave and good,
> We link your memory;—martyred ones!
>   Ye died as brave men should;—
>
> Your good swords in your hand,
>   Your faces to the foe;
> Oh, sainted heroes! it was grand,
>   'Twas glorious to die so!
>
> A grateful land uprears
>   Her tribute to your praise;
> Yours are the holiest of her tears,
>   The greenest of her bays.

Then followed an invocation by Rev. S. A. Collins of Fitchburg, and reading from the Scriptures by Rev. Mr. Hatch, of Fitchburg. A second hymn was sung, after which Rev. Henry L. Jones, rector of the Episcopal Church, delivered the funeral oration.

The present, he said, was an occasion truly solemn; still it had been said it was "better to go to the house of mourning than to the house of feasting." In allusion to the many excellencies in the character of the departed officer, he said there were some who lived, not for themselves, but for others and the great interests of humanity. He hoped their spirit might be caught by others, who would emulate their example. The day, he said, was peculiarly fitting for the occasion which called for the expression of their feelings. The 19th of April,—the anniversary of two of the most memorable events in American history,—the first blow for freedom, and the dastardly attack on Massachusetts men who were hastening to the defence of the national life. The speaker gave a brief sketch of the history and life of the departed hero. George E. Marshall, was the son of Abel Marshall, and was born on the 15th day of Jan. 1837. His early education was acquired in Fitchburg. Subsequently he removed to Chelsea, where he remained till the act which inaugurated the war, when he enrolled himself, as a private, in the 13th Massachusetts regiment. After following the young soldier through the fearful scenes of his experience, and referring to the well merited promotion which was awarded him by his appreciative superiors, he closed his address with a high and touching tribute to the character and qualities of the subject of his oration.

Rev. Mr. Jones was followed by his Excellency Governor Bullock, who spoke eloquently as follows:

"*Friends of Colonel Marshall, and Citizens of Fitchburg:*

It has been to me a melancholy pleasure to attest by my presence the representative interest of the State in these services. A pleasure, indeed, because it is a duty to bid hail and farewell to those whose triumphant deaths have brought to us the double victory of Union and humanity. And a pleasure of melancholy, most surely, that even such rich results, so national and so enduring, should have made four years of war a continuous funeral, and should lengthen the train into the years of peace. But such has been the providence of God, which brings this community to-day to one of the closing scenes.

These ceremonies, this solemn service, this martial attendance, make fit tribute to the memory of Lieut. Col. Marshall. His friends, his neighbors, the whole people of this town of his residence and love, are out to reclaim his dust and to pay honors to him. This is simple justice to the soldier, and the best possible expression of the heart of the community which knew and cherished him. I have traced his record out of the peaceful pursuits of this town. I have followed him, when he left you, and after he left you, from Virginia to Fort Wagner, from Fort Wagner to Florida, from Florida to Drury's Bluff, and onward over all the field and through twenty-four battles, to Coal Harbor, where at last he fell. The manner and measure of his military service crowned his life with public praise, and the circumstance and the place of his death shed upon the close of that life a positive effulgence of glory. The battle of Coal Harbor was so barren of any appreciable advantage, that I would inscribe on the headstone of every Union soldier who laid down his life there, for his epitaph of renown, *that he fought and died in obedience to orders, and for the sake of his example.* Many of our best young men are entitled to that great distinction; for they passed thence to their sleep, and witnessed not in their last moments, the possible benefit of the battle. It is to render the tribute of official honor and personal sympathy in commemoration of the gallant service and glorious death of such a hero, that I am pleased to unite my presence and voice with yours. Nor is it for the brave departed Marshall alone. I do not forget, in the thick-coming memories which this scene enforces upon me, that this ancient and beautiful town of Fitchburg—to which by neighborhood, ties of birth and youthful residence, my heart ever draws me, and ever will—distinguished herself by the promptness, by the alacrity, by the prodigality of means and of men, with which she entered upon the opening, solemn drama in the early days of the war. Not many towns in the State matched her record, and few, if any, surpassed her. My friend and predecessor in office, who is present, (Governor Andrew) knows only too well and too sadly, how many of these brave boys went forth from this town, to uphold the flag of the government, and breathed their last sigh in triumphant death under its folds. This day of local observance, with reversed arms, and muffled drums, and the lengthened train, and the sorrowful assemblage, belongs to Marshall, and to all of them. This day, the nineteenth of April, in a broader and more historical sense of the earlier and the later baptism, belongs not only to them, but to all the sons of the Commonwealth, who laid down their lives, that the country might live. It is my privilege, in the present instance, to pronounce the thanksgiving and the benediction of Massachusetts, over their scattered ashes, and over their common graves. All generations shall commemorate their valor and their patriotism. No ties of kindred can impose limitations upon the grief and gratitude in which they shall be held and treasured. The country shall be their monument.

> "There is a tear for all that die,
>   A mourner o'er the humblest grave,
> But nations lift the funeral cry
>   And freedom weeps above the brave.
>
> For them is sorrow's purest sigh
>   O'er ocean's heaving bosom sent;
> For them are tears in every eye;
>   All earth becomes their monument.
>
> A theme to crowds that knew them not,
>   Lamented by admiring foes,
> Who would not choose their glorious lot,
>   Who would not die the death they chose?"

At the conclusion of his Excellency's remarks, prayer was offered by Rev. Alfred Emerson, who closed the services by a benediction. The casket was then conveyed to the hearse, and the procession formed in the following order: Escorts—Fitchburg Fusiliers; pallbearers—Colonels Upton, Hawkes, Cunningham and Barker, Lieutenant Colonels Foster, Goodell and Barrett, and Major Brown—with the hearse, which was followed by the body servant of the deceased, leading the horse formerly used by him; carriages containing immediate relatives, and the former officers of the 40th Massachusetts regiment, the Governor and staff in barouches, city government of Chelsea, members of the Legislature, citizens and friends. Following in the rear of the line of carriages, were the army and navy associations, and the fire department, headed by the chief engineer. The procession moved directly to the cemetery, amid the tolling of the bells. On arriving at the entrance, the casket was deposited in the receiving tomb, and the long line of carriages passed by between the tomb and the military escort, who stood in the position of "parade rest." After the last carriage had passed, the customary salute was fired, the procession returned to the Town Hall, where the escort was dismissed. The guests from Boston returned in the five o'clock train. They were accompanied by Hall's Cornet Band, which furnished the music on the occasion.

IN PRISON.

During the war but few comparatively, of our citizens were so unfortunate as to be held prisoners in the hands of the rebels. Probably the largest number at any one time, was twelve or fifteen of the Fifteenth Regiment captured at Ball's Bluff, October 21st, 1861, and who were held through the winter. But this was before the days of extreme barbarity to prisoners, and their prison was a palace compared with the foul "pens" of Florence, Andersonville, and Belle Isle. Seven only, so far as we have been able to learn, died victims to the systematic *devilish* treatment of the rebel authorities. Their names are John H. Prichard, Charles E. Goodrich, Wm. H. Hayden, Wm. T. Peabody, Henry K. Hill, George P. Cotting and Cyrus Putnam. But little is known of their terrible experience after falling into the hands of these "demons" in human form.

John H. Prichard, formerly of the Fifteenth, and afterwards of the Second Heavy Artillery, was captured at Plymouth, N. C., April 22d, 1864; he was carried to Andersonville, and remained there until his death, January 18th, 1865. This was his second capture, as he was taken prisoner at "Ball's Bluff" when a member of the Fifteenth Regiment, and held seven months. Of this captivity he has left an interesting account which we shall insert in full.

He was last seen by any of his townsmen, on the 14th of Sept. following his capture. At that time a squad were coming to Charleston to be exchanged. Prichard was one of them and started with the rest, but so weak had he become, that he could not reach the outside of the stockade, and was obliged to turn back again to misery. His comrades thought he could not survive many days, but if the record is correct, he lived some four months. His grave is identified, and is numbered 12475, in the Andersonville cemetery.

CHARLES E. GOODRICH, another victim, was one of our youngest soldiers, having enlisted at the age of sixteen, as drummer in the Twenty-first Regiment. He was captured at the battle of the "Wilderness," May 6th, 1864, and carried to Andersonville. He was one of the most robust young men in his regiment, and of that happy temperament which can bear great troubles and privations, and outlive them. But what constitution could bear up under the treatment received in these rebel prisons? Gradually his fair, round, pleasant face grew long and thin, and his strong frame wasted slowly but surely to decay. On the 14th of September, when he was far enough gone to be thought by these *fiends* to be useless for further service, they sent him to Charleston to be exchanged, but through some fatality the exchange did not take place, and he, with others, was sent to another "prison pen," at Florence, S. C., where he died in the month of October.

So perished this brave boy,—foully murdered, yes, murdered by slow degrees. For his friends have the sworn statement of an officer who was with him, that nothing caused his death but the slow, deliberate process of starvation. And this, only one of thousands.

WILLIAM T. PEABODY and HENRY K. HILL, also taken prisoners at the Wilderness, had a similar experience to that of those we have related. The former died at Andersonville, September 1st, 1864, from sheer starvation, as we are informed by a reliable witness who saw him die. The number of his grave in the Cemetery in Andersonville is 7556. Hill went to Charleston with others, and from there to Florence, where he too, succumbed to the terrible exposure and privation he had undergone. He was buried with the multitude, and his grave is unnoted and unknown.

GEORGE P. COTTING was a member of Company F, Twenty-fifth Regiment, and was taken prisoner at the engagement at Deury's Bluff, May 16th, 1864. He was carried to Andersonville, and underwent all the horrors of that terrible imprisonment, and gradually wasted to a perfect wreck of a man. He, too, was thought to be a fitting subject for exchange, and with others, was sent to Charleston and exchanged. He was brought to Annapolis, Md., and was too weak to proceed farther. He was placed in the hospital, tenderly cared for, his parents sent for to come to him, but he died before they reached him. The treatment he had undergone was too sure in its result, and he died after a very few days, another victim of the merciless cruelty of the rebels towards their captives.

WILLIAM H. HAYDEN enlisted in the Navy, and was aboard the "Hatteras" when she was sunk by the notorious Alabama. He was afterwards attached to the gun-boat "Granite City," which, with the "Wave," it will be remembered, was captured when cruising up one of the bayous of Texas. He was taken prisoner with the rest of the crew, May 8th, 1864, and was carried to Galveston. Although but little has been said of the condition of the prisoners at Galveston, we have the best authority for saying that the systematic cruelty of Andersonville, Salisbury, Florence and Belle Isle was practiced there. Willie soon fell a victim to scorbutic disease, brought on by the miserable quality as well as scanty supply of rations issued to the prisoners. He was placed in what they called a "hospital," but we have the authority of an officer of the Navy that it was but little better than a "slaughter pen," where the "let 'em die policy" was carried out to the fullest extent. Under such circumstances as these, suffering untold privations, surrounded by companions whose miseries had driven them to selfishness and despair, this noble sailor-boy died on the 16th of Sept., 1864, after an imprisonment of a little over four months.

CYRUS PUTNAM, the last we are called upon to mention in this connection, was a soldier of the Twenty-fifth Regiment. He was wounded and captured at the battle of "Drury's Bluff." He was carried to Richmond and subjected to the miseries of rebel imprisonment. His privations, the sufferings he was forced to undergo, with the neglect of his wounds, soon carried him to his grave. We know not just how long he lingered; we only know that he perished there by degrees, as thousands of others had perished. He was a good soldier and deserved a better fate. He was buried at Richmond, and we do not know that his is not a "nameless grave."

Such is the brief, sad history of these "our martyrs." It is impossible for us properly to depict to ourselves the terrible sufferings of their incarceration. Oh, the long, dark, weary days, weeks and months of their captivity! Oh, the visions of homes and friends and comfort and plenty! Oh, the longing and the waiting, and the watching for that deliverance which they had prayed for until hope deferred had made the heart indeed sick, and they were almost ready to believe that they were really forsaken by God Himself.

The horrors of the prison pens of Salisbury, of Andersonville and Florence, *have* never been, *can* never be half told. Miss Clara Barton, who was known in the Army of the Potomac, as the "angel of the battle-field," and whose name is a "household word" in many a soldier's home, visited Andersonville soon after the close of the war, and to her are the friends of the soldiers buried there indebted for causing their graves to be identified, and properly marked. In her report of the expedition, addressed to the people of the United States, she says:

"But after this, whenever any man who has lain a prisoner within the stockade of Andersonville, would tell you of his sufferings, how he fainted, scorched, drenched, hungered, sickened; was scoffed, scourged, hunted and persecuted, though the tale be long, and twice-told, as you would have your own wrongs appreciated, your own woes pitied, your own cries for mercy heard, I charge you, listen and believe him. However definitely he may have spoken, know that he has not told you all. However strongly he may have outlined, or deeply he may have colored his picture, know that the reality calls for a better light, and a nearer view than your clouded, distant gaze will ever get. And your sympathies need not be confined to Andersonville while similar horrors glared in the sunny light, and spotted the flower-girt garden fields of that whole desperate, misguided, and bewildered people.

Wherever stretched the form of a Union prisoner, there rose the signal for cruelty and the cry of agony, and there, day by day, grew the skeleton graves of the "nameless dead."

Would that we might draw the curtain and forever hide the picture, even for the sake of our common humanity. But no—forget these scenes we cannot, though *possibly* there may be enough of christian forbearance in our natures to forgive the wicked perpetrators of their atrocities. How many thousands of brave young men, were thus cruelly murdered. Dreadful to think of, this long, lingering death by starvation. Easy is it for the true soldier to face death upon the field of battle, to charge up to the very cannon's mouth, to do and dare everything for the righteous cause, but to languish and die, as these, our own brave fellow citizens died, victims of a barbarity that savages would scorn to practice, this is indeed terrible. Oh, martyred ones; though yours was not the death of those who fell fighting in the van, yet it is none the less honorable than theirs. As your trials and sufferings were great, so shall your memories be precious, and a grateful people shall ever hold your names in fond remembrance.

The following account of prison life at Andersonville, is furnished, at our request, by Dr. A. K. Gould, of this town, who was for several months a prisoner there:

RECOLLECTIONS OF ANDERSONVILLE.

"Well do I remember when I first arrived in sight of this terrible place, on the 29th day of May, 1864, and of my first interview with the rebel officer in charge of it, Capt. Henry Wirtz, a most savage looking man, and who was as brutal as his looks would seem to indicate. He offered us all the abuse he was capable of, and then marched us into prison. It was no uncommon thing for this brute to strip the prisoners of their clothing, and everything of value about them, before sending them inside the stockade. The stockade in which we were confined, was made by setting logs upright in the ground, as closely as they could be driven, standing above the ground about fourteen feet, and enclosing about nineteen acres of land, about half as wide as it was long. Running through or across this lot, was a brook about four feet wide, and generally, two or three inches in depth, thus giving us water to use, but of the filthiest character, on account of there being just above us, a camp of three thousand rebels, and as many more negroes, (serving as guard over us) all of whose filth and refuse was emptied into the brook and swept down to us. In addition to this, the land on either side of the brook, to the extent of six acres, was a complete swamp. A portion of this was used by the thirty thousand prisoners, more or less, for "sink" purposes, and its effect upon the water, can better be imagined than described.

When I entered the prison, May 29th, the number of prisoners was about nine thousand, which was gradually increased to thirty-two thousand, in the fore part of July. Their condition was enough to make one sick, on first entering the place, but it was nothing in comparison with what I experienced afterwards. To see my fellow men suffering for the want of food and clothing as I did; to see them stretching out their bony hands for the merest morsel to eat; to hear their piteous inquiries, "shall we ever go home;" to see how they died, poor fellows, wasting away, little by little, exposed to the scorching rays of a Georgia sun; this was enough to break the hardest heart.

It may be interesting to know how we lived. We dug holes or burrows, in the ground, thus forming a little shelter for us. Once a day we had brought in to us our rations, which consisted of one-half pint of cob corn meal, coarsely ground, or its equivalent of beans or rice, or sometimes bacon, and all of these of the poorest quality. One of the most dreaded things in this dreadful place was the "dead line." This was a furrow turned up, about twenty feet from the stockade all around, and was called the "dead line," and if a man dared to step over this line, or cross it by mistake, he was at once shot by the guard, without a word being said. It was sickening to see the dead as they lay in prison. It was the custom to carry them out every morning, the prisoners being hired to do this, their pay being an extra ration and a chance to bring in an armful of wood when they returned; and these inducements were so great, that sometimes one squad would steal a dead body from another, in order to get a chance to go out to get wood and more to eat. Others were detailed for that purpose, and they also got extra rations, and when the guard came for any such purpose, how eager the men were to get a chance to go, and how savagely they were treated when refused. So many of these barbarities crowd themselves upon my mind, that I hardly know where to stop.

Some of the prisoners thought they might escape if they got out, but the bloodhounds were too much for them. A pack was kept for the purpose of hunting all such, and very savage they were too, so that few escaped them who ever tried. I found in the prison several men from Fitchburg, and vicinity. Wm. T. Peabody, was captured with me, and remained with me until he died, Sept. 1st, 1864, poor fellow, literally starved to death, no disease about him, but reduced to a living skeleton, as was the case with thousands there. Also John H. Prichard, Geo. E. McMaster, who died after I was released. Also H. K. Hill, Charley Goodrich, and David Wallace, who all died at Florence, S. C., after my release. These men were all in my mess, or in the same "one thousand." There was also there, Mr. Geo. Phillips, who was released and came home.

There are many incidents which might be of interest, had I time or space to write them. There was one scene I shall always remember, and that was the hanging of six of our comrades. Their crime was raiding upon and murder of their fellow prisoners. Their plan was to fall upon any of us they thought they could plunder from. They would steal clothing or anything else, which they could bargain to the "Rebs." The rebel authorities allowed the prisoners to try them and hang them, glad even to have some of us killed off in that manner.

Another feature of this place was the damnable "stocks." I never suffered in them, but have often seen my fellows tortured by them. The pain was excruciating in the extreme. The men were put into a hellish machine that would stretch them all their muscles and cords would bear, and with their faces turned up to the scorching sun, they were left from twenty-four to forty-eight hours. This was the most barbarous act of all, and this to men already completely emaciated by sickness. I have seen men taken from the "stocks" only to expire in a few minutes. All this was done by authority of the officers in charge. All I have to say is, let just retribution be their reward. There were many other wicked cruelties practiced upon the prisoners, but I have not time to dwell upon them. We were taken from this place to the city of Charleston, September 14th, where we were kept under fire of our batteries for three weeks, but fared much better than elsewhere, being fed and cared for by the "Sisters of Charity." From there we were taken to another most damnable prison pen—a second Andersonville, called Florence.

Here the same usages, the same fare and treatment were dealt out to us, but there was one new phase presented to us, and that was, the compulsory movement to make our men enlist into their service. This was done by extra starvation, in some cases depriving us of food for three days at a time.

Who can say that the leaders and instigators of these outrages should not be punished?

I was finally released December 15th, having been in prison seven months and two days.

(Signed)   A. K. GOULD.

The following interesting account of prison life is from the pen of John H. Prichard, who was twice a prisoner, and who died a victim to the barbarities of Andersonville. It was written soon after his release from Salisbury, but we think it has never been published:

LIFE IN THE SOUTH.

BY A PRISONER.

At the close of the battle of Ball's Bluff, those who were captured by the enemy were taken to Leesburg, Va. Those who were able to travel, were marched immediately to Manassas. As the writer was totally blind from the passage of a ball beneath his eyes while lying upon the ground to avoid the enemy's bullets, he was obliged to be led by his companions to Leesburg, about one and a half miles from the field of battle. He remained at Leesburg in the hospital, while his comrades continued their compulsory march through mud and rain, to Manassas Junction. At the hospital a good supper was served of coffee, bread, butter and meat. The wounded were cared for in the kindest manner until the next day, when such as were able, also proceeded to Manassas in company with those prisoners who were taken after 9 o'clock of the day preceding, amounting in number to some hundred and seventy-five. As I had then recovered the use of my eyes, I constituted one of the number. Starting late, on the first day we made about twelve miles, to Goose Creek, where we encamped in a covered bridge for the night. A small allowance of corn bread and boiled bacon was served out to the prisoners, and to most of us it was a sweet morsel, as we had had nothing since the commencement of the fight, saving those who were taken the day previous, like myself. In the morning the march was resumed at an early hour, and continued until we reached Manassas Junction, where we passed by files, through the head quarters of General Beauregard, while the clerks registered our names, and regiments. Here we were obliged to wait for over an hour at the door, and at the close of the registration, were chilled through, as well as tired, lame, sore and hungry. We were then marched to the guard-house, which was at that time occupied by the turbulent and rebellious ones of their own forces, confined for their misdemeanors. As a previous lot of the prisoners had, as they said, robbed them of their blankets, dishes, &c., they, (the rebels in the guard-house,) would not permit us to enter the sheds there erected, but forced us to remain in the yard. Here the mud was from a quarter to half an inch in depth, owing to the heavy rains. However, we had three or four fires built, and lying down on the wet ground, with our feet to the fire, we alternately roasted and shivered the whole of the bitter night. About an hour after our transfer to the guard-house, a loaf of bread was served to each man, and several sides of raw bacon were brought in, which, at our option, we devoured raw, or smoked and burnt over the fire. The lucky ones who managed to get a slice, did so by struggling and fighting for it, as it was each man for himself, and many were so tired and sleepy they could not, or would not, even make an effort for themselves; some had it, but many went without. After a most uncomfortable night, during which few slept for the cold, we were marched to the depot without any breakfast, the food served the previous night being calculated for both supper and breakfast for us. There we were put aboard cars, some passenger, some cattle, and started for Richmond. At various stations where the cars stopped on the road, among which were Gordonsville and Orange Court House, the cars were surrounded by negro women selling cake, fruit, pies, and other refreshments, at exorbitant prices, to those who had money to purchase. Some of them were quite intelligent, and appeared to be house servants to the various white families.

At every station were crowds of ladies and gentlemen, full of curiosity to see the "Yankees." Most of them were civil, and seemed to feel that though by the fortune of war, we were prisoners, that we were yet men; others jeered at, hooted, and taunted us with our misfortunes. The most frequent questions asked were "What did you come down here for?" "Come down to steal our niggers, ravish our wives and daughters, and burn our houses, didn't ye?" "Think ye can whip us, hey? didn't do it, did ye, hey?" Some few seemed to pity our misfortunes, and hoped we should be treated well and kindly, others were fierce for hanging and shooting us.

Upon arriving in Richmond, we were marched under a strong guard to the tobacco factories, or warehouses, which were to be our home for the remainder of our stay in Richmond. During our passage from the cars to the prison, the streets were crowded to their utmost capacity, by the curious inhabitants, who for the major part were very abusive, and scandalous in the abuse and epithets applied to the d——d yankees, as their favorite term was for us. In fact, had it not been for the guard, we should probably have been sacrificed to the popular hatred. After arriving at the prisons, we were placed in the third story, as the lower stories were occupied by prisoners taken at Manassas, and citizens arrested for loyalty to the Union, in Western Virginia. No communication between the several floors, was allowed, although we had to pass through them to get to the yard. Only two at a time were allowed to pass to the yard from each floor, and in the morning, a line of forty or fifty, would be formed on the lower floor, awaiting their turn to go to the hydrant to wash. It was worse than a barber's shop or a California post office. After several weeks had elapsed, General Winder removed these restrictions, and we were allowed freely the use of the small yard. We were formed into squads of about fifteen, under a corporal or sergeant, elected by vote among ourselves, and who received and divided among us, our daily rations, consisting for the most part, of boiled fresh beef and bread, in the morning, with the addition of beef broth at night. Only two meals per day were allowed. Breakfast about nine, A. M., and supper about five, P. M. A few potatoes and some rice and cabbage, were served occasionally. Worms in the rice, and beef whose "offence was rank and smelt to Heaven," were among the common incidents of our living. We were not allowed to approach the windows, under penalty of being shot by the guard. Seven men were shot dead, in the various Richmond prisons, and several wounded, for this criminal offence. The room which I was in was fired into twice, but fortunately no one was injured. We slept on the bare floor for six weeks of the coldest part of the season, with no covering but our clothes, which we happened to have on at the time of our capture. The facilities for keeping clean being entirely inadequate, and we having no change of clothing, all were soon covered with vermin, which abounded in the prison. Toward the latter part of our stay in Richmond, the members of Co. B, from this town, received a large box of clothing, blankets, etc., from the good people of Fitchburg, and a more acceptable present was never sent to men. The tear of gratitude rolled down more than one of their sunburnt manly faces, as they thought of those who had so kindly remembered them in their captivity, and three cheers for old Fitchburg, were given with a will. Soon after, abundance of clothing was sent us by our noble old "Bay State," and we were proud that we came from old Massachusetts.

On the 22d of December, an order was issued from the S. C. War Dept., to transfer the prisoners taken at Bull's Run, and Manassas, and the citizens under arrest, to Salisbury, N. C. After they had transferred the above, there was accommodations for about one hundred and seventy-five more men at Salisbury, and there being nearly that number on the floor where I was confined, we were sent on the 24th of Dec., to fill up the desired complement. Of the Fitchburg company, there were but three members able to go, out of four in that room. Geo. S. Gilchrist, Maynard, of Winchendon, and myself. J. L. Moody, being very sick, was left behind. We bade farewell to our comrades, and took the cars under guard of a company of Georgia soldiers, on return to their State. At Petersburg, we changed cars for Raleigh, where we arrived on Christmas morning, this day being a holiday, and the special train not running, we remained at Raleigh until the next day. The officer in charge of us, Lieut. Col. Winder, son of Gen. J. H. Winder, was one of the very few educated, refined, kindly-hearted and gentlemanly men we had to deal with while in the South. He was the best sample of the chivalric honorable Southerner, and almost the only one we met. He showed us every courtesy and kindness which laid in his power, and has been severely reprimanded for his leniency to the prisoners who have been under his charge at various times. At Raleigh, he gave us full liberty to walk about wherever we pleased, without restraint, previously running the cars back from the city about a mile, to avoid a crowd, and the soldiers who were encamped there, lest from conversation on political subjects, difficulties might arise. We enjoyed more liberty that day than any other one during our imprisonment. In the evening, we returned to the city, and several of us obtained permission of the Col. to go up town, accompanied by a guard.

The city is composed mostly of wooden buildings, and bears the marks of antiquity. The people were very civil, on the whole, and we received none of the insults offered us at Richmond. Early the next morning we started for Salisbury, where, after a long and tiresome ride, we arrived at about seven, P. M. We were received by a deputation of the guard, and marched to the garrison, an enclosure of about thirteen acres, containing a large cotton factory, and other buildings fitted up as a prison. There were about one hundred prisoners already in confinement there, taken in the early part of the war, from the steamship Union, wrecked on Bogue Island, and from three or four prizes taken by the enemy's privateers. These, our fellow prisoners, furnished us with some supper, and gave us a welcome. There were no facilities for cooking the food for so many, and it was nearly midnight before we were all served. The next day, and in fact for several days, we were obliged to cook rations for two hundred men, in a common cooking range, with not nearly enough boilers or other utensils. After a few days, a second cooking range was procured, and we got along better, but even then we had to cook day and night.

After enduring this as long as possible, our numbers augmenting every day, by the accession of prisoners, we took hold ourselves, and built ovens, and set nine large kettles, of twenty or thirty gallons each, so that we could have raised bread, and save much labor, we having had nothing but biscuit, resembling a solid compound of putty and lead, previously. The kitchen was built on at the back of the factory, and connected with the various floors by a dumb waiter. The building was of four stories, we occupying the third, until the prisoners sent to New Orleans and Tuscaloosa returned on their way home as far as Salisbury, when we were transferred to the fourth story, which was much the pleasantest and healthiest. We were very closely confined from the first, and not until the surgeons had repeatedly represented to the authorities that we should all die of scurvy, and other diseases, if not allowed more exercise and air, were we allowed to remain in the yard over five minutes at a time. We did finally obtain from these representations, the use of about five or six acres of ground, including a grove of huge oak trees, for a play ground. After a few weeks, fresh provisions gave out, and all the meat issued was the rank, oily, smoked bacon, and the soup from the same, thickened with rice or corn meal, this being made our unvarying food, and having but one way of cooking, viz: boiling, nearly every one of our number were made sick with jaundice and scurvy.

The hospital arrangements were totally insufficient—from twenty to thirty men with various complaints, placed in a room 16 by 20, many without beds, lying on the floor on a single blanket—if it had not been for the constant care of our own comrades, many would have died from sheer neglect and exposure. One man in particular, deserves honorable and grateful mention for his unremitting care and attention to his sick comrades in arms. His name is Cornelius Lowe, of Whitehouse, Huntingdon Co., New Jersey. When it came his turn to leave for home on parole, he said he could not go and leave his sick comrades, and staid till all were safely on their route home, and then attended them as kindly as a woman, till they were received into the U. S. hospitals at Newbern and New York.

He will ever hold a place in the hearts of his grateful fellow prisoners as a a *man*, a *true*, *noble hearted* and *unselfish man*, well worthy of all the honor, respect and love he so well deserves. After a time, however, a new hospital building was built, accommodating about one hundred fifty to two hundred patients, and this was full, nearly all the time during the latter part of our stay. The major part of our sickness was caused from the food, and having no vegetables whatever for months; sour bread and bacon continually, without change. Scurvy, jaundice, erysipelas, fever and rheumatism were the more common complaints. Out of fifteen hundred men there were not fifty but what had the scurvy, more or less; some were unable to walk without crutches. The medicines used in the hospitals were very few except mineral and vegetable poisons, as calomel, opium, ipecac, &c.; a little salts (Epsom,) quinine, rhubarb, spirits nitre, turpentine, sulphur and cream of tartar, comprising about everything, and most of these being gone before our release, and no means of replenishing. The Confederate Surgeon was a well meaning man, but rather ignorant and conceited, in fact, we had to do our own doctoring, as a general thing, according to our own judgment. Our mortality at Salisbury was about one-fifth that of the secesh who guarded us—out of fifteen hundred prisoners, on an average of three months, nine died; out of five hundred guards, average of three months, seventeen died, showing conclusively, that in spite of confinement, bad food, and want of fresh air and exercise, "Yankees" can stand the climate and hardships of the South better than the Southerners themselves.

The guards themselves, were the most ignorant, degraded, dirty looking lot of men I ever saw. Not one in ten could read or write. Even some of the officers, who belong to the better class, were nearly as ignorant as the "poor whites" who compose the rank and file. Out of sixty-three men from Salisbury and vicinity, taken at Roanoke Island, when called up to sign a parole, fifty-four had to make their mark, could neither read nor write. Some of the officers treated us as kindly as could be expected, others were surly, cross and disagreeable, insulting us in every way possible, and loading us with opprobrious and scurrilous epithets. During our captivity in Richmond, we had the city papers freely, if we chose to purchase them, this however, was before the reverses of the confederate arms at Roanoke, Newbern, &c. When removed to Salisbury, no papers were allowed in the garrison, and all we obtained there were smuggled in, nevertheless we managed to keep informed as to the general movements of both armies. Reading matter of any kind was very scarce. A Mrs. Johnson, a New England lady, sent in quite a number of books to the prisoners. One of our number received a couple of dozen of Harper's novels, which were read as long as anything of them was legible. We whiled away the hours in making pins, rings, tape and crotchet needles, penholders, badges, &c., out of the beef bones we could obtain from the kitchen, wooden pipes, &c., playing cards, dominoes, chess, checkers, backgammon, &c., all the implements but the cards, being the work of our hands; writing to our friends, composition, &c. We were only allowed to write one half page of letter paper, and that was of course read before being sent to our friends north.

The weary months dragged on, and finally an order came for our release, and we were sent off in squads of two or three hundred at a time, in alphabetical order, by way of Raleigh and Goldsboro', to Tarboro', on the Tar river. There we staid a day or two, quartering in the Courthouse, a fine looking building of brick, in form of a Maltese cross. The village was one of the pleasantest we passed through, during our journeyings in the Southern States, the streets being wide, and lined with shade trees of different kinds, and the houses neat and in good repair. From here we proceeded down the Tar river, in flat boats, towed by a little tug boat, the Col. Hill, to Washington, N. C., where we were received by Gen. Burnside. When the prisoners saw the old United States flag, three rousing cheers burst forth, and the happiest day of our lives was when we stepped on board the U. S. boat, and felt that we were *free*. Gen. Burnside shook hands with each of us, and welcomed us back, and the cheer after cheer, from the boys on the shore, rang out on the air, welcoming us back to life and liberty. From Washington we went by boat to Newbern, where we remained until all the prisoners arrived, when we left for Hatteras Inlet, and there taking an ocean steamer, we came to Governor's Island, N. Y. The first two lots of prisoners dispersed to their several homes, without waiting for pay or ration money, the remainder staid for two or three weeks at Governor's Island, until paid off. I myself, being too weak to stand the voyage to New York, stayed at Newbern, with the members of the Twenty-first and Twenty-fifth regiments, until I had regained my strength in a degree, before coming on, and I owe my thanks to the officers and members of Co. D, Twenty-first, and Co. F, Twenty-fifth, for their kindness to me while at Newbern, also to the Quartermaster and Colonel of the Twenty-fifth, and their assistants, for the many favors received.

Thus ends a very hasty and imperfect sketch of the experiences of prison life in the South. It is brief, and does not enter into detail as much as might be desirable for the purpose intended. The imprisonment commenced Oct. 22d, 1861, and all were released May 31st, 1862.

May none of the readers of this hasty sketch ever be obliged to experience the misfortune of confinement in a Southern prison, is the last wish of

A. PRISONER.

RECEPTION OF REGIMENTS.

Public receptions were given to two of our regiments only, by the people of Fitchburg, the Fifteenth and Fifty-third, full accounts of which are given here, and for which we are indebted to the *Fitchburg Reveille*.

Other receptions would doubtless have been as heartily extended to the returning veterans, but for the reason that no other regiments or companies arrived in town under any organization, as they were generally mustered out at remote points, and scattered to their homes. Our citizens would have been glad to extend to all of our soldiers as hearty a greeting as was given the two organizations referred to.

RECEPTION OF THE FIFTY-THIRD REGIMENT.

The reception, at Fitchburg, Monday, Aug. 24th, 1863, of this noble regiment, on its return from an arduous and successful campaign, was an affair so characteristic of the high spirited, patriotic and appreciative people of Worcester North, and so indicative of the love and esteem in which the brave men of the Fifty-Third are held by their fellow citizens, that it will not soon be forgotten by those who had the privilege to witness or take a part in it. It is estimated that upwards of eight thousand people were present from other towns represented in the regiment. These towns were Barre, Petersham, Athol, Royalston, Winchendon, Templeton, Gardner, Ashburnham, Westminster, Lunenburg, Leominster, Lancaster, Sterling, Clinton, Groton, Shirley, Townsend, Pepperell, and Ashby. During the whole day, from an early hour in the morning, Main street was thronged by the vast multitude.

Many of the public buildings, stores and dwellings were elegantly decorated, most of them by Mr. Yale, of Boston. Among these were the Fitchburg Hotel and American House, the Fitchburg Depot, the stores of L. Sprague & Co., J. J. Hardon, D. Jennison, L. W. Warren, the Reveille office, the office of C. H. B. Snow, the dwellings of Alvah Crocker, E. T. Miles, Mrs. Willis, Amasa Norcross, W. W. Comee, H. J. Lowe, C. E. Pratt, and others.

The music was furnished by the Germania, Brigade, and Gilmore Bands, of Boston, the Ashburnham, Winchendon, Townsend, and Pepperell Bands, and the Fitchburg Cadet Drum Corps, of some twenty lads, whose performances were very creditable to them and their instructor, Mr. E. H. Frost.

Col. Edwin Upton acted as Chief Marshal, assisted by his aids, Wm. Kimball, Francis Buttrick, Jr., W. W. Comee, Joseph Tufts, C. L. S. Hammond of Fitchburg, and Col. Henry Smith, of Templeton.

Dr. Alfred Hitchcock and Messrs. Hale W. Page and James P. Putnam had been appointed to receive and provide for the sick, and under their direction, the Lower Town Hall was fitted up with comfortable beds, washing apparatus, and other conveniences, and the attendants engaged from among the ladies.

It had been at first arranged that the regiment should go to Camp Stevens to be furloughed, but on representation being made to Quartermaster McKimm, of the proposed reception, the order was changed, and Hon. Alvah Crocker was chosen by the committee of arrangements to meet the regiment at Albany or Buffalo, and inform them of what had been done.

The regiment reached South Fitchburg between six and seven o'clock Monday morning, where they stopped two or three hours to bathe and wash, and partake of hot coffee and a hastily prepared breakfast. In the meantime, the sick belonging to Fitchburg, were taken home by their friends, and those from the towns above Fitchburg, were conveyed to the Town Hall, where wine, broth, and such other refreshments as they needed, were administered by Dr. Hitchcock and Messrs. Page and Putnam, and the ladies in attendance. There were twenty-four taken care of here. The same attention was received by some twelve men who remained in the cars, until they could leave for Clinton, Lancaster, and other places below. The whole number of sick with the regiment was about fifty.

The regiment was received on the Common near the depot, at about half past nine, where, after prayer by Rev. J. M. Heard, the following address of welcome was delivered by Amasa Norcross, Esq.:

Col. Kimball, Officers and Soldiers of the Fifty-Third Regiment:

Welcome! Welcome to the State you have honored—Welcome to familiar scenes—to home and friends.

It is with a new experience I give you greeting in behalf of this vast assemblage. It has not happened to us ever before to greet friends under similar circumstances. To-day the heart fills with new emotions. Words of mine are indeed inexpressive utterances, when they attempt to measure the depth of that out-gushing sympathy, mingled with patriotic pride and affection, which the hearts of all who have awaited your coming, now fully experience.

You return to us after a lapse of nearly twelve months. A period, on the part of those who surround you, of thoughtful solicitude, characterized by intervals of intense anxiety, yet of earnest hope. You come, the worthy recipients of that honor which manly courage, faithful performance of duty, heroic endurance, and success in arms in a just and noble cause, may rightfully bestow.

We recur to the time when impending danger summoned you to the field. When voluntarily you sundered the ties that bound you to the active pursuits of peaceful civil life and impelled only by a sense of duty, left all for the service of your country.

When your ranks were filled, and we witnessed your bearing in camp, we then believed that the future had in store for you no holiday experience. The determined character of the men composing this Regiment, was enough to satisfy citizens who remained at home, that yours would be a field of active service. And when with unanimous voice you welcomed as your leader and commander, one who took his early baptism in this great struggle against treason at the ever memorable Ball's Bluff, and who fearlessly stood in the thickest of the fight through the weary days of the campaign of the Peninsula, who was commended for his gallant bravery at the battle of Fair Oaks, and through the desperate conflicts of South Mountain, and Antietam—we knew it signified that such a commander but realized your conceptions of what should be expected of Massachusetts men.

Soon after bidding adieu to home and its attractions, you encountered sufferings not soon to be forgotten. Thrown upon Long Island, tentless and shelterless, you passed a season so inclement that, chilled and frozen, some of you were for a time disabled. Your position changed for quarters in the city of New York. Before entering upon your destined voyage, there came sickness, which seemed to threaten prolonged delay. But the part you were to take in this great contest was not then to be determined. Convalescence ensued, the sick recovered, and it now seems as if these early privations and sufferings were designed but to prepare you for more trying experiences.

Embarking for your place of destination, you accomplished a passage of more than seventeen hundred miles, at times tempestuous, during which sickness and peril at sea were added to the sufferings already endured upon land.

Such were the experiences, such the unaccustomed privations you were called to endure before entering upon the brilliant campaign through which you have since passed. From the hour of your arrival at New Orleans until the expiration of your term of enlistment, few regiments, if any, had seen severer service, and none have more fully earned the gratitude of their country.

Time would fail me to recount in detail, the hardships encountered. The sanguinary contests with a vigilant enemy; the subjugation of an extensive territory where now the flag of freedom floats securely; your long and weary marches, traversing a distance of more than six hundred miles; the suffering and exposure on the march; the effect of an unaccustomed pestilential climate, sapping at the foundation of many a strong constitution, all these form but a part of the material of a history yet to be written, of that eventful campaign.

Yet, passing through all this, there still remained unaccomplished, the crowning work of your gallant army—the reduction of Port Hudson—the opening of that vast river which gave to loyalty unobstructed possession thereof, from the Falls of St. Anthony to the Gulf.

This event, occurring only after terrific assaults, in which it was reserved to the Fifty-third regiment to take so distinguished a part, must forever stand out in the clear light of history, as one of the most important achievements of the loyal armies.

And, while we gladly recognize this glorious success, we are not unmindful of the cost, or the means employed for its accomplishment. Shoulder to shoulder stood the sons of New England and the brave men of the West, and while the maintenance of a common flag, and the support of a common government was the chief concern of all who fought, and all who fell in the struggle before Port Hudson, I cannot doubt that our countrymen of the West will ever remember that the best blood of New England was shed to open up to them more immediately, an undisputed communication between their vast possessions and the Gulf.

Hereafter, if the enemy of his country shall dare suggest the possibility of separation between New England and the West, let him know that his words are vain, for at Port Hudson and Vicksburg a bond of Eternal Union between the East and West, was sealed with the commingled blood of the sons of each. That bond of unity thus cemented in blood, cannot be broken as long as the banks of the Mississippi shall be hallowed by the memory of New England's heroic dead.

But there remains one subject which presses with sorrowful weight upon many hearts, and extends its shadow over us all. All have not returned. Your ranks are thinned; by sickness and wounds many are prevented from participating in the joys of this occasion. The faces of some we shall see no more on earth—they have fallen. They have placed upon the altar of their country the richest gift that loyal devotion can offer. They have sacrificed their lives in defence of her integrity and her honor, for the perpetuation of Republican Liberty, and for the cause of humanity among the nations everywhere. Enshrined in our hearts, and among our most sacred memories, shall incidents of the lives of each find a place.

I would not trust myself to make personal allusion to each of your fallen comrades, their memory requires no words to invoke a common gratitude—

> "High on the world's heroic list,
> Shall every name be seen;
> And time among the cherished dead
> Shall keep their memories green.
>
> The patriot's heart shall warmer glow,
> When standing by their grave;
> And dearer still shall be the flag
> They welcomed death to save."

Thus shall it be—and to you who remain, permit me to say, that the consciousness of important duty well performed; the preservation of a government better than any other; the gratitude of a great people, are among the compensations that await those who have braved the dangers of the battle-field in defence of that priceless inheritance it was the aim, but not within the power of treason to wrest from our hands.

But I will not add another word to prolong the interval that separates you from the tender recognition of waiting friends.

Col. Kimball responded with an earnest expression of the thanks of the regiment for the cordial reception they had met, and gave an extremely interesting statement of the experience of the regiment during its campaign. A procession was then formed on Summer Street, and marched through Main Street, to the Common in front of the Unitarian Church, where a bountiful repast had been provided for the regiment, by the ladies of Fitchburg.

The procession was led by a cavalcade of eighty-three men, from Leominster, under the command of Capt. Leonard Woods, followed by the various delegations, fire companies and military, consisting of a fine company in uniform, from Ashburnham, commanded by Capt. Asa Wheeler, and accompanied by the Ashburnham Band; the Washington Guards, Capt. Lawrence, and the Fitchburg Fusiliers, Capt. Day, of Fitchburg, two fire companies from Templeton, one fire company from Pepperell, four fire companies from Fitchburg, and delegations from Townsend, Winchendon, Leominster, Ashby, and Lunenburg.

Several banners were in the procession, among which was one with the following mottos, borne by the delegation from Leominster: "Leominster honors her brave soldiers. Victors of Bisland and Port Hudson." The following was borne by the delegation from Winchendon: "Welcome home! The memory of the fallen, the heroism of the living, alike sacred to us."

After the collation on the common, the regiment was escorted to the depot, where the different companies composing it departed in various directions, to their homes, pleased, we trust, with the efforts made by the people of Fitchburg and vicinity to show how much they honor all of its brave members, and rejoice in their return, and how deeply they sympathize with their neighbors who mourn over the fallen, called as they are, almost every day, to weep anew over the remains of their own sons, who come home still and cold in the narrow house, or reach their hearthstones only to die there.

RECEPTION OF THE FIFTEENTH REGIMENT.

(FROM THE REVEILLE OF JULY 23D, 1864.)

The remnant of this gallant regiment, with the exception of eighty-two who are prisoners, arrived in Worcester, Thursday afternoon, July 21st, and were formally received there the next day. A large number gathered to join in a cordial welcome to these brave men. Gov. Andrew and staff, with the Boston Cadets, and the Fitchburg Fusiliers, Capt. E. T. Miles, with the Ashburnham Band, were present. The *Spy* states that a procession was formed, and marched down Main street to Lincoln square, and countermarched to the common, where the arrangements for speaking were provided, near the Bigelow monument. The whole route of the procession was thronged with spectators, and the stores and public buildings were profusely decorated with flags and streamers of red, white and blue, the whole forming a brilliant and exciting spectacle. The returning veterans were greeted with cheers throughout the line of march, and the spontaneous tribute of the people's gratitude and praise was all that could be desired.

On arriving at the speaker's stand, the regiment and escort were ranged in front of the stand, and the veterans were welcomed back from the fields of war by an eloquent and appropriate speech by his Honor, Mayor Lincoln, who was followed by Gov. Andrew, who addressed the regiment with his usual earnestness and enthusiasm. Major Hooper responded for the regiment to the words of welcome spoken by the representatives of the city and State, and in behalf of the officers and men of the regiment tendered their thanks for the reception.

At the close of the entertainment at Worcester, the Fitchburg Fusiliers took under their especial charge the remnant of Co. B, and proceeded in the cars for Fitchburg. We give the names of the returned heroes, Lieut. Beaudrey, of Winchendon, in command.

FITCHBURG SOLDIERS.—F. A. Brown, H. L. Sheldon, W. F. Griswold, G. H. Cunningham, G. A. Harwood, D. R. Pierce, H. D.

McIntire, J. K. Hosmer, J. R. Ring, J. H. Tenney, A. C. Plaisted, J. E. Morse, Orlando Wetherbee, F. Scott.

WINCHENDON SOLDIERS.—A. Fisher, N. B. Bruce, E. Chase, D. W. Scott, E. W. Kendall, W. E. Taylor.

WESTMINSTER SOLDIERS.—L. C. White, L. Nichols.

On arrival at the Fitchburg depot, a procession was formed, and escorted by the Ashburnham Cornet Band, marched through Main street, the little squad of war worn veterans receiving at every point demonstrations of congratulation and joy at their safe return; while at the same time, feelings of grief and sadness were manifest on comparing *now* with *then*, when three years ago, this gallant company, with elastic step and buoyant hopes, under command of Capt. (now Colonel) Kimball, marched to the battle field.

At the Town Hall, the soldiers were welcomed by Hon. Alvah Crocker, in one of his hearty, whole-souled and pleasant addresses, and other highly interesting exercises followed. At eight o'clock, the company was summoned to supper at the Fitchburg Hotel, where Mr. Day and his active associates had spread a bountiful repast, and where the large assemblage gave every indication that they enjoyed the good fare set before them. At the close of the feast, the intellectual banquet was commenced by Mr. Crocker, who presided at the table. He was followed in short and appropriate remarks by Rev. Kendall Brooks, Dr. A. Miller, A. P. Kimball, Esq., Maj. F. B. Adams, Rev. Mr. Jones, Capt. Miles, and Adjutant Willis, who read a letter from Capt. Charles L. Eager, formerly an officer in Co. B, regretting his inability to be at the reception. Three cheers were here given for Col. Kimball, and Capt. Eager. Lieut Beaudrey, in a neat and appropriate speech, thanked the audience in behalf of himself and the soldiers, for the generous and courteous reception received at their hands. The pleasant hour at the table was also enlivened by singing and sentiment, and some excellent music by the Ashburnham Cornet Band. It was a rare and delightful occasion, and will not soon be forgotten by those who were present.

TOWN ACTION, PUBLIC MEETINGS, INCIDENTS, CORRESPONDENCE OF SOLDIERS, &C.

RESOLUTIONS ADOPTED AT TOWN MEETING,
April 14th, 1862.

The following Resolutions were submitted by L. H. Bradford, Esq., and were accepted and adopted by acclamation and a rising vote:

Resolved, That the thanks of the town be extended to our own citizens, the officers and privates of General Burnside's Division, who have done themselves and the town so much honor in the late battles of Roanoke and Newbern, thus maintaining by valor and bravery, their right to the position accorded them for discipline and soldierly bearing.

Resolved, That we extend our thanks to Captain Clark S. Simonds and his command, for gallantry on the Heights of Ball's Bluff, and especially to George L. Boss, Walter A. Eames, Fred. H. Sibley and Alvin A. Simonds, our own townsmen, for swimming their Commander, Colonel Chas. Devens, across the bloody waters of the Potomac, on the night of the 21st of October last.

Resolved, That we extend our heartfelt sympathy to Captain Theodore S. Foster, and all of the wounded soldiers from Fitchburg, who have so nobly maintained the bravery of Massachusetts soldiers by pouring out their blood on the battle-field.

Resolved, That we extend our unfeigned sympathy to the families of our brave townsmen, Charles D. Munroe, George C. Taylor, Ai D. Osborne, John M. Whittemore and Harrison W. Battles, who have laid down their lives in defense of their country's honor, that it is due to their memories that their heroism be commemorated by the enduring granite of their own native Rollstone.

Resolved, That copies of the above resolutions be transmitted to Colonel Upton, Captains Foster, Foss and Simonds, and entered on the Records of the Town.

Copies of the foregoing were sent to the field, and the following responses from Colonel Upton and Captain Simonds, were received:

HEADQUARTERS, 25TH REGIMENT, MASS. VOLS., }
Newbern, N. C., April 24th, 1862.

John T. Farwell, Clerk of the town of Fitchburg:

DEAR SIR:—With feelings of gratitude, I received from you the resolutions passed by the said town of Fitchburg at their annual town meeting, on the 14th inst. While absent from our New England homes, and the bosoms of our families, where we have come *not* from *choice,* but to do our *duty* to *God* and our *country,* in aiding to restore the Stars and Stripes that have been torn down by wicked and unprincipled persons calling themselves men, it is gratifying to know that we are not forgotten by our friends that we have left behind; that we still live in their memories, and are considered worthy of so high a mark of respect and confidence by them, for the part we have acted in the conflicts thus far for the supremacy of the law, and maintainance of our glorious Union. In the two battles that we have been in, at Roanoke and Newbern, I can say of a truth, I felt comparatively no fear for myself, but only anxious to do the best possible thing for the men under my command consistent with the accomplishment of the work of defeating the enemy. And now that they are passed, I think I can look back with the greatest degree of satisfaction that I have performed my duty in a manner which proved for the interests of the Union forces, and to the regiment under my command. But I cannot forget to tell you how much we need the sympathies and prayers of all our friends at home, both for ourselves and those loved ones we have left behind, as I often think they have the most trying part of all, and are as much entitled to the sympathy of our friends as we who have left them, although not exposed to the dangers themselves, but in a constant uncertainty about their friends, which we all know is very unpleasant.

Oh, that the Lord might continue to smile upon us, as he has in these few months that are past, and that this unholy war may soon be brought to a close, and we be returned to our homes, in our happy New England, is the ardent desire of him who has written these few lines to you.

We are still at Newbern the Twenty-fifth guarding the town, and have been since we first came here, on the 14th of March. We cannot advance from here until reinforced, which I think will not be until something decisive takes place at Yorktown and Richmond. I think our force sufficient to hold this place, but not sufficient to hold the place and make an advance at the same time, and therefore we had much better wait a few weeks than to make an attempt that we could not carry through. I suppose that by to-day the bombardment of Fort Macon will commence, and therefore you may expect to soon hear of its surrender. Our forces have been some four or five weeks getting ready, under command of Gen. Parke, and we feel that we may look now for the speedy accomplishment of the work, and hope without much loss of our brave soldiers.

Give my best respects to the friends in Fitchburg, and retain a share for yourself.

I am very respectfully, your obedient servant,

EDWIN UPTON.

"CAMP WINFIELD SCOTT,
near Yorktown, April 23d, 1862.

Mr. Farwell, DEAR SIR:

With pleasure I acknowledge the receipt of a copy of the resolutions passed at the Annual Town Meeting in Fitchburg, and forwarded by yourself as Town Clerk. It is exceedingly gratifying to those of us who are actively engaged in the services of our country to receive such testimonials of confidence and respect from our fellow townsmen at home; and while honoring the living, it is still more gratifying to me, sir, to know that the memory of those who have laid down their *lives* in defence of their *country's honor*, is *sacredly* cherished, and finally, that the gallantry of those who *periled their own lives* to save that of their Colonel's, is *acknowledged* by those *at home*. In closing, accept my thanks for your own *personal* testimony of respect and confidence. And may I ever merit it, is the wish of

Yours truly, C. S. SIMONDS,

Capt. Com'g Co. B, 15th Reg't M. V."

RESOLUTIONS OFFERED BY L. H. BRADFORD, ESQ., AT ANNUAL TOWN MEETING, APRIL 13TH, 1863.

Whereas, since the date of our last annual meeting, several of our citizen soldiers have sealed their devotion to their country with their lives, it seems fitting that we should make record of the fact, and thus stimulate the living by commending the example of the patriotic dead. And therefore

Resolved.—That we bear in memory, and cherish the names and virtues of all those heroic dead who have fallen in the service of their country the past year, viz: Capt. Clark S. Simonds, Lieut. Henry A. Beckwith, Calvin E. Tolman, Alvaranzo Bigelow, Jefferson Lakin, John Campbell, D. Carpenter, W. S. Boynton, Horace R. Barker, Geo. F. Howe, John L. Lamson, Charles M. Whitney, Simon F. Marshall, James T. Townsend, Amos W. Lawrence, Orwell L. Stockwell, Michael Kavanaugh, Patrick C. Sullivan, Michael Spencer, Henry D. Brigham, Wm. S. Bardeen, Henry S. Woodbury, and any other brave men who have fallen, which we may not have named.

Resolved.—That we do extend our sympathies to those who have been bereaved in the loss of beloved friends and relatives, whether by death on the battle field, or by disease in the camp.

Resolved.—That we bear in our hearts, those of our citizens who are now absent in the service, who have gone forth to defend our beloved country, and to subdue the Rebellion, that we will continue to follow them with our wishes, our sympathies and our prayers, and in due time will welcome them home with increased honors.

Resolved.—That as citizens, and as a town, we will continue our means, and our influence, to sustain our Government in its measures, until every traitor has disappeared from the land.

RESOLUTIONS OFFERED BY L. H. BRADFORD, ESQ., AT TOWN MEETING, APRIL 11, 1864.

Resolved, That we extend our heartfelt and tenderest sympathies to all of the families and relatives of the following soldiers, our own fellow townsmen, who have fallen the past year in defense of the flag of our common country, viz.: Captain George H. Bailey, Captain Jerome K. Taft, Captain John Murkland, Lieut. George G. Nutting, Lieut. Fred. H. Sibley, Thomas Bartlett, Chas. P. Battles, George L. Boss, Horace M. Churchill, E. L. P. Cochran, Israel Cummings, Henry J. Cutting, Samuel F. Dadmun, Edward P. Farwell, David A. Harrington, Francis D. Hill, J. Henry Kendall, Henry L. Joslin, George E. Knight, Alvin G. Lamb, Wm. H. Shattuck, Wm. H. Simonds, Charles W. Stewart, Solon W. Spooner, Sam'l Stearns, N. Bradley Upham, George G. Winchester, Wm. Wooldridge, Frederic L. Works, Benj. R. Wiley, Albert C. Wilsey; that we will remember with gratitude their noble sacrifice, and embalm their memory in our heart of hearts;

> "So shall they all forever rest,
> By all their country's wishes blest.
> When Spring, with dewy fingers cold,
> Shall come to deck their hallowed mould,
> She there shall dress a sweeter sod
> Than Fancy's feet have ever trod.
> There Honor, too, a pilgrim gray,
> Shall come to bless their honored clay;
> And Freedom shall awhile repair
> To dwell a weeping hermit there."

Resolved, That we place upon the Records of the Town, our thanks to those soldiers who have re-enlisted for the war, and also, to Col. John W. Kimball, of the Fifty-third Massachusetts nine months volunteers, his officers and men, for the noble record they have made for themselves and for us, their fellow citizens.

Resolved, That we remember with patriotic pride the late heroic action of our young townsman, Captain George E. Marshall, of the Fortieth Massachusetts Mounted Infantry, who, with forty-nine of his men, captured and held Gainsville, Florida, against treble the number of the enemy, meriting and receiving the thanks of General Seymour, his commanding officer, and every lover of our beloved country, and we are happy to congratulate him upon his prompt and deserved promotion.

Resolved, That we remember with gratitude, and appreciate the noble patriotism of all our citizens who have taken part in the conflict through which we are now passing.

SUMMARY OF EXPENSE INCURRED BY THE TOWN, ON ACCOUNT OF THE WAR.

The figures given below approximate very closely to the amounts actually paid out by the town, as shown by the books.

Bounties paid to soldiers direct, by vote of the town,	$36,868.00
Amount refunded by vote of town to subscribers to "bounty fund,"	34,758.25
Amount paid to individuals who voluntarily furnished substitutes,	4,375.00
Recruiting expenses,	1,017.65
Amount paid families of soldiers, reimbursed by the State,	60,727.79
Amount so paid not reimbursed (estimated)	1,600.00
Contingent expenses, clothing, supplies, funeral expenses, &c.	2,890.93
Total,	$142,237.62

The total debt of the town in 1861, was $58,240.09; and in 1866, $110,278.88; an increase of $52,038.79. It is difficult to state just what portion of this increase is directly chargeable to the war, but a very large proportion of it, to say the least.

As a thriving and rapidly growing town, our debt is quite likely gradually to increase, but we apprehend that whatever charges of extravagance our descendants may have occasion to bring against us, that portion incurred in the suppression of the Rebellion will be considered as money well expended, and will be deemed no burden to those who live to enjoy what *we* were obliged to fight for, to preserve.

SOLDIER'S MONUMENT.

At the annual Town Meeting in April, 1862, the subject of a monument to our fallen soldiers was considered, and a Committee chosen to report at a future meeting, on some plan for such a memorial. The following constitute the Committee: Alvah Crocker, L. H. Bradford, Stephen Shepley, E. T. Miles, Geo. E. Towne, A. P. Kimball, and H. A. Willis. This Committee has held many meetings, and will be prepared to submit to the town, at the next Annual Meeting, one or more plans for the proper commemoration of our "fallen heroes." It is certainly very desirable that the town should do something in this direction worthy of its dignity, and with a liberality corresponding to its practice toward the soldiers through the whole war, and we doubt not that when the subject is presented in a tangible form, that there will be no stint in the appropriations, and that the "memorial," whatever form it may take, may be a fitting and generous tribute to the memory of those of our young men who fell while nobly fighting to uphold our institutions, and the honor of our flag.

REJOICING AND MOURNING.

While the war was in active progress, our people, as well as the whole country, lived in a constant state of excitement. Now jubilant over the glorious news of some great victory; now depressed by accounts of defeats and disaster. On many occasions, public demonstrations were made over the good news from the "field," but it remained for the occasion of the surrender of General Lee, with his entire army, to bring out the general enthusiasm to its fullest extent.

The news of this last great and final victory was received on the morning of April 10th, 1865, while our citizens were assembled in Annual Town Meeting. The following extract from the records of the town will show how it was received:

Voted, To take a recess of ten minutes to hear read the glorious news received by the morning papers, when the Moderator read the official despatch from the Secretary of War, announcing the surrender of the Rebel General

Lee and his whole army, whereupon it was requested that the meeting rise and give loud and long cheers for Lieut. General Grant and his noble army, and immediately three times three were given ; also, General Sheridan and his brave and fearless army received their due share of the loud and long, enthusiastic cheers of the meeting.

The meeting then resumed its business, and the following Resolution, offered by L. H. Bradford, Esq., was unanimously adopted by a rising vote.

Resolved, That the thanks of the citizens of this town be reverentially offered unto Almighty God for the signal success with which he has crowned our arms, in the capture of the rebel Capital, and the whole army of Northern Virginia.

Notice was given to the people to illuminate their dwellings in the evening, and a large amount of money was at once subscribed for firing salutes, a band of music, and a general jollification, which was pretty thoroughly kept up all day, and nearly all night. The town was illuminated from one end to the other, and presented a most beautiful appearance. A procession paraded the streets in the evening, with music and fireworks, calling out some of our citizens who made speeches suitable to the occasion. Everybody seemed overjoyed, for all could see that now was indeed the "beginning of the end," and that peace would soon return to bless us. And so it proved, but ere it should come, we were destined to receive a shock more terrible by far, than we had yet experienced. Our joy had indeed been great, and who could have dreamed that in less than one week, we would be thrown so suddenly, so terribly to the other extreme.

The news of the murder of Abraham Lincoln came upon us on the morning of Saturday, April, 15th 1865, like a terrific peal of thunder in a cloudless sky. Upon receiving the news, the Selectmen at once posted a call for a gathering of the people, to take place the same afternoon. All business was suspended, and our community gave itself up to mourning for a loss to which all the previous disasters of the war seemed as trifling. The outward emblems of mourning so generally displayed, the blanched faces, the tearful eyes and tremulous voices of the citizens, as they met and discussed the great calamity, gave token of the deep love the people bore our martyred President. We give an account of the afternoon services:

In response to the invitation of the Selectmen, a meeting was held at the Town Hall, at two o'clock, P. M., at which time the hall was filled to overflowing with grief-stricken men and women. The following list of officers was chosen:

President, Geo. E. Towne; *Vice Presidents*, Moses Wood, Alvah Crocker, Ebenezer Torrey, Jonas A. Marshall, Alfred Emerson, Stephen Shepley, Otis T. Ruggles, L. H. Bradford, J. W. Kimball, T. R. Boutelle, Alfred Hitchcock, Amasa Norcross, Nathaniel Wood, John T. Farwell, T. S. Wilson, L. B. Jaquith, E. T. Miles, Wm. O. Brown, Lyman Patch, G. M. Steele, Kendall Brooks, H. L. Jones, T. K. Ware, Wm. Kimball. *Secretaries*, John J. Piper, C. H. B. Snow.

Mr. Towne briefly addressed the meeting, remarking that nations, as individuals, have their seasons of joy and of mourning, and that within one short week we had been raised to the highest pitch of joy and exultation, and cast down to the lowest depths of grief. He eloquently portrayed the many virtues, the pure life, the eminent public services of the great and good man, more loved and revered by the people than any benefactor of his country save Washington, and closed with the remark that words were too feeble to adequately give utterance to the grief which possessed all hearts. The services were continued by the singing of hymns by the choir, reading of the scriptures by Rev. Mr. Jones, and prayers by Rev. Mr. Brooks, and Rev. Mr. Steele.

The following resolutions were submitted and unanimously adopted:

By the people of Fitchburg, assembled at the call of the Selectmen of the town, on the 15th of April, 1865:

Be it Resolved, That we have heard with a shock of inexpressible sorrow of the death by assassination, of the President of the United States:

That such an event, fitted under any circumstances, to fill the hearts of all good citizens with anguish, seems far more disastrous when we remember the character of the President, and the exigencies of the times;

That we recognize in him a man whom God had qualified for a great service in a crisis of unsurpassed importance, by giving to him singular practical sagacity, and great influence with others, and especially with the masses, by maturing in him a deep sense of justice, and all those convictions and sentiments, and traits of personal character which awaken the confidence of the people, which rendered him a fitting representative and leader of the nation in the terrible conflict of right and wrong;

That his clear perceptions of great principles, and his steady purpose to maintain them, his sympathy with the oppressed, and his largeness of soul, peculiarly qualified him for leading not only in the suppression of the rebellion, but also in the more serious, and scarcely less difficult work of reconstruction;

And that the loss of such a man, at such an hour, is an immeasurable calamity, which the Providence of God alone can rule for good.

Resolved, That while receiving this sudden and stunning blow, we will remember that the Lord God Omnipotent reigneth; that we will call upon Him in the bitterness of our distress, to preserve our Nation; to interfere with the plans of wicked and traitorous men; to guide by His own wisdom, in the re-establishment of the National authority in all the rebellious States, and in the securing of peace and justice and all human rights to all the people of this Republic;

And, that we have faith in God, the Ruler of the world, whose plans cannot be disappointed, and who, as He has often caused the wrath of man to praise Him, can make use of the assassin's hand to set forward the interests of Truth and Justice and Right.

On the Wednesday following the day of the President's funeral at Washington, by request of President Johnson to the people of the country, funeral services were held in memory of the great, and honored, and beloved dead. Business was suspended, and a service held in the Congregational Church, which was appropriately draped in mourning. Rev. Mr. Emerson preached a very able and impressive funeral discourse, giving a sketch of Mr. Lincoln's character, and setting forth the lessons to be drawn from the horrid event. A universal feeling of sorrow pervaded all classes, and terrible forebodings for the future of our beloved country were indulged in, for our Vice President had already shown he was not the man for the position which this sad event had elevated him into. Every loyal heart felt itself dedicated anew to the great work of extirpating treason from the land, and the feeling universally prevailed that no leniency should be shown to the plotters and abettors of the great conspiracy against the government, of which this wicked murder was the legitimate result.

THE ESCAPE.

A story of the adventures of two soldiers of the Fifteenth regiment, who escaped from the enemy while being marched to Andersonville, and after wandering in the mountains of Virginia for twenty-three days, and travelling four hundred miles, reached our lines at Harper's Ferry, written for this history by Alvan A. Simonds of this town.

"On the 22d of June, 1864, the remnant of the Fifteenth Massachusetts regiment was captured by Gen. Mahoney's Division, of the Rebel army. Roland E. Bowen and myself found ourselves inside the rebel lines with plenty of " grey backs " wishing to trade jack-knives, watches, &c., &c. We stopped in Petersburg two days, and were thence taken to Richmond, to Libby prison, where for two days we had the pleasure of looking through the grated windows. In Libby they searched us for money, each man being required to remove all his clothing, except his under garments, the rebels taking the liberty to confiscate all money found. Bowen and I had divided our money, and had about seventeen dollars each. I sewed mine very carefully into my pants and blouse in four different places, and they succeeded in finding only two dollars of it, but my friend was more unfortunate, as they took all but three dollars from him. From Libby we were taken to Belle Island. The rebels with *great generosity* gave us some tents, which although they would shelter from the sun, were worthless in the rain. Our stay here was short, for in three days they started us for Andersonville, Ga., travelling by rail to Lynchburg.

Bowen and I had resolved to improve any opportunity given us to escape. We left Richmond in the morning, and arrived in Lynchburg in the evening. We were kept in the crowded cars during the night without water, and as they had given us none during the day, which had been exceedingly hot, we suffered much from thirst. At Lynchburg they gave us four days' rations, consisting of sixteen hard crackers and a small piece of bacon, this to last until we reached Danville, seventy miles south of Lynchburg, to which place they intended to march us. When they issued the rations, some very mouldy bread was thrown on the ground. Of this we took all we could carry in our haversacks, resolving we would make our escape before we reached Danville. A few moments before we left Lynchburg, I improved an opportunity to step into a store and buy four bunches of matches, paying for them one dollar in Confederate money. The first night out we were on the watch to make our escape, but no favorable opportunity was offered. But the second day about eleven o'clock, the prisoners had got well strung out in attempting to get water at a house in our way, and the head of the column was halted in a road leading through a piece of woods. It being very hot and dusty, every man made for the shade. This was an opportunity not to be lost. Before we reached the woods we had so planned as to have a guard about a rod in front of us, but none for several rods in the rear. We then slipped into the woods. When we were safely past the guards, we ran for half a mile or more, until we come to a brook, where we stopped and quenched our thirst and had a good wash, which was a luxury we appreciated after our travels. We rested here for a short time and then started for the Blue Ridge of the Alleghany mountains, taking the sun for our guide, travelling northwest as near as we could calculate. The mountains were not in sight the first day. The second morning while passing the woods, we came suddenly upon a man dressed in gray, with brass buttons upon his jacket, and a gun over his shoulder; as we could not avoid him, we walked up to him, and the relief of our minds may well be imagined when he informed us after a few minutes conversation, that he was not a rebel picket, and had no authority to stop any one, but was out hunting squirrels.

In the afternoon, about one o'clock, I should judge, (neither of us having a watch) we came in sight of the Virginia and Tennessee railroad. We were quite a distance from it, but the country being very open we could see men upon the road, but could not tell whether they were friends or foes. After holding a "council," we concluded to keep in the woods until dark, and then cross the railroad. We soon found a little brook and proceeded to make ourselves comfortable. The mosquitoes were plenty, and comfort not to be had. At about ten o'clock we proceeded on our way, and succeeded in crossing the railroad in safety. Several trains of cars passed us during the afternoon. We then attempted to travel by taking the north star for a guide. This did very well until we came to the woods; while in the woods we found it impossible to keep it in sight, so we laid down for the night. In the morning we resumed our travels, but the country being very open, we thought we were running too much risk, and stopped until night, when we again took the north star for our guide. We were more fortunate than the night before and travelled several hours, but before morning we had to stop on account of the woody country. Next morning we proceeded, stopping at a house where there was a negro woman with several children. She told us she had nothing to eat, but if we would go up to "Massa's house" he would give us something. We asked if she knew who we were? She said she did not. We told her we were yankees. She said we had better keep away from "Massa's" then. She told us where a woman lived whose husband was in the rebel army, some half a mile away. To her house we went. Bowen stopped outside in the woods, and I went to the house. I rapped, a woman came to the door, I asked her if she could get me anything to eat. She invited me into the house and gave me a large piece of bread. She asked about the army, (rebel of course) for her husband had been conscripted, and was serving under Lee at Petersburg. I could give her but little information, but told her I was going home on a furlough, over the mountains. I left her with thanks for her kindness, and we proceeded on our way, after dividing the bread.

At noon we came to the foot of the mountains, but thought it not best to attempt to ascend without more rations. A short distance from us was a field of wheat in the stook. Of this we took as many bundles as we could carry, threshed it out, went into the woods, and soon had it boiling in our cups over the fire. This, without salt, and a little mouldy hard bread was our food for the next four days.

We reached the top of the mountains before sunset, but as we wished to take observations, concluded to spend the night there. At sunset we took a stick, pointed it toward the setting sun and placed it across a stone. We then lay down to rest. When I awoke, my friend was placing a stick across the other, thus pointing to the North Star. This showed us how much north of west the sun set, and the knowledge was of great advantage to us in traveling, the next three weeks. We traveled near the top of the mountains the greater part of the day, until thirst compelled us to go down for water. We always found good water by following down the ravines. The mountains were covered with scrub oak and other small brush, which made it very hard traveling, and we did not make very rapid progress, but we kept on, up and down mountains, traveling by the sun. In three days we reached the top of the mountain which overlooked the James river at what is known as Balcony Falls.

The river did not look deep, and we thought we might easily ford it, so we walked down a ravine until we came to the water. We here boiled some wheat which we had brought with us, then took off our stockings, and tried to cross, but found the current so deep and swift that we could not. On the banks of the river we found a small garden which some one had planted, in which we dug a few small potatoes, and went back into the woods and boiled them. We slept well that night notwithstanding our great disappointment. At sunrise we started up the river, going a mile or more, when we came to a dam. A high bluff overlooked it, to which I climbed for a view farther up. While on this bluff, two rebel cavalrymen passed up the tow-path of a canal on the other side of the river. Soon after, three boys came out in a boat just below the dam, and we called them to take us across, which they did. Still, there was the canal between us and the mountains, but we soon found a lock where we crossed. Once more we were in the mountains, having crossed the only river in our course. After travelling three or four days up and down the mountains, we came to a log-house, where a man sat at the door. We stopped an hour or more with him, and he gave us a dinner of boiled potatoes and string beans. For the next three or four days nothing of note transpired.

We got our food by digging potatoes, and taking wheat from the fields. July 14th we came to a neat looking frame house. As it was a much larger one than we had previously visited, we held a "council," whether to go to it, but after walking round so that we could examine all sides, I ventured. Found a young lady with two children at home, and a negro servant; told her I was a yankee, had made my escape, and would like something to eat. She gave me half a loaf of bread, a pie, some bacon, and some milk. I asked permission (after eating what I wished) to take the remainder to my companion. She granted it, and gave me another large piece of bread. She also gave me a Richmond Examiner, of July 12th. I returned to Bowen, and we went on a mile or more when we stopped to examine the paper. We learned that Gen. Early was in Maryland with a large force. Whether to change our course by crossing the valley and mountains, to Beverley, Western Va., or keep on northeast, was a question in our minds. At our present rate of travelling, it would be a week or ten days before we could reach Harper's Ferry, and the latest news the paper gave was already a week old, so we concluded that Gen. Early, would be further north or else back into Virginia before we could get to the Potomac. We had now passed through the counties of Campbell, Bradford, Rockbridge, and were now in Augusta. We left the village of Waynesboro' on our left, and crossed the railroad running to Staunton. In the afternoon we overtook a negro with a wooden leg, out picking blackberries.

He asked us to his house and his wife cooked us a johnny-cake. We spent two hours with them, then went on, the negro with us for a short distance, telling us all about the country for several miles. He gave Bowen a canteen, which was very useful to us, as we did not have to hunt up water so often; also some meal and pork. We next passed Brown's Gap, but here we had to wait for some rebel scouts to pick what blackberries they wanted to eat, before we could cross the road.

We kept on our way into Rockingham county, getting our living by going to log houses, near the foot of the mountains, which were occupied by the poorer classes, who seldom refused us food. We crossed the mountains into Green county, through Madison, and back over the mountains into Page, down the Luray valley into Warren county. We were informed that Gen. Early was back in Virginia, that there had been a fight at Snicker's Gap, and the rebel cavalry were picketing Chester and Manassas Gaps, as the yankees were expected down on the east side of the Blue Ridge. We continued on to the road leading to Chester Gap. When we came in sight of the road, only a few rods off, we saw an old man passing on horseback. Before he was out of sight a boy came along, then two rebel cavalrymen. After they had passed we pushed on, crossing the road and into the woods. We soon came to the road leading to Manassas Gap, which we crossed and kept on through the woods near the road, passing through an open field. When within a few rods of the woods we looked up and saw a squad of rebel cavalry in the road. We ran into the woods and looked around. The rebels had not seen us. We watched them pass, there were thirteen. We passed Manassas Gap railroad that day, and succeeded in crossing in safety Paris Gap. The next day we passed Snicker's Gap, but not without an adventure. For just as we were in the middle of the road, two of Mosby's men came around a bend in the road. They saw us. We ran for the woods, the rebels putting spurs to their horses, and as they came up to where we crossed the road, we were in the woods up the side of the mountain. They sent a pistol ball after us, and just as it whizzed past our heads, I stumbled and fell. My companion thought I was wounded, and cried out "we surrender!" No we don't, said I as I jumped up. We ran until out of breath, and then lay down in the bushes. If the guerrillas followed us we have the satisfaction of knowing that they had their labor for their pains. I lost my quart dipper, but we were about through with that, as we arrived at Harper's Ferry the next day and were once more among friends. It was a happy day for us. It was twenty-three days after we made our escape before we arrived inside the Union lines. We had travelled about four hundred miles, and although foot sore and weary, rejoiced that we had so providentially made our escape from the horrors of a Southern prison.

INCIDENTS OF THE BATTLE OF BALL'S BLUFF.

It will be remembered that at the terrible defeat at Ball's Bluff, our men were driven into the Potomac, and obliged to escape by swimming the river, Col. Devens of the Fifteenth, and Lieut. Eager of our Co. B, could neither of them swim, and were taken across the river by four of the members of Co. B, Walter A. Eames, Geo. L. Boss, Fred H. Sibley and Alvan A. Simonds. This gallant action on their part, was duly acknowledged by Lieut. Eager, in the following extract from a letter of his which was published at the time. We regret that we cannot give similar acknowledgment from the pen of the other officer.

"You asked me for an account of my escape from the "sacred soil of Virginia" on the night of the 21st of October. I must say I feel decidedly delicate in furnishing any items relating to myself, but it will give me pleasure to put on record the acts of those four brave fellows (God bless them!) who took me safely across, at the risk of their own lives, and but for whom, I might now have been confined in some Southern prison. After the order had been given to retreat, we rallied in a kind of *bridle path* under the Bluff, and near the river, when Colonel Devens ordered us to throw our arms into the river and take care of ourselves as best we could. There were a good many of the Company who said they could not swim, or did not dare undertake it. I told them I could not swim, but we would keep together as much as possible, make our way up the river, and perhaps find a boat in which we could cross. Geo. L. Boss upon hearing me say I could not swim, said two or three of them could take me across, and soon appeared with Corporal Fred. H. Sibley and Alvan A. Simonds, who insisted upon my going with them. I told them I might be the means of drowning them all, and they had better go without me, but they still insisted, and seemed so confident of success, I told them if I could find anything that would float, I would make the attempt. Upon going to the river edge, we found a limb some six inches through at the butt, and perhaps ten feet long, and in pulling that out, pulled up a common *floor joist* about the same length. Upon seeing that, I told them I could "make the trip" with it, on my own hook, and not endanger their lives, but they would not hear a word to that, and said I must go with them. At this point Walter A. Eames offered his services in assisting us across, and which proved to be very valuable. I certainly think without his help we should have had hard work to have reached the opposite shore. Just as we were about to embark, Colonel Devens came to the water's edge stripped of his equipments and clothing, when Eames asked him if he could swim. He replied that he could not. Eames said to him, "Hop on to our craft, and we will take you across too." After satisfying himself they were all swimmers but *me*, he *waded in*.

In spite of all our efforts, we drifted quite a distance down stream, the current being strong, and finally landed on a small island, separated from Harrison's Island by a stream some twenty-five yards wide, which proved to be fordable, only about waist deep. When we arrived at the *old barn*, we learned that no soldiers would be allowed to cross, as they were very busy getting the wounded from the Island to the Maryland shore. We found our overcoats and blankets which we had left there in the morning, wrapped ourselves up and laid down by some wheat stacks till there was an opportunity for us to come over. We reached Poolesville about 12 o'clock at night, some barefooted, others bareheaded, and some with nothing but *shirt* and overcoat."

SOLDIERS' CORRESPONDENCE.

We select a few of the many letters of our own, and from the newspapers, received from soldiers in the field belonging to the different regiments, in which we had companies, believing they will be of interest to the reader, as conveying the best idea of a soldier's life in camp, on the march, and amid the perils of battles. Of the many at hand, it is difficult to make selections, and we regret that our space will permit us to give so few of them. Some were written with a view to publication, but the most of them with no expectation of it. They are none the worse however on that account, and although they are used without permission, we trust we shall be pardoned for the liberty taken. We commence with a letter from private (afterwards Lieut.) Geo. B. Simonds, giving his experience at the battle of Ball's Bluff:

"LUNENBURG, JAN. 4th, 1862.

Dr. Hitchcock,

  DEAR SIR: Since you have desired me, and I have promised to write what I saw and experienced at the battle of Ball's Bluff, I will try and do so in this letter. It would be impossible for me to write what is called "a glowing account" of that disastrous affair, but if a plain statement of a few facts, as they came under my observation, will be acceptable, you shall have them. About half past one on the morning of the 21st of October, we were all startled by that soldier's warning, the long roll. "To the river, take your blankets, overcoats and one day's rations," were the orders.

To throw on our accoutrements, roll up our blankets and overcoats, and fill up our haversacks and canteens, were duties quickly performed; this done we were immediately ordered to march.

I think we never marched six or seven miles easier than we did that morning. We all knew and felt that "*something* was up." We all hoped that before the next morning, *something* would be *done*.

We arrived opposite Ball's Bluff about four o'clock; were here ordered to halt; found that those five Companies of our Regiment which had lately been stationed at the river as pickets, had already crossed, under Col. Devens. We waited until about seven or half past, before receiving any orders to cross. A short time before this we had heard irregular firing in the direction of the Bluff; it lasted however, but a few minutes, but our impatience was only equalled by our eagerness to learn its cause and effect. Harrison's Island lay between us and the opposite shore. As this island is over two miles long, we were obliged to cross it. The only means of transportation which we had on this side of the island, consisted of two flat bottomed boats not capable of holding more than thirty-five men apiece. Arriving at the island, we found that the firing we had heard, was no boys' play. Quite a number of Company H's men lay wounded in the only house there was. It was then and there that we first witnessed the horrors of war.

Leaving our blankets and overcoats in the ruins of an old barn, we embarked, or rather, my Company (B,) crowded itself on to the only boat there was for conveying us to the Virginia shore. Notwithstanding the miserable and insufficient means of crossing, we landed safe at the foot of Ball's Bluff. We were now fairly on the "sacred soil," to us it was the "land of promise"; the great battle-field where the fate of our country was to be decided, and, *this* decided, we should return to our never forgotten homes.

Following a narrow and rather circuitous bridle path, we proceeded through the woods, up the Bluff, across an open space, again into some woods to within a few rods of another open space. Here we found Colonel Devens and that part of the regiment that had crossed in the night. We were about a mile from where we landed, and in the direction of Leesburg. The roll was now called and sixty-five of our Company responded to their names. As this was the number that started from camp, it proved that with us, all was thus far, well.

After waiting impatiently some time, and finding that we were not likely to move soon, I came to the conclusion that it would be well to look out for breakers ahead. Accordingly, I sat down on the ground, the order being "rest," and thoroughly refreshed the *inner* man with salt beef and hard bread, and the *outer* with a short nap.

While we were here waiting, our skirmishers, or advanced guard, who were nearly one-fourth of a mile in advance, exchanged shots with those of the rebels. That those shots did not always fall short of their mark, the wounds of the injured, who passed us on their way back to the island, too plainly told. Sergeant (now Lieutenant,) Jorgerson of Company A, passed about eleven o'clock, wounded in the arm.

The ground in the open space in our front, rose gradually for about one-fourth of a mile, to where our skirmishers were deployed. This space was bounded by woods on the left, and partly so on the right.

Soon after twelve o'clock, my brother, Captain Clark S. Simonds, Co. B, was ordered to take his platoon and relieve Company A's skirmishers. As we filed out of the woods I heard some one say, "Good Bye, George," and turning met the look, and shook the hand of my friend, Andrew Cowdry, of Company A. It was the last time I ever saw him. That day "he fought his last battle"; he now "sleeps his last sleep." He was severely wounded in the main fight, and died in the hospital a few days after.

From our new position we could see a part of Leesburg, and what was of more importance to us, quite a large body of rebel infantry. They were however, out of reach of our guns, we being armed with that *very modern* invention, the smooth bore muskets.

Perhaps I should tell you that when deployed as skirmishers, each man is about five paces from the next, consequently our first platoon of only thirty-two or three men, were extended over a line of as many rods. We had not been in this position long when we saw an officer ride in front of their infantry and wave his hand. Immediately the infantry advanced, and at the same time a rushing sound was heard in the woods on our left; some one said "cavalry," and sure enough, the next minute a large body of them dashed upon us. It was impossible for so few of us, situated as we were, to withstand such a force. We fired upon them and did our best to get back to the reserve. As I turned to retreat, I saw Geo. Taylor a few rods from me, making his way off the field, but as he did not get back to the reserve and has not since been heard from, I conclude that he was shot dead; being the only one that was killed in that skirmish, although two of our boys who were wounded and taken prisoners have since died from the effects of their wounds. I had not proceeded more than five rods on my retrograde march, when I experienced a peculiar sensation in my right thigh. There was not much chance to doubt what hurt at that time; the balls were whistling on all sides, and I believed that I was carrying an ounce of lead besides the forty in my cartridge box. Such proved to be case, for in a minute or two my shoe was full of, and my pants saturated with blood. Although wounded, I still kept on, resolved to get back to friends or die. A body of the rebel infantry had got into the woods on the left, and cut off our retreat through the open space; we therefore took to the woods on the right, which we knew led round to the reserve. Before I reached them I saw Ai Osborn and Albert Litchfield sitting behind a corn stook, both I believe were wounded, and both soon after taken prisoners. Stopping behind a little house, which was about three rods from the edge of the woods, for a moment, I found Geo. Daniels wounded in the wrist and shoulder. Lowell, another of our boys, was also there. I saw him go to the corner and fire. "There," says he, I've *fixed him*, I saw him fall." Lowell went through the fight and still lives to tell his own story.

Leaving the house, I reached the woods, and was now comparatively safe, but I was very faint. Before this I had thrown away my musket, and was now about to throw away all my trappings, when Corporal Fisher, seeing that I was wounded, kindly offered to assist me. With his assistance, I reached the river, passing on our way the regiment, which had fallen back to the open space, and was now forming in line of battle.

Here ends my personal knowledge of the Ball's Bluff fight.

Geo. Daniels and myself were taken to a house on the Island. Here we remained until evening, of course not far from where the fighting was going on. The awful volleys and the great number of them, told how bravely that field was contested.

Of course I was anxious to know how the battle was going and until it was fairly ended, the invariable answer to my many questions concerning it was, "our men are slowly driving them." About dark the firing ceased entirely, and then came the bitter news that we were defeated. I thought the wound was bad enough and the extraction of the ball painful enough, but when this word came it proved a "*miserable comforter.*" About this time the only boat there was on the Virginia side of the river sank, and the poor boys had no chance to retreat except by swimming the river. It was an awful evening, and a heart-rending sight to see the wounded, and those shivering, benumbed comrades, who had swam that river; they were seven miles from camp, nearly all of them barefoot and with only their shirts and drawers on. It was one of the coldest nights we had had, and several of our boys were so chilled as to be almost unable to move. No one *thought* of asking whose blanket or overcoat that was, if it was needed it was taken. I succeeded in getting to the Maryland shore, in one of the boats. After lying on the ground some time, Corporal Fisher, who after helping me down to the river, went back, was in the whole fight, and escaped uninjured, obtained a chance for me to ride up to Poolesville in an ambulance, arriving at the hospital about twelve o'clock. I will not write you my experience of hospital life in the succeeding week, suffice it to say, that "there was lack of woman's nursing, there was dearth of woman's tears." At the end of that time you saw me there, and assisted by Messrs. Kimball and Shepley, kindly brought me home. By this act I believe you saved my life, and I *know* that I can *never* cancel the debt of gratitude I owe to you and them. May the Great Author of all good remember and reward you.

Yours, with respect

GEORGE B. SIMONDS,

Co. B, 15th Regt. Mass. Vols.

PORTION OF A LETTER FROM "I. B. G." TO FITCHBURG REVEILLE.

"HEADQUARTERS 1ST BRIG. 1ST DIV. 9TH A. C.,
Before Petersburg, Va., August 5th, 1864.

MR. EDITOR: The movement so long anticipated, has come off. The attack has been made, and resulted in nothing save a little rough experience, which should be very beneficial to those who direct the movements of the armies. Our loss has been very heavy, as also, has the enemy's. I propose to give you and your readers, a short narrative of the fight, as seen by me. Arrangements having been completed on the previous day, and the lead in the charge decided by lot, and the positions of the troops assigned to them, early on the morning of the 30th, the Ninth Corps and one Division of the Eighth were massed in the rear of General Wilcox's front, near the left centre, and then awaited the signal for the charge. A mine which run beneath a fort of the enemy's in front, was to be exploded. Everything being in readiness the match was applied, but it was extinguished twice, and it was not until 4.40, A. M., and daylight had fully come, that the explosion was heard, and the brown earth was seen rising in a towering cloud to the height of several hundred feet. The explosion was not loud, but deep, and shook the earth quite sensibly where we were standing. As soon as the explosion was heard the batteries on our lines at once opened, and a most terrific firing commenced.

At the same time the First Division, Ninth Corps, with General Bartlett at the head, started over our breastworks and toward the enemy's. The charge was successful. The rebels were partially surprised and at once gave way, leaving many prisoners in our hands, and two stands of colors.

Our supports came quickly up, and the line was held. Meantime, the enemy was vigorously shelling the captured fort from his batteries on either flank, but without much effect.

To take these batteries, however, was next in order. and the colored division was ordered up. They went in in gallant style, and their appearance and conduct seemed to promise much for their performance of duty. They were formed in front of our main line, and were about to charge, when a line of rebels *charged them*, and the inexperienced contrabands at once broke in extremest confusion, running into and over the white troops in their rear. A panic ensued, terrible in its consequences, for their dense masses, jumbled together in inextricable confusion, and pierced through and through by the terrible fire of musketry and cannister poured into them. The day was lost; the troops fell hurridly back in their original line, and all attempts to rally them were fruitless until too late. Gens. Bartlett, Griffin and Hartsauft, however, succeeded in rallying a few men, and they held the "crater" of the captured fort for some time, until, seeing that there was no hope for a renewed assault, and knowing that to remain long would be impossible, the men were ordered to save themselves if they could, as the fort must be surrendered. Gens. Harnsauft, with many men, succeeded in running the terrible gauntlet from the fort to our own lines in safety, and thus escaped; but Gen. Bartlett having in some manner injured his artificial leg, could not escape, and surrendered the fort. Thus ended the operations of the day. That some one was blamable for gross mismanagement, there is little doubt, but it is not my intention now to discuss that part of the question. One thing is generally conceded to be true, that is, that the *plan* of the assault was faultless. I know not whose it was, whether Grant's, Meade's, or Burnside's. But whosoever it was, had it been *executed* properly, it could not have failed of success.

A SOLDIER TO HIS PARENTS.

NEWBERN, N. C., *Mar.* 19*th*, 1862.

Dear Parents:

Last Friday (13th,) we landed in the mud, as usual, and started off through the woods along the road toward Newbern. We soon came to some barracks which had been vacated a few moments before by about fifty cavalry. They left in a hurry. On we marched through the mud ankle deep, preceded by our Generals and Aids, one of which soon reported that the rebels had left their first Battery, also, that we had obtained possession of the railroad; we soon came to a long breastwork mounting seven guns, with which they intended to protect the railroad. This was a *masked* battery, and the rascals might have bothered us some and fell back to their stronger one, for we should have driven them just as sure as they had made a stand. But on we marched until dark, and at last lay down in the woods, on the wet ground, with nothing but our rubber blankets over us. It rained quite hard most all night, and it was something of the rough side of the soldier's life. We built fires, however, and made out to endure it patiently until morning. As soon as it was light we marched along for perhaps a mile and a half, and saw before us the Twenty-fourth and Twenty-seventh formed in line of battle, in the edge of the woods. We filed behind them to the right and were to flank the enemy. We marched up until the head of our column was within ten rods of the left of their battery. The land was wooded and we could not see them, but they could see us, or at least knew where we were, from the sound of our voices. We soon advanced toward the opening, and the rebels gave us a raking fire from a pivot gun on the corner. We immediately lay flat, and the grape or canister went over us, hitting a few of our regiment. In this position we lay and received six or seven charges, and retired about five or six rods into a hollow. After a little while orders came to go down in front of the battery, which was done in good order. Previous to this movement we were formed in divisions. The rebel gunners saw us and let fly charges of grape and canister. We lay down as before, and the iron hail passed over us. These were moments of awful suspense. The ammunition for our artillery was all expended. The gunner (whose men had been all shot from the guns,) said, give me six hundred men and I will take the Battery. General Burnside's Aid told us to charge, and the Colonel gave the order, which was promptly obeyed. The rebels gave us a volley of musketry and one charge of grape, but we rushed on, and with a loud cheer entered the battery. Massachusetts had the State colors on first, but I believe the Pennsylvanians had up the Stars and Stripes first. Very soon we marched on about forty rods, and formed in line of battle. Here we were sometime, continually annoyed by the rebel sharpshooters. At last General Foster gave orders to *charge*, which we did, and fired a volley into the woods which made them leave. I think this was the last firing which was done. We marched up the railroad until, arriving at the burning bridge, we were obliged to stop. Here we remained about three hours, then crossed into the city by steamboats. The Twenty-fifth Massachusetts were the first to enter the city, and have a chance to "look around." I went to a rebel camp and picked up a number of small articles which I shall send home some time if I have an opportunity. The black people seem delighted to "see de wite people."

Co. F landed in the city about five o'clock, and the Captain dismissing us, we at once went out to pick up trophies. I picked up a rifle, miniature cup, &c. Company F took up quarters in the Mercantile Bank building, but has since removed to a fine two story house once owned by Benj. Ellis. It is lighted by gas, and very comfortable. Soldiers seldom get such quarters. Fifty rebel cavalry rode into the city the other day, without arms, with a flag of truce. Some think the rebels will try to recapture the city, but they will require a large force to drive us out. There are quite a number of cannon to guard the outposts, and about five regiments to support them, besides as many more just across the river. I enjoy talking with the secesh; some are a little cross. Truly God was with our forces in this battle, else how did we take these fortifications? They had the advantage, three to one, in position, with an equal number of men. Let us praise God for these great victories. Let us pray for the continuance of His favor, without which we shall not conquer.

Your affectionate son, ——.

The following letter from a member of Co. B, Fifteenth regiment, will give some idea of army life on the Peninsula, in the famous and fated McClellan campaign:

CAMP ADVANCE, NEAR YORKTOWN, *April 7th* 1862.

FRIEND W.—Your favor of the last of February, did not come to hand until after our return to Washington, or I should have attended to it sooner. We embarked on board the steamer "Argo," for Fortress Monroe, on Saturday, the 29th ult. and arrived there Monday following. Were not allowed to land there but laid at anchor till morning, then run up to Hampton, and encamped there until Friday morning, at seven o'clock, when we marched for Great Bethel and camped near the ground where the battle was fought last summer. Marched at six next morning, and during the day passed over the ground occupied by Gen. Magruder the day previous, arrived at this point just at night. There is a force of some thirty thousand in advance of us, which looks very much like our being a portion of the reserve. Yesterday was Sunday, and a splendid day it was too. There were several regiments out scouting, but not a gun fired from our artillery, although there are over one hundred pieces already in position. Saturday there was some fighting. Gen. Keyes was making an effort to throw a bridge across a stream (where the rebels had burned one) under fire. We lost only three men and seven horses killed, and very few wounded. There are thirteen of the Massachusetts regiments in this movement, including the 16th at Fortress Monroe. The 1st, 7th, 9th, 10th, 11th, 15th, 16th, 17th, 18th, 19th, 20th, 22d, 29th. I heard Gen. Porter's force were in advance of all, so Massachusetts will be represented by the 9th, and from all accounts they expect a good report from them. Sedgwick's Division is temporarily detached from Sumner's Corps, perhaps we shall join him at Richmond if success attends us, as we have faith to believe it will. I assure you we have had a rough time of it since we left Poolesville. Our trip to Berryville and Winchester was decidedly severe. We have no tents now, but instead, long India rubber blankets, and a long rain would be very disagreeable in those. The weather generally has been quite cool since we landed in this section.

Tuesday Morning.—We are having a cold rain storm; commenced about five o'clock last evening and continued through the night quite severe. There is some prospect of its clearing up to-day. Sedgwick's Division is still here and we may remain for three or four days. It was the general impression that we should have a fight on Monday. The truth of it is, *we know little about the business any way.* When we get orders to march, we march where they lead us, and stop when ordered. It is almost impossible to ascertain where we have been, at least to find a name for the place. At Great Bethel we found an old church (from which it takes its name) and two or three deserted houses. Hampton is truly a desolate place. Magruder did his work well—did not spare a dwelling within sight of the road for miles back into the country. We passed their fortifications at three different points after leaving Bethel; some three miles out, there were quite extensive earthworks, and good barracks for eight or ten thousand troops. About three-fourths of a mile back from where we are now camped, there are some splendid barracks, equal to anything the yankees could get up. The *Regulars* now occupy them. By the way, we have portions of the 2d, 3d, 4th, 10th, 12th, 14th and 17th U. S. Infantry with us, a few companies from each, should say there were between three and four thousand men all told. They are held in reserve I believe—are considered *more reliable* than *volunteers*. All is, I hope the first sharp fight we are in there will be a regiment of them along side of us, we will see how much *later they stay* than volunteers. All above the 10th regiment have been recruited since last summer, and have seen no fighting whatever. Most of them have been in barracks all winter, and look accordingly. They evidently feel above the volunteers, at least feel that they can fight a little better, but I can't *see the point*, particularly between *new recruits* of the regular army and volunteers.

* * * * * * * *

Truly yours,

The following letter was written by a member of Company D, Twenty-first Regiment, during its connection with the Burnside Expedition to North Carolina:

STEAMER NORTHERER, HATTERAS INLET,
JAN. 21, 1862.

Dear Friend W.

Thinking that a few lines from me may be acceptable, I will venture to write to you, that you may know how we are getting along. * * * * * At last the Burnside Expedition has sailed, and the Twenty-first is with them. Of our movements at the present time you are doubtless aware, as far as the press can inform you, but if you were here to observe with your own eyes all that takes place, I fear that your opinions would not be very high. Certainly there is mismanagement somewhere, for often I hear Regimental and Brigade Officers complaining of inefficiency, but I assure you the *military* portion of the expedition is not included in their complaints. Every day vessels are getting smashed up by collisions and by being wrecked. Already a large steamer, the City of New York, loaded with ordnance stores, and the steamer Pocahontas, with ninety horses, have been lost by being driven ashore by the high winds and rough waters of this dreaded North Carolina coast. We have now been on board ship for sixteen days, and expect to be for at least over three weeks yet, and the boys are naturally very anxious to get on dry land again, even though they have to fight for a foothold. * * * Our passage here from Fortress Monroe was a very rough one, and our vessel was considered a very unsafe one for the waters we were in. In consequence of the high seas which prevailed, we had it anchored one night near Cape Hatteras. We doubled the Cape, and were obliged to retrace our steps for about ten miles, to a place of safety. The next morning we made the Inlet, thankful that we were safe and sound. We arrived here on Monday morning, the 13th instant. The weather is very unsteady here, being most of the time cloudy or else high winds prevailing.

Of the two Forts here you probably understand the position as well as I can describe it to you. The point of land on which Fort Clark is built is very sandy, and is a desolate place for one to look upon. All of the boys are cheerful, and are anxious to see a fight soon, and if need be, to engage in it themselves. Doubtless before many days we shall have had a conflict somewhere, and many of our Regiment may find a grave upon North Carolina soil. Who are to be the first victims of the enemy's bullets is not for us to tell. May be one of my father's children will be called for, to go to another world, and perhaps all of us will be spared to return to our homes

again. If any of us three should perchance have to lay down our lives in this war, all I can ask is that those who are left behind us, dependent upon our efforts for their livelihood will be properly cared for, and not be allowed to come to want in this world. I shall, if called upon, go to battle determined to do my whole duty, like a good and faithful soldier. If wounded, the wounds will be my pride and glory in future years. If killed, I shall die cheerfully, and hope to meet my companion and friend, Serg't. Geo. C. Taylor, of the Fifteenth, who has died before me. Taylor was a noble boy and of a brave and cheerful spirit. Any mother should be proud of such a son, any sister of such a brother. For nearly three years I worked side by side with him, and I loved him as a brother. * * * * *
All of us are in the best of health, and we ask that you will soon write to us, if convenient. Your friend, ———

The following are extracts from a very long letter from Lieut. Fred. H. Sibley, of the Thirty-sixth Regiment, to his family, bearing date July 28th, 1863, at Vicksburg, Miss. He lived but three weeks after the letter was written, falling a victim to the climate of Mississippi and the hardships of the campaign:

"It has been a long time since I have written a letter home, and now I propose to write a long one, giving you a full and detailed account of this month's campaign here in Mississippi. I suppose the old Ninth Corps will term it the Mississippi campaign, and taking into consideration the short allowance of rations we were on, the hot and dusty marches and the scarcity of water, I think it rougher than the Peninsula campaign, and those who passed through that can imagine a little what this has been. We read in the history of the Russian campaign, of men freezing and dying by the roadside. Here in Mississippi we see men drop dead in the ranks while marching along, caused by the excessive heat.

The old Ninth Corps arrived back at our old camp yesterday, with only about one-third of the men fit for duty. The remainder are sick, demoralized and "played out." We need rest and must have it. I never experienced the want of water so much as I did on the march from here to Jackson. I will give you a kind of a diary of the month, commencing July 4th, the time we commenced our advance on Jackson. Saturday, July 4th—Went on picket on the advance post about three miles from camp. While on picket reports came in to us that Vicksburg had surrendered, but I could not believe it until about two o'clock, when the Adjutant came out with an order for me to draw in my pickets as the regiment was about to move. He said General Pemberton had surrendered Vicksburg and the whole garrison to General

Grant. Grant immediately put his army in motion after Johnson, the Ninth Corps having the advance on the left. I immediately drew in my pickets, and on arriving back at camp found the regiment ready to move, and waiting for me, and an order temporarily assigning me to Company H, as the officers of that company were sick—Captain Sawyer sick with fever, and Lieutenant Howe with small pox, of which he has since died. Lieutenant Chipman was in command of the Company at the time, and you can imagine something how agreeable it was to me to go into Company H, but the easiest way to get along in Military is to obey orders and not grumble, and I did so accordingly.

The regiment did not get away from camp till five o'clock. The officers left their baggage and everything behind, taking only rubber blankets with them. The Brigade which was encamped some five or six miles in advance of us, did not wait for us to come up. We marched about ten miles before we halted for the night. We took the wrong road once, and traveled round four or five miles more than there was any need, trying to find water. It was about eleven o'clock when we camped down tired, dirty and sleepy. The march had been a hot and dusty one. Before going further you must know that there are not springs and brooks in Mississippi, as in the Northern States, and it is hard getting water in the best of times, and at this present time it was very dry, as we had not had rains for a long time, and we suffered much for want of water. The dust was horrible, being from five to six inches deep. We received a large mail at this place.

Sunday, July 19th—Were up at three o'clock this morning and got our breakfast, then went to work destroying the railroad. Our Brigade destroyed about three miles of track, and then burned the depot. Our Corps has destroyed the track some ten miles from Jackson north.

It will cost somebody something to repair it. We got through with our work about noon, and then returned to Jackson, making out a pretty hard day's work for us, especially for Sunday. But the soldier does not know of any such day as Sunday. His days are all working days. The men are living mostly on green corn and fresh beef. They have had only quarter rations of bread dealt out to them lately. We arrived at Jackson about sundown with orders that we should take an early start to-morrow morning for Vicksburg.

* * * * * * *

July 28th—We still lay here (at Vicksburg,) in camp, waiting for transports. A part of the Second Division has gone aboard, and I think perhaps we shall go aboard sometime this week.

F. H. S.

In Camp, Co. A, Fifty-third Regiment,
Baton Rouge, La., March 13, 1863.

Editor Reveille.—Although ordered to be ready to move with three days rations in our haversacks on the 9th inst, we did not leave here until yesterday morning. At four o'clock, A. M., "reveille" was beat, and at five A. M., the order to "fall in." Soon the 53d regiment (with the exception of Company K, which was detailed on the 10th for special service at the city) under Col. Kimball, marched to the levee at Baton Rouge, where together with twenty mounted riflemen, they went aboard the steamers "Iberville" and "St. Maurice," which, with a gunboat as convoy, immediately steamed up the Mississippi river to a point of land some eight miles above Baton Rouge. Here the expedition landed, and after a short address by the Colonel, in which he reminded the men that they had the honor of Worcester North in their hands, and if they met the enemy the *order to retreat* never should be given unless overpowered by an overwhelming force, we marched into the interior. At the landing we siezed a rebel and a rebel "signal flag," both of which we took with us. Immediately upon the moving of the regiment, Co. A was thrown out as flankers to the right and left, and the cavalry scouted in front. After proceeding about two miles inward, and thoroughly scouring the country without seeing the enemy, we came to the road leading from Baton Rouge towards Port Hudson, down which the riflemen went, encountering the cavalry pickets of the enemy, firing at and driving them in. But as the expedition had no orders to proceed further in that direction, we returned by the Baton Rouge road, having been within a dozen miles of Port Hudson, passing our most remote pickets some five miles from the city. One of them informed me that two nights previous one of their companions was dangerously shot by one of those mounted rebels, whom he challenged and stopped, and who upon his advancing, immediately fired and fled, but not without his discharging his gun, and as two rifles were found near by next morning, it is thought with some effect. On our return we passed through the city, where we halted, and Colonel Kimball went and reported to Gen. Banks. We arrived at camp at five P. M., well satisfied that we had marched far enough, and were well tired, but as we received a large mail from home on our return, the men soon forgot the march, but were reminded of it again, for orders came to strike our "wall tents," and put up our shelter tents instead, which we had to do before retiring. This morning all our extra clothing, wall tents, &c., have been sent to the city, and we have orders to have three days rations in haversacks and be ready to march at any moment. It is rumored here and in the city to day, that Port Hudson has been evacuated. B.

FRONT OF PORT HUDSON, *Friday A. M. May* 29, 1863.

—— —— Although I have just sent a letter down to division headquarters this morning, I will write again that you may know what have been our labors. I will go back one week to Friday, the 22d. On that day we were stationed at Simsport, on the Atchafalaya river. Friday evening we were ordered aboard the "Laurel Hill," bound for Port Hudson. Most of us laid down without unrolling our blankets, using the wet deck for our mattress and the moon and stars for our coverlet. Saturday morning, May 23d, when we awoke, we were at anchor in the "Father of Waters," by the bayou Sara. We disembarked at daylight, and our regiment, (the other regiments of our brigade has been sent on before us,) acted as a guard to a supply train. On this day's march toward our division, on the road in advance, we came up with our brigade before dark and reported ourselves, immediately pitched our tents in a cornfield, and after making our coffee, laid down to rest. About ten o'clock we were called out and stationed behind a rail fence on one side of the road, the 31st Massachusetts being on the other side, and a battery across it, behind a thick hedge of underbrush. You see we had no idea of letting the rebels skedaddle in the night. We slept on our arms that night without any cause for an alarm.

Sunday morning we were called in, and after we had cooked our breakfast, we were ordered out as skirmishers for the whole Division which had started onward. During the afternoon we came across a deep ravine, with a small brook running through it. Part of the boys in our Company had laid down their guns, and were just on the point of getting some water, when we received a volley from the enemy concealed on the other side. This made the boys jump in a hurry, regardless of water, blankets, canteen, or anything else. Strange to say, no one was wounded. We did not attempt to cross the ravine, but were ordered back again. That night our regiment went on picket, and passed the night without much trouble, except being pretty well worn out by losing our sleep. Monday forenoon we rested ourselves. In the afternoon we advanced with the rest of our Brigade. The rebels were posted in the woods, and our advance had driven them back about a quarter of a mile by dark. The Fifty-third was ordered to relieve the Ninety-first New York, who were in the advance. Soon after, the rebels opened upon us, and their fire was immediately returned by two regiments in our rear. From front and rear we received volley after volley resulting in several casualties. Captain George H. Bailey was shot in his left side during this fire; Mason Harrington had a ball just touch him over his eye, and a ball pass through his cup and canteen; Bradley Upham had a ball pass through his coat sleeve. As soon as I found they were firing from behind, I laid flat on the ground and so escaped uninjured, though I never did hear such a buzzing around my head as there was for a few minutes. As soon as the firing ceased, the picket line was corrected, and we had but little firing in the night from the rebels, although the balls did buzz occasionally.

Saturday Afternoon, May 30th.—At three o'clock Wednesday morning, we were called up, filled our haversacks with three days' rations of hard tack, coffee and sugar, rolled our blankets and piled them against a tree, and at half past five o'clock stood in line of battle ready to go forward and meet the enemy. Colonel Kimball spoke a few words to us, telling us that he expected every man to do his duty, and after asking if he could rely on us, there was a unanimous *yes*, passed the whole length of the line. We advanced in the second line of battle, supporting a battery through the woods, with the shot and shell flying thick and fast around. One of the enemy's solid shot struck a tree about as big as a peck measure, but a little distance from us, and cut it completely in two. I used to think it would be hard work to pick out a place for a battle, but it seems that the battles take place in the roughest places. We have to march over ledges, stumps, brush and ravines. We advanced in line without any one being wounded until twenty minutes of nine, when I heard the order, "Company A, right face, forward, march, by file right, march." Obeying these orders took us to the rear, where we learned that we were detailed as provost guard, whose duty is to drive forward all stragglers, guard the hospitals and prisoners, &c. Of course we could not but be thankful that we were detailed, for no one wishes to go into battle, yet I believe that every man of us had made up his mind to meet the enemy like a hero, and fall nobly if fall he must. During Wednesday wounded men were brought in continually, and it was heart-rending to hear the shrieks of the wounded. I never should have supposed that I could have been so little affected, but I have seen so much suffering that I stood without even so much as a shudder, and saw legs and arms cut off. One man was brought in with his knee all shattered, and he talked and laughed with us, yet within an hour after, he had breathed his last. Another came in who was shot through his mouth, the ball passing out of his cheek. He could not speak, and he would walk around us with the blood streaming out of his mouth. I pitied the poor fellow, and hoped I never should be in like situation. How many were killed on Wednesday I do not know, but I heard one of the hospital nurses say a few minutes ago, that up to this time, there were about eight hundred in all. But very many have been wounded since Wednesday, as the principal action since, has been artillery against artillery.

Thursday, Friday and to day, we have been getting some heavy pieces into the best positions, while the infantry are remaining in about the same position as on Wednesday night. The rebels are posted in rifle pits, and our boys in deep ravines almost under their big guns. Our Company still act as provost guard, and I am satisfied to remain in this position for the present. As far as I can judge, we are surely going to bag the rebels here, though probably they will hold out for a number of days. We have them entirely surrounded, and it is merely a question of time when the fort will fall.

SURRENDER.

As a fitting close to this field correspondence, the following letter from Mr. Frank H. Snow of this town, (an agent of the Christian Commission) is given. It is a clear and interesting account, by an eye witness, of the surrender of Gen. Lee's Army of Northern Virginia, an event which terminated hostilities and brought the war to a close.

Sunday, April 9th, 1865.—The most brilliant page in the military history of our nation has been written to-day in characters that shall never be effaced. The Rebel Napoleon has surrendered his entire command to the Wellingtonian Grant, and the rebellion is virtually brought to a close. The enthusiasm of our troops to-night knows no bounds. The air is filled with the sound of glad huzzas as the great news spreads like wild-fire from regiment to regiment. All along the lines hundreds of military bands are discoursing martial music, and naught seems lacking to complete the happiness of all. For the first time since the opening of the war, a hundred thousand Union soldiers lie down to rest with the certainty that they will not be summoned to arms before morning.

It has been a proud day for the Army of the Potomac, which, now unchallenged, takes the foremost place among the armies of American history. The movement of the last twenty-four hours, attended with such glorious results, have evinced the most masterly military genius.

Appomattox Court House, the scene of the surrender, is by rail forty-five miles northwest from Burkesville, one hundred miles west from Petersburg, and twenty-four miles east from Lynchburg.

At Farmville, yesterday, we received intelligence that Thomas was rapidly approaching Lynchburg from Tennessee, with a force that could easily hold that city against the whole of the rebel army. The circle was being rapidly completed, and the army of Northern Virginia seemed already doomed to destruction. There was, however, one avenue of escape remaining. Two miles west of Appomattox Court House, the turnpike road branches off toward Danville. Could Lee reach this outlet before Grant, he might be spared the humiliation of a surrender. But not thus was the death blow of the rebellion to be averted. While Meade with the 2d and 6th Corps followed closely upon the rear of the rebel columns, Sheridan and the 5th corps together with Ord's detachment of the army of the James, were dispatched to the left by a circuitous route in order to anticipate Lee's arrival at the last loophole of retreat.

By a forced night march of nearly forty miles Sheridan's advance arrived at the critical spot almost simultaneously with the vanguard of the rebel army at an early hour in the morning. A sharp fight ensued in which the cavalry were repulsed, the infantry supports not having yet come up. The rebels had already started their wagon trains through the open gap. At this critical juncture the 5th and 24th corps troops arrived, having pressed forward upon the double quick for the last three miles of their march. The rebel wagon train was captured, and their advancing columns brought to a sudden halt by the fatal celerity of the Union soldiers. The circle, some six or seven miles in diameter, was now complete. Its circumference consisted of a hundred thousand Northern veterans, and the rebel army was its centre. Three hundred and eighty pieces of artillery were in position, ready to concentrate a fire of annihilation upon the confederate host.

Lee's only alternative was—surrender, or death. Under the circumstances he deemed it best to choose the former course. The articles of capitulation were made out by General Grant, and signed by General Lee at the house of Wilmer McLean, who, singularly enough, is also, the owner of the first Bull Run battle-field. The negotiations were completed at twenty minutes to four o'clock this afternoon. At that time the two Generals-in-Chief came out from the house and rode away each to his own army. I was so fortunate as to be within a rod of General Grant, when he dismounted from his horse. Some traces of satisfaction were visible even upon his usually inflexible countenance. He filled a tin cup with water from a pail near by, and allayed his thirst. Then cutting off a twig from a little bush at his feet, he sat down in General Gibbon's camp chair and began to whittle. In about half a minute he coolly turned to Major General Gibbon and remarked, "General, I think we'll begin to go home to-morrow." Gibbon replied with enthusiasm, and the conversation soon became general.

The whole impression of Grant's character conveyed by his conduct on this remarkable occasion, was that of a great military genius, whom no reverse could discourage, no victory unduly elate, and no obstacles deter from the successful accomplishment of his plan.

Amid the general rejoicings which followed the announcement of the surrender, one incident occurred which deserves to be recorded.

When the good news first came in, Mr. G. S. Chase, the agent of the Christian Commission, of the Fifth Corps, remarked to Brig. Gen. Gregory, by whose side he chanced to be standing, that no event in American history demanded more hearty thanksgiving to Almighty God, than this glorious termination of the Great Rebellion. General Gregory immediately ordered his brigade to be drawn up in solid column, and then those scarred and bronzed veterans, the heroes of a score of battle-fields, sang together, and with impressive effect, that familiar doxology—"Praise God from whom all blessings flow."

Such was the fitting termination of the bloody scenes which for four years have been enacted on the soil of Virginia. God grant that the sword need never again be drawn in defence of Liberty and Union!

CONCLUSION.

We have attempted to the best of our ability, with such resources as we could command, to prepare in a form to be preserved, our "war history." We cannot but feel that it is in many respects deficient, but any omissions must be excused in part at least, on the ground of the very meagre records that have been preserved. If as in many towns, a systematic plan had been adopted and carried out, of collecting from month to month, to be preserved, such records and items concerning our soldiers as might be of interest in future years, the work of the historian would have been comparatively an easy one. Some efforts were made in this direction, as will be seen by what follows.

At a town meeting held Dec. 14th, 1861, the following resolutions were presented by Hon. Alfred Hitchcock, and unanimously adopted.

Resolved, That the Trustees of the Public Library be required to take immediate measures to preserve in their Archives in some permanent form, all the interesting facts, correspondence, narratives, incidents, memorials, trophies, or patriotic sentiments and sacrifices which may illustrate and perpetuate to future generations, the history of the service in which the Fitchburg volunteers have been or may be engaged.

Resolved, That this request of the town, through the Trustees of the Library, be extended to the citizens generally, and especially to the regimental and company officers, asking their contributions in making a correct history of their services in the war.

The Legislature of 1863, with the same view, passed an Act making it the duty of the Clerk of every city and town, to make out a full and complete record of the names of all soldiers, with their rank, company and regiment; "to add to and note any changes from time to time, as may be necessary to make said record perfect and complete."

But little was done under either of these plans. So far as relates to the Public Library, a few subscription papers and letters from soldiers in the field, are all that its archives afford. With reference to the town record it is but just to say, that the work was well begun, as we find a list of something more than half the names of soldiers who enlisted from this town, giving the military records of a portion of them. But unfortunately the record was not kept up. We speak of these not to throw censure upon any one, for we well know that there was no wilful neglect in either case, but it is only a result of carelessness which is very apt to occur in cases where there is no one person directly responsible for the work. Had the case been different, this history might have been far more complete and satisfactory.

But we think that the records which the preceding pages have given, show a result of our share as a town in the great work, which we may well look upon with pride.

Few, if any, communities have sent into the service so large a proportion of their own citizens, and have as large a surplus to their credit over all calls. Few have done more for the relief of the soldiers and their families. Our whole people, with hardly an exception, have given liberally of their means, and the busy hand of woman has incessantly labored for their benefit. All can claim some share in the work that has been done. We say all; but we remember in sadness and mortification, that there were a few exceptions. It would seem that in a community like ours, where public sentiment was so overwhelmingly loyal that any outspoken sympathy with rebels would be quite unknown. But such was not the case. A few rare specimens of the genus "copperhead" were found here; men who had no heart in the great cause; no sympathy for those who went to fight its battles; who had no joy in our successes, but who secretly exulted over our reverses; who gave nothing for the relief of the war's victims, or gave grudgingly; who were continually croaking over the causes which brought on the conflict, or venting gloomy forebodings of the future; and some of whom, when we were crushed by the great national sorrow, could ill conceal their delight that our beloved President, whom they hated, had been removed by the hand of the assassin. A few such we had, and they are so few that they might easily be designated. But this is unnecessary. The present generation *knows* them and will remember them; the next will be only too happy to forget that they ever existed. We leave them to the reproaches of their own consciences, which should be more bitter than any execration we might heap upon them. The world is wide enough, and there is room for them, but what true man can respect the secret enemies of his country?

> "Living shall they forfeit fair renown,
> And doubly dying shall go down
> To the vile dust from whence they sprung
> Unwept, unhonored and unsung."

But while nearly all have done so well, yet to those who actually went forth to fight our battles, chiefly belongs the credit. The *true* hero of this war is the *private soldier*; he who at the call "to arms" has given up all and gone forth to toil, hardships and privations, for the mere monthly pittance and bounty, and the opportunity to fill a soldier's grave. To all who have so gallantly served us in the field, and helped to achieve the splendid victory, we owe a debt of gratitude we can never repay. While we live, "like the poor, we shall always have them with us." Let us never forget what they have done for us. Let us cherish them as the benefactors of their country. Let them have the respect that is due them, so long as they shall not forfeit it by any bad conduct. Let any among them who are needy be tenderly cared for.

Surely, we, fresh from these years of war and bloodshed, cannot forget to be just to those whose courage and gallantry we are so familiar with. They were well cared for during the war; let them not be neglected now that peace has come. We cannot doubt that the present generation will do them all justice—Nor can we doubt that in future years, when most of us have passed away, and this valley shall be filled with substantially another people, the few "veterans" who shall go down from us to them —"spared monuments" of this great struggle—will be as tenderly cherished as were the old "Revolutionary fathers." Some of them will have a competence, and their declining days will glide smoothly on, and in their happy old age they will live over anew their younger days in rehearsing again and again, to the delighted children of another age, the "stories of their battles."

Others, less fortunate, crippled old men, (for they are already crippled in their youth,) who have buffeted the seas of life a half century beyond this present time, will be poor, feeble, forlorn, helpless. These are the legacies we shall leave our descendants. Oh, may they tenderly guard them, and prevent suffering and poverty from visiting them; may their lives be made happy, for they will soon pass to their rest, leaving no living witnesses of these "our days of trial"; even as the last "Revolutionary hero" has already been gathered to his fathers, and *we* are forced to feel that the last connecting link between us and the birth-time of our Republic is broken forever.

Such as they are, and may be, we commend them to the benevolent hearts of their present and *future* fellow citizens.

Peace has again come to us, and prosperity reigns among us. True it is, that at the present time, (the Autumn of 1866,) the political horizon is obscured by clouds, and it would appear that the fruits of four years of hard fighting may yet be lost. The spirit of treason is still abroad in the land. The people of the South, who at the close of the war, acknowledged themselves so completely whipped, and were willing to abide any terms that would give them their lives and liberty, have, (through a mistaken policy of leniency towards them,) become rampant, and are fast assuming an attitude of defiance. But the signs of the times are auspicious, and there are indications that the elections which have taken place, and are about to occur, will speak in such "thunder tones" to the rebels at the South, and their sympathizers at the North, proclaiming the will of the people, (that the great question of Reconstruction shall only be settled upon the principles of Justice and Right,) that the plotters of Treason and Anarchy will desist from their hellish schemes.

Yet there are those who predict another outbreak at no distant day. God grant that we may be spared the horrors of another Civil War! But if it should come, our people would remain no idle spectators. Fitchburg, in the future, as in the past, would be a unit against treason in whatever form it appears. Our young men would again rush to the conflict, which, though it might be brief, yet long enough to teach the guilty that the *people* can punish treason and "make it odious," if their officials cannot. But this conflict need not occur if the people of the country do their duty. The battle is to be fought out at the polls, and the ballot is the silent, all powerful weapon.

To us, and especially to the young men of the country who are just coming to the exercise of their privileges as citizens, is to be the keeping and preserving of all that has just been gained by successful war. The next few years are to try the strength of this Nation. The issue is between loyalty and disloyalty—whether the government can be carried on by those who will be true to its best interests, and the welfare and peace of the country, or whether it shall pass into the control of its enemies whose hands are red with the blood of the victims of the Rebellion.

Let us see to it, as far as in us lies the power, that the "Temple of Freedom" is securely guarded, that no "traitor" again pollutes the Capitol; and that none who *have* been "traitors," either North or South, be permitted to have any part in the government until they have done works meet for repentance.

True to our instincts, let no uncertain, temporizing policy ever receive any encouragement, from whatever quarter it may originate.

The war has settled the question that "Secession" is impossible, and State Sovereignty is a fallacy, and that the States lately in rebellion are subject to all the consequences of the war, the abolition of slavery in *fact* as well as name; the repudiation of their debts incurred in carrying on the rebellion; and to such other conditions as Congress, within the Constitution, has a right, and thinks fit to impose for the future protection of the Government. The work is going on—let us keep fully awake to the emergency.

As we stand around the fresh graves of the thousands of heroes who have laid down their lives in this great contest, filled with gratitude to them and the brave survivors for what they have done, let us solemnly resolve that we will fight out the battle to the end, that we will be swayed from our purpose by no political expedients, but stand firmly forth for the right, and insist on those guaranties for the future peace of the country which justice and the welfare of the whole people of all races and conditions alike demand. With these secured, we shall have a peace which will be abiding, when liberty and equality shall prevail throughout the land to all the people. Then shall our government be enduring, because established upon the sure foundations of Truth and Justice, and the Eternal Laws of God.

NOTE.

The Roster of Commissioned Officers and Roll of all Soldiers from this town which follow, have been prepared with great care from the Records of the Town, and Adjutant General's Office, and from information obtained from many different officers and soldiers belonging to the different Companies we have sent into the service. The list of Commissioned Officers contains fifty-seven names. The whole number of names in the roll, officers and enlisted men, is eight hundred and twenty-four, of which *seven hundred sixty* were Fitchburg men, and sixty-four were substitutes, who went to our credit. The list also includes the names of the few men we had in the Naval service. Of our own men all but twenty-one are accounted for. No effort has been made to account for the substitutes. The list is submitted with the feeling that there must necessarily be some inaccuracies, but no efforts have been spared to make it as complete as possible. The compiler would respectfully request all soldiers and others, who may notice any omissions or errors, to communicate the same to him, as it is probable that a corrected list will be made for the Town Records.

LIST OF COMMISSIONED OFFICERS FROM FITCHBURG.

COLONELS.

NAMES.   DATE OF COMMISSION.

Edwin Upton, 25th Regiment, Sept. 9, 1861.
John W. Kimball, 15th and 53d Regiments, Major, Aug. 1, 1861 ; Lieut. Colonel, April 29, 1862 ; Colonel, Dec. 6, 1862.
Thaddeus L. Barker, 36th Reg't, Capt., Aug. 19, 1862; Major, May 6, 1864; Lt. Col., Oct. 12, 1864 ; Col. Nov. 13, 1864.

LIEUTENANT COLONELS.

George E. Marshall, 40th Reg't, Capt., Aug. 15, 1862 ; Major, March 10, 1864 ; Lieut. Col., April 20, 1864.
Theodore S. Foster, 21st Reg't, Capt., Aug. 21, 1861 ; Major, May 17, 1862 ; Lieut. Col., Sept. 2, 1862.

MAJORS.

George Jewett, Asst. Surgeon 10th and Surgeon 51st Reg't, 1st Lieutenant, Jan. 21, 1862 ; Major, Nov. 4th, 1862.
Wm. M. Barrett, Asst. Surgeon 53d and Surgeon Colored Reg't, 1st Lieut., Dec. 4, 1862 ; Major, 1863.

BREVET MAJORS.

Edward A. Brown, 53d Reg't and Gen'l Staff, 1st Lieut., Dec. 4, 1862; Capt., May 18, 1864 ; Brev. Major, Mar. 15, 1865.
Alfred O. Hitchcock 57th Reg't, 2 Lt., Oct. 13, 1863; 1st Lt., Oct. 7, 1864; Capt., Nov. 11, 1864; Brev. Maj., Mar. 15, 1865.
Henry S. Burrage, 36th Reg't, 2 Lt., May 16, 1863; 1st Lt. Nov. 17, 1863; Capt. June 19, 1864 ; Brev. Maj. Mar. 15, 1865.
Albert H. Andrews, 19th U. S. I., 1st Lieut. May 14, 1861, Capt. Jan. 30, 1862, Brevet Maj. March 13, 1865.

CAPTAINS.

Clark S. Simonds, 15th Reg't., August 1, 1861.
John Murkland, 15th Reg't., September 18, 1862.

Charles H. Eager, 15th Reg't, 2d Lt. Aug. 1, 1861 ; 1st Lt. May 11, 1862 ; Capt. Oct. 15, 1862.
James May, 15th Reg't, 2d Lt. Oct. 28, 1862 ; 1st Lt. March 30, 1863 ; Capt. Nov. 22, 1863.
Charles H. Foss, 25th Reg't., Capt. Oct. 12, 1861.
Joseph A. Marshall, 36th Reg't, 2d Lt. Nov. 22d, 1862 ; 1st Lt. Sept. 1, 1863 ; Capt. April 23, 1864.
Joseph W. Gird, 36th and 57th, 1st Lt. May 19, 1862 ; Capt. Dec. 31, 1863.
Eugene T. Miles, 53d. Reg't, Capt., mustered on old Militia Commission, Oct. 17, 1862.
George H. Bailey, 53d Reg't, Capt. May 21, 1863.
Jerome K. Taft, 53d Reg't, 1st Lt. May 21, 1863 ; Capt. June 10, 1863.
Jonas Corey, 53d Reg't., Capt., mustered on old Militia Commission, Oct. 17, 1862.
Levi Lawrence, 25th and 57th Reg'ts., 1st Lt. Oct. 12, 1861 ; Capt. Feb. 11, 1864.
Charles Barker, 21st and 57th Reg'ts., 1st Lt. Aug. 21, 1861 ; do. Feb. 11, 1864 ; Capt. Nov. 11, 1864.
George B. Proctor, 36th U. S. Reg't (colored,) 1st Lt. July 14, 1863 ; Capt. Feb. 29, 1864.
George E. Goodrich, 21st and 24th Reg'ts., 2d Lt. Aug. 6, 1862 ; 1st Lt. Sept. 6, 1863 ; Capt. Oct. 15, 1864.
David H. Merriam, Provost Marshal 9th District, April 29, 1863.
Eben T. Hayward, 21st and 4th H. A., 2d Lt. Aug. 21, 1861 ; 1st Lt. March 3, 1862 ; Capt. Aug. 16, 1864.

FIRST LIEUTENANTS.

Joseph M. Goddard, 15th Reg't, Aug. 1, 1861.
George B. Simonds, 15th Reg't, July 30, 1863.
Henry A. Beckwith, 21st Reg't, 2d Lt. March 3, 1862 ; 1st Lt. June 19, 1862.
Ira B. Goodrich, 21st, Reg't., 2d Lt. Sept. 2, 1862 ; 1st Lt. Jan. 15, 1863.
Julius Whitney, 21st Reg't, 1st Lt. June 18, 1864.
William O. Brown, Quarter-master 25th Reg't, 1st Lt. Sept. 20, 1861.
John Simonds, 25th Reg't, 2d Lt. March 10, 1865 ; 1st Lieut. June 29, 1865.
George L. Chipman, 36th Reg't, 2d Lt. Aug. 13, 1862 ; 1st Lt. Aug. 22, 1862.
Frederick H. Sibley, 36th Reg't, 2d Lt. Aug. 22, 1862 ; 1st Lt. Aug. 2, 1863.
Edward F. Emory, Quarter-master 36th Reg't, 2d Lt. Aug. 1, 1863 ; 1st Lt. Feb. 21, 1864.
Samuel Osborn, 36th Reg't, 1st Lieut. July 7, 1864.

NAMES.	DATE OF COMMISSIONS.

George G. Nutting, 53d Reg't, mustered on old Militia Commission Oct. 17, 1862.
Henry T. Pratt, 53d Reg't, 1st Lieut. June 10, 1863.
Carlos B. Wilson, 53d Reg't, mustered on old Militia Commission Oct. 17, 1862.
J. Henry Richardson, 25th and 4th H. A., 2d Lieut. Oct. 12, 1861; 1st Lieut. Aug. 16, 1864.
Henry A. Willis, 53d Reg't, 1st Lieut. and Adjutant, Dec. 6, 1862.
Alphonzo Marsh, 53th Reg't, 1st Lieut. July 25, 1863; 1st Lieut. June 9th, 1864.
George Lawrence, 1st Reg't, 2d Lieut. Aug. 30, 1862; 1st Lieut. July 2d, 1863.
Frank A. Brown, 15th Reg't, 1st Lieut. Feb. 6, 1864.
Gilbert Thompson, 4th Cavalry, 2d Lieut. Nov. 15, 1864; 1st Lieut. Apr. 7, 1865.

SECOND LIEUTENANTS.

James Graham, Jr., 25th Reg't, Jan. 27, 1864.
Daniel W. Tuttle, 53d Reg't, mustered on old Militia Commission, Oct. 17, 1862.
Oscar A. Battles, 53d Reg't, mustered on old Militia Commission, Oct. 17, 1862.
Daniel C. Putnam, 25th Reg't, May 71, 1865.
Fred. A. Hale, 53d Reg't, May 21, 1863.
Martin F. Becker, 59th Reg't, Sept. 20, 1865.
Gilbert W. Greene, 4th Cavalry, July 8, 1865.

OFFICERS IN THE NAVY.

John M. Whittemore, 3d Assistant Engineer, Gunboat Mohican.
Milton B. Cushing, Assistant Paymaster, Gunboat Seneca.

Alphabetical Roll of all Soldiers from Fitchburg.

NAMES.	COMP. & REG'T.	RANK.	DEATH.	DISCHARGED.	REMARKS.
Abbott, Caleb T.,	E, 1st Cavalry.	Private.		for disability.	
Adams, George	B, 15th Reg't.	Private.	Of w'nds, Gettysb'g Va.		
Adams, Ephraim	D, 21st "	Private.		with reg't.	
Abbott, Henry S.	D, 21st "	Private.		with reg't.	Wounded.
Andrews, Frederick A.	F, 25th "	Private.		for disability.	
Atherton, Edwin D.	A, 53d "	Principal Musician.		with reg't.	
Alvord, Francis A.	A, 53d "	Private.		with reg't.	Wounded.
Aldrich, Nathan H.	B, 53d "	Musician.		with reg't.	
Atkinson, Joseph P.	B, 53d "	Private.		with reg't.	
Arnold, Chas. F.	B, 53d "	Private.		for disability.	
Alden, George	D, 2d "	Private.		exp. of serv.	
Ackley, Edward W.	H, 4th H. A.	Private.		with reg't.	
Aldrich, Frank S.	H, 4th "	Private.		with reg't.	
Aldrich, L. C.	H. 58th Reg't.	Private.		with reg't.	
Adamson, William	F, 4th Cavalry.	Private.		with reg't.	
Andrews, Albert H.	19th U. S. Inft.	Capt. & Brev. Maj.			Still in service.
Bigelow, Daniel R.	F, 13th Reg't.	Private.		exp. of serv.	
Bradley, Thomas	Engineer Corps.	Private.		exp. of serv.	
Becker, Thomas J.	54th Reg't.	Hospital Steward.		with reg't.	
Becker, M. F.	55th "	2d lieut.		with reg't.	
Bennett, Stephen S.	A, 15th "	Private.		for disability.	
Butler, Eli H.	H, 4th H. A.	Private.		for disability.	
Brown, C. H. 2d	22d Reg't.	Private.	Disease, at home.		
Boyle, Thomas	Vet. Reserves.	Private.			Drafted man.
Buckley, John	30th Reg't.	Private.		with reg't.	
Brown, John 2d	13th Reg't.	Private.		with reg't.	

NAMES.	COMP. & REGT.	RANK.	DEATH.	DISCHARGED.	REMARKS.
Battles, Harrison W.	D, 21st	Private.	Killed at Roanoke.		
Barker, Horace R.	D, 21st Regt.	Private.	Disease, Newbern, N. C.		
Bigelow, Frank W.	D, 21st	Private.		with regiment.	
Brownson, James	D, 21st	Corporal.	Disease, Newbern, N. C.		
Beckwith, Henry A.	D, 21st	1st Lieut.	Wounds, Chantilly, Va.		
Brack, Andrew M.	D, 21st	Corporal.	Disease, Annapolis, Md.		
Boynton, Wm. S.	D, 21st	Private.	Killed, Antietam, Md.		
Brooks, Benj. V.	F, 25th	Private.		for disability.	
Burrage, Henry S.	A, 36th	Capt. & Brevet Maj.		with regiment.	
Brick, Charles A.	A, 25th	Musician.		for disability.	
Bass, Orlando P.	F, 25th	Private.		with regiment.	
Battles, Wm. E.	F, 25th	Private.		with regiment.	
Brown, Edward A.	3d & Gen. Staff.	Capt. & Brevet Maj.		exp. of service.	Was wounded, taken prisoner, and exchanged for Roger A. Pryor.
Barrett, Wm. B.	3d & Col'd Regt.	Surgeon.		resigned.	
Bailey, Geo. H.	A, 53d Regt.	Captain.	Wounds, Port Hudson.		
Bruce, John F.	A, 53d	Corporal.		with regiment.	
Bartlett, James F.	A, 53d, F, 57th	1st Sergeant 57th.		with regiment.	Wounded.
Barnum, Alonzo P.	A, 53d, Regt.	Private.		with regiment.	
Barthel, Thomas	A, 53d	Private.			Died soon after discharge.
Bemis Daniel W.	A, 53d	Private.	Disease, at home.		
Bosch, John H.	A, 53d	Private.		with regiment.	
Bowen, Peter M.	A, 53d	Private.		with regiment.	
Brown, Joseph W.	A, 53d	Private.		with regiment.	
Brown, Charles H.	A, 53d	Private.		with regiment.	
Bardeen, Wm. S.	A, 53d	Private.	Disease, at New York.		
Battles, Charles P.	B, 53d	Private.	Disease, at New Orleans.		
Belcher, Alfred W.	B, 53d	1st Sergeant.		with regiment.	

FITCHBURG IN THE REBELLION.

Name	Regt.	Rank		Discharge	Status
Barnes, Willard F.	F, 57th Regt.	Private.		with regiment.	
Bonney, Daniel	B, 15th "	Private.		for disability.	Wounded.
Babbitt, C. W.	F, 57th "	Private.		for disability.	Wounded.
Barker, Charles	F, 57th "	2d Lt. 21st Cpt. 57th		for disability.	Wounded.
Brown, Robert	F, 57th "	Private.		with regiment.	
Bartlett, Geo. A.	F, 57th "	Private.		with regiment.	
Beckwith, Herbert D.	F, 57th "	Private.	Disease, Petersburg, Va.		
Brigham, O. A.	F, 57th "	Private.	Killed, Petersburg, Va.		
Burke, John	F, 57th "	Private.		with regiment.	
Brannan, Patrick	F, 57th "	Private.		with regiment.	
Benson, Wm. G.	F, 57th "	Private.		for disability.	
Baker, Henry	H, 4th H. A.	Private.		with regiment.	
Barrell, Elmer C.	H, 4th H. A.	Private.		with regiment.	
Bennis, Jos. C.	H, 4th H. A.	Private.		with regiment.	
Bolton, Alonzo D.	H, 4th H. A.	Private.		with regiment.	
Babbitt, Caleb H.	H, 4th H. A.	Private.		with regiment.	
Bigelow, Alvaranzo	D, 21st Regt.	Private.	Killed, Chantilly, Va.		
Butters, Henry W.	A, 36th "	Private.		for disability.	
Brown, John	A, 36th "	Private.		with regiment.	
Bowker, Geo. H.	Navy, "Itasca."			exp. of service.	
Bischee, Charles F.	D, 2nd Regt.	Private.		exp. of service.	
Booth, Alvin C.	D, 2nd "	Private.		by spec'l order.	
Booth, Edward	E, 15th "	Private.		exp. of service.	
Ballou, Philetus	I, 15th F, 2d H. A.	Private.		for disability.	
Bliss, Frederick G.	A, 32d "	Private.		with regiment.	
Bruce, Abel Jr.	B, 15th "	Private.		for disability.	
Brown, Frank A.	B, 15th Regt.	1st Sergt. 2d Lieut.	Killed, Gettysburg, Md.		
Bose, Geo. L.	B, 15th "	Corporal.		exp. of service.	Prisoner.
Britton, Fred A.	B, 15th "	Corporal.		for disability.	
Brown, Cyrus	B, 15th, H, 4th H. A.	Sergeant.		exp. of service.	

FITCHBURG IN THE REBELLION.

NAMES.	COMP. & REGT.	RANK.	DEATH.	DISCHARGED.	REMARKS.
Battles, Oscar A.	B, 53d Regt.	2d Lieut.		with regiment.	
Bigelow, Calvin A.	B, 53d F, 57th	Sergeant, 57th.		with regiment.	
Browning, Silas W.	B, 53d "	Private.		with regiment.	
Bacon, Joseph E.	B, 53d Regt.	Private.		with regiment.	
Bagley, Charles H.	B, 53d "	Private.		with regiment.	
Bagley, Moses	B, 53d "	Private.		with regiment.	
Black, Charles H.	B, 53d "	Private.		with regiment.	
Blanchard, Benj. Jr.	B, 53d "	Private.		with regiment.	
Bickford, Charles	B, 53d "	Private.		with regiment.	
Bickford, Wm. O.	B, 53d "	Private.		with regiment.	
Bailey, Ezekiel G.	C, 25th "	Private.		for disability.	
Boutwell, Warren P.	B, 53d "	Private.		for disability.	
Ballon, Ira T.	navy 'Aroostook				
Brigham, Henry D.	B, 53d Regt.	Private.	Disease, New Orleans.		
Battles, F. C.	A, 36th "	Private.		with regiment.	In Invalid Corps.
Barber, Charles S.	A, 36th "	Private.			Deserted.
Barnett, John	navy 'Vermont.'				
Baxter, Adam	K, 36th Regt.	Private.		exp. of service.	
Bixby, Aaron B.	A, 36th "	Private.		exp. of service.	
Bardeen, C. W.	1st "	Corporal.		exp. of service.	
Billings, W. R.	D, 4th N. H.	1st. Lieut. Q. M.		exp. of service.	
Brown, Wm. O.	25th, Staff.	Private.		by spec'l order.	
Blood, Charles	B, 5th Regt.	Private.		with regiment.	Taken Prisoner.
Bruce, George	D, 2d "	Private.		with regiment.	Prisoner and wounded.
Coughlin, John	F, 57th "	Private.		with regiment.	
Casey, John	F, 57th "	Private.		with regiment.	
Clason, Henry	F, 57th "	Private.		with regiment.	

Name	Co./Regt.	Rank	Notes	Status
Changyou, Levi	F, 57th	Private		
Costello, Thomas T.	F, 57th	Private	with regiment.	
Changyou, Joseph	F, 57th	Private	with regiment.	Deserted.
Changyou, Wm.	F, 57th	Private		Deserted.
Caswell, Almon	H, 4th H. A.	Private	with regiment.	
Caswell, Herbert C.	H, 4th H. A.	Private	with regiment.	
Chase, Andrew	H, 4th H. A.	Private	with regiment.	
Cooledge, Louis W.	H, 4th H. A.	Private	with regiment.	
Cushing, Sewell G.	H, 4th H. A.	Private	with regiment.	
Cushing, Charles S.	H, 4th H. A.	Private	with regiment.	
Cane, John	D, 1st H. A.	Private	with regiment.	
Carey, James	F, 57th Regt.	Private	with regiment.	
Collins, James B.	4th H. A.	Private	with regiment.	
Cooledge, Henry W.	1st H. A.	Private	with regiment.	
Cheney, Gilbert	D, 2nd Regt.	Color Corporal	Wounds, Antietam, Md.	
Clark, Caleb	F, 57th	Private	for disability.	Deserted.
Church, Alfred B.	B, 15th	Corporal	with regiment.	
Corey, Jonas	B, 53d	Captain	with regiment.	
Clark, James E.	B, 53d and 5th H. A.	Corporal	with regiment.	
Chase, Alvin B.	B, 53d and 4th H. A.	Sergeant	with regiment.	
Cochran, Nathaniel L.	B, 53d Regt.	Private	with regiment.	
Colbourn, Manly	B, 53d	Private	with regiment.	
Childs, J. Ward	B, 53d	Private	with regiment.	
Clark, Eber F.	B, 53d	Private	with regiment.	
Cochran, Edward L. P.	B, 53d	Private	Disease, at Home.	
Callahan, James	K, 36th	Private		Deserted.
Chase, Joseph W.	A, 36th	Private	Wounds, Coal Harbor.	
Chipman, George L.	A, 36th	1st Lieut.	Resigned.	
Cook, T. J.	A, 36th	Private	exp. of service.	
Coyle, Andrew	A, 36th	Private	exp. of service.	

NAMES.	COMP. & REG'T.	RANK.	DEATH.	DISCHARGED.	REMARKS.
Cutting, H. J.	36th	Private.	Disease.		
Carter, George.	A, 34th	Private.		exp. of service.	
Conner, Thomas.	I, 34th	Private.		with regiment.	
Collins, John.	H, 21st	Private.			
Caswell, Charles M.	K, 21st	Private.		for disability.	
Crehore, Charles W.	A, 30th	Private.	Disease, New Orleans.		
Cunningham, Geo. H.	B, 15th	Corporal.		with regiment.	
Carpenter, Daniel	B, 15th	Corporal.	Killed at Antietam, Md.		
Clark, Benj. F.	B, 15th	Private.		for disability.	Wounded.
Campbell, John.	B, 15th	Private.	Killed at Antietam, Md.		
Carter, Rufus H.	D, 21st	Private.	Killed, Petersburg.		
Cummings, Israel	F, 21st	Sergeant.	Wounds, Knoxville, Tenn		
Corting, Geo. P.	F, 25th	Private.	Disease, Annapolis, Md.		Wounded, Prisoner, Starved.
Collins, Richard.	F, 25th	1st Sergeant.			
Chancy, Wm. B.	A, 53d	Sergeant.		with regiment.	
Carlton, Merrill	A, 53d	Corporal.		with regiment.	
Conner, P. Charles.	A, 53d	Private.		with regiment.	
Caldwell, Charles H.	A, 53d	Private.		with regiment.	
Caldwell, Wm. M.	A, 53d, F, 57th	Private.	Killed, "Wilderness."		
Churchill, Horace M.	A, 53d Reg't.	Private.	Disease, New York.		
Cushing, Milton B.	navy, "Seneca."	Asst. Paymaster.			Still in service.
Davis, Oscar D.	F, 57th Reg't.	Private.			Deserted.
Dolan, Timothy	E, 57th	Private.		with regiment.	
McDowell, James	F, 57th	Private.		with regiment.	Wounded.
Delaney, John	F, 57th	Private.		for disability.	Wounded & Prisoner.
Dunn, Wm. S.	F, 57th	Private.		for disability.	Wounded.
Dailey, Charles	F, 57th	Private.		for disability.	Wounded.

FITCHBURG IN THE REBELLION.

Name	Regt.	Rank	Notes	Discharge	Remarks
Dudley, Stephen W.	H, 4th H. A.	Private.		with regiment.	
Davis, Geo. A.	H, 4th H. A.	Private.	Disease, Washington.		
Davis, Edwin J.	H, 4th H. A.	Private.		with regiment.	
Davis, Charles H.	H, 4th H. A.	Private.		with regiment.	
Downe, Romanzo	navy 'Catalpa.'	Master's Mate.	Accidentally shot.		
Drake, L. P.	Vet. Reserves.	Private.		with regiment.	
DeCoursey, Tim	B, 61st Regt.	Private.		with regiment.	
Dame, Geo. H.	2d Cavalry	Private.		with regiment.	
Donlan, Edward	E, 25th Regt.	Private.		with regiment.	
Duffey, Charles P.	H, 11th "	Corporal.		for disability.	Wounded.
Daniels, Geo. T.	B, 15th "	Private.		with regiment.	Wounded.
Delaney, Dennis	D, 21st "	Private.		for disability.	Wounded.
Deane, Nathaniel C.	D, 21st "	Private.			
Dadmun, Samuel F.	F, 25th "	Private.	Disease at home.		
Dailey, James	A, 53d "	Private.		with regiment.	
Daisey, Henry H.	A, 53d "	Private.		with regiment.	
Dineen, Patrick	A, 53d "	Private.		for disability.	
Demsey, John C.	B, 53d "	Private.		with regiment.	
Drake, Jason W.	B, 53d "	Private.		with regiment.	
Danley, John	B, 53d "	Private.		with regiment.	
Delaney, Daniel	F, 9th "	Private.		with regiment.	
Derby, Edwin A.	F, 1st R. I.	Hospital Steward.	Disease, Harrison's Landing, Va.		
Doe, Edgar J.	F, 57th "	Private.		exp. of service.	
Derby, Edward M.	Conscript.	Private.	Killed, Spotsylvania, Va.		
Downes, John	B, 15th Regt.	Sergeant.		for disability.	Wounded.
Eames, Walter A.	B, 15th "	Corporal.		exp. of service.	Lost one arm.
Edgell, Stillman W.	B, 15th "	Captain.		Resigned.	
Eager, Charles H.	F, 25th "	Private.	Wounds, Coal Harbor.		
Ellenwood, Artemas W.	A, 53d "	Corporal.		for disability.	
Eaton, Wm. H.					

NAMES.	COMP. & REGT.	RANK.	DEATH.	DISCHARGED.	REMARKS.
Eddy, Amasa T.	B, 53d	Sergeant.		with regiment.	
Eaton, Abel.	B, 53d	Musician.		with regiment.	
Emery, Edward F.	A, 36th	1st Lieut.		with regiment.	
Earle, Edward O.	H, 4th H A	Private.		for disability.	
Eager, John W.	C, 25th Regt.	Private.			
Eastman, Amos S.	D, 21st	Private.	Disease, at Home.		
Ellsworth, George R.	E, 57th	Private.	Killed, Roanoke.		
Elson, Wm. E.	4th Cavalry.	Private.		with regiment.	Taken Prisoner.
Frederick, G. H	A, 36th Regt.	Private.			Deserter.
Fitzpatrick, Joseph	E, 25th	Private.		with regiment.	
Farnsworth, Joseph W.	C, 57th	Private.		with regiment.	Lost left leg.
Flagg, Joseph H.	H, 25th	Private.		for disability.	
Frederick, Elisha F.	A, 36th	Private.		with regiment.	
Fitzgerald, Richard	Ssg, "R. B. (ttr."	Private.		with regiment.	
Friar, Henry Allen	E, 53d Regt.	Private.	Disease, Chattanooga.		
Farrell, Wm H	B, 53d	Private.		with regiment.	
Farnsworth, John M	B, 53d	Private.		with regiment.	
French, J. A.	A, 36th	Private.		From Hospital.	
Flynn, John	A, 36th	Private.	Killed, Coal Harbor.		
Farwell, Geo. G.	A, 32d	Private.	Killed, Petersburg, Va.		
Fay, Stephen	G, 28th	Private.		exp. of service.	
Fergeson, James	A, 33d	Private.		for disability.	
Friar, Rawson	N. H.	Private.			
Farwell, Abel, Jr.	D, 2d	Private.		exp. of service.	
Farrell, Martin	F, 57th	Private.		with regiment.	Wounded.
Fuller, Henry A	F, 57th	Private.		for disability.	Wounded.
Farnsworth, Rufus G.	F, 57th	Private.		with regiment.	

FITCHBURG IN THE REBELLION. 261

Flagg, Edwin A.	F, 57th Regt.	Private.		with regiment.	Wounded.
Fortin, David	H, 4th H. A.	Private.		with regiment.	
Freeman, Charles N.	H, 4th H. A.	Private.		with regiment.	
Fuller, Dana L.	H, 4th H. A.	Private.		with regiment.	
Fuller, Marshall R.	H, 4th H. A.	Private.		with regiment.	
French, Geo. A.	H, 4th H. A.	Private.		with regiment.	
Farnum, John R.	B, 15th Regt.	Corporal.		with regiment.	Prisoner.
Farmer, Charles H.	B, 15th "	Private.		for disability.	
Fletcher, P. H.	B, 15th "	Private.		for disability.	Wounded.
Fay, Charles E.	D, 21st "	Private.		for disability.	
Flint, S. W.	D, 21st "	Private.		with regiment.	
Foster, Theodore S.	P, 21st "	Lieut. Colonel.		resigned.	
Farwell, Artemas S.	E, 25th "	Sergeant.			Wounded.
Foss, Charles H.	F, 24th "	Captain.	Disease, Newbern, N. C.		
Farrar, Ephraim E.	A, 53d "	1st Sergeant.		with regiment.	Wounded.
Farrar, Francis F.	A, 53d "	Private.		with regiment.	
Farrar, Morris	A, 53d, 4th H.A.	Private.		with regiment.	Wounded.
Flynn, Patrick	A, 53d Regt.	Private.		with regiment.	
Forister, Arthur	A, 53d "	Private.		with regiment.	
Farwell, Edward P.	A, 53d "	Corporal.	Disease, Port Hudson, La.		
Farmer, Sherborn B.	B, 53d "	Private.		with regiment.	
Foster, Geo. W.	A, 36th "	Private.		for disability.	
French, Increase H.	B, 53d "	Private.		with regiment.	
Farmer, O. Franklin	B, 53d "	Hospital Steward.		for disability.	
Green, James S.	21st "	2d Lieut.		exp. of service.	
Green, Gilbert W.	4th Cav.	Private.		with regiment.	
Green, M. D. E.	H, 4th H. A.	Private.		with regiment.	
Gunnison, Horace A.	H, 4th H. A.	Private.		with regiment.	
Gibson, Daniel O.	H, 4th H. A.	Private.		with regiment.	
Gillis, James	A, 36th Regt.	Private.		with regiment.	

262 FITCHBURG IN THE REBELLION.

NAMES.	COMP. & REGT.	RANK.	DEATH	DISCHARGED.	REMARKS.
Griffin, Thomas 2d	3d H. A.	Private.		with regiment.	
Gibson, Luther R.	B, 53d Regt.	Private.		with regiment.	
Granger, C. S.	E, 22d "	Private.		with regiment.	
Glacker, John	K, 61st "	Private.		with regiment.	
Gilmore, Thomas	B, 20th "	Private.		with regiment.	
Glennon, James	A, 47th "	Private.		with regiment.	
Gilchrist, Warren F.		Musician, 2d Corps.		exp. of service.	
Green, Andrew J.	A, 53d Regt.	Corporal.		with regiment.	
Gates, Edwin	A, 53d "	Private.		with regiment.	
Green, Henry D.	A, 53d "	Private.		with regiment.	
Griswold, Albert	A, 53d and H, 4th H.A.	Private.		with regiment.	
Gilmore, D. Alfred	B, 53d Regt.	Sergeant.		with regiment.	
Gill, Frank C.	B, 53d "	Corporal.		with regiment.	
Gould, Alonzo	B, 53d "	Corporal.		with regiment.	
Goodrich, Harrison	B, 53d "	Private.		with regiment.	
Gould, Austin K.	B, 53d, F, 57th	Private.		with regiment.	Prisoner.
Garfield, Silas	B, 53d Regt.	Private.		with regiment.	
Gibson, Andrew C.	A, 36th "	Private.		for disability.	
Gerry, H. A. D.	I, 25th "	Private.		for disability.	
Griswold, Wm. W.	A, 36th "	Private.		for disability.	
Gould, G. A.	A, 32d "	Private.		for disability.	Wounded.
Goodall, Robert	H, 4th N. H.	Private.		with regiment.	
Gale, Darius M.	H, 4th H. A.	Private.		with regiment.	
Garfield, Warren	H, 4th H. A.	Private.		with regiment.	
Gilchrist, George S.	B, 15th "	Corporal.		for disability.	Prisoner.
Gilson, Artemas A.	B, 15th, and H, 4th H.A.	Corporal.		for disability.	
Gilson, Wm.	B, 15th, " " "	Corporal.		for disability.	

FITCHBURG IN THE REBELLION.

Name	Co. & Regt.	Rank	Remarks	Discharged	Status
Griswold, Wm. T.	B, 15th Regt.	Private.		with regiment.	
Griswold, Charles E.	B, 15th "	Private.		for disability.	Wounded.
Gibson, Lemuel W.	B, 15th "	Private.		for disability.	
Goddard, J. Myron	B, 15th "	1st Lieut.		for disability.	
Goodrich, Charles E.	D, 21st "	Drummer.	Disease, Florence, S. C.		Prisoner, starved.
Green, Charles T.	D, 21st "	Private.		for disability.	Wounded.
Goodfellow, David W.	D, 21st "	Private.		with regiment.	
Goodrich, George E.	D, 21st & 34th R.	Captain.		with regiment.	
Goodrich, Ira B.	D, 21st "	1st Lieut.		with regiment.	
Graham, James Jr.	F, 25th "	2d Lieut.	Killed, Coal Harbor.		
Gardner, James F.	F, 25th "	Private.		with regiment.	Wounded.
Girl, Joseph W.	F, 25th, & 57th.	Captain.	Killed, Wilderness.		
Gibson, Appleton M.	F, 25th Regt.	Sergeant.		for disability.	
Goodrich, Herbert	E, 5th "	Private.		with regiment.	Wounded.
Hagar, Wm. S.	F, 25th "	Private.		for disability.	
Hale, Fred A.	F, 25th "	2d Lieut.		with regiment.	
Harrington, Mason A.	A, 53d "	Private.		with regiment.	
Harrington, Cornelius.	A, 53d "	Private.		with regiment.	
Harris, Edwin A.	A, 53d "	Private.		with regiment.	
Hastings, John M.	A, 53d & 57th.	Private.	Killed, Spottsylvania.		
Hartshorn, Geo. F.	A, 53d Regt.	Private.		with regiment.	
Harri, Charles T.	A, 53d "	Private.		with regiment.	
Hartwell, James A.	A, 53d "	Private.		with regiment.	
Harwood, Junius.	A, 53d "	Private.		with regiment.	
Henry, William E.	A, 53d & F, 5th.	Private.		with regiment.	
Hitchcock, Alfred O.	A, 53d & F 57th.	Capt. & Brevet Maj.		exp. of service.	Wounded.
Hill, Francis D.	A, 53d Regt.	Private.	Disease, at home.		
Harrington, David A.	A, 53d "	Private.	Disease, at home.		
Hosmer, Stephen C.	B, 53d and H, 4th H.A.	Corporal.		with regiment.	Wounded.
Harris, Wm. H.	B, 53d Regt.	Private.		with regiment.	

NAMES.	COMP. & REGT.	RANK.	DEATH.	DISCHARGED.	REMARKS.
Hemenway, Frank F.	B, 53d Regt.	Private.		with regiment.	Wounded.
Harrington, John N.	B, 53d, H. 4th H. A.	Private.		with regiment.	
Hadley, Alzah A.	B, 53d Regt.	Private.		with regiment.	
Hill, Thomas	B, 53d "	Private.		with regiment.	
Hanniston, Sam'l G.	B, 53d F, 4th H. A.	Private.		with regiment.	
Hamilton, James R.	A, 36th Regt.	Corporal.		for disability.	
Hancock, Joseph	A, 36th "	Private.			Deserted.
Hughes, John	Navy "Sabine."				
Harrigan, Jerry	A, 36th Regt.	Private.	Killed, Petersburg, Va.		
Hennessey, N. R.	" 28th "	Private.		with regiment.	
Harrigan, Owen	" 28th "	Private.		for disability.	Wounded.
Henry, Geo. A.	C, 28th "	Private.		with regiment.	
Hennessey, John	F, 57th "	Private.		with regiment.	
Hall, Rodney	F, 57th "	Private.		with regiment.	Since died from disease contracted in service.
Hayward, Chas. E. F.	H, 4th H. A.	Private.		with regiment.	
Holman, Edwin	H, 23d, Regt.	Private.	Disease, Newbern, N. C.		
Hayward, H. P.	D, 2d & B 53d.	Private.		exp. of service.	Deserted, wounded.
Hayes, Michael	I, 9th Regt.	Private.			
Howe, Geo. H.	B, 21st "	Private.	Disease, Roanoke.		
Hudson, George	G, 25th "	Private.		with regiment.	
Hartwell, Edwin	D, 26th "	Private.	Disease, at home.		
Hirsh, Wm. E.	C, 32d "	Private.		for disability.	
Harwood, Kilburn	B, 15th "	Corporal.		exp. of service.	Wounded.
Harwood, Geo. A.	B, 15th "	Principal Musician.		with regiment.	
Hosmer, Granville C.	B, 15th "	Private.		for disability.	Prisoner.
Hosmer, Henry J.	B, 15th "	Private.		for disability.	Prisoner.
Hosmer, Joel K.	B, 15th "	Private.		exp. of service.	Wounded.

Name	Co., Regt.	Rank			
Hunkins, Harrison M.	B, 15th Regt.	Corporal.		for disability.	Wounded.
Hildreth, Frank A.	B, 15th "	Corporal.	Disease, Poolesville, Md.		
Hayward, Eben T.	D, 21st "	Captain.		with regiment.	
Hall, Charles	F, 25th "	Sergeant.			
Henshaw, Dexter	F, 25th "	Private.	Killed, Coal Harbor.		
Haynes, Sylvester	F, 25th "	Private.		for disability.	Wounded.
Hunter, Charles H.	F, 25th "	Corporal.		with regiment.	
Hodgman, Wm.	D, 21st "	Private.	Killed at Roanoke.	with regiment.	
Herrick, Noyes B.	H, 4th H. A.	Private.		with regiment.	
Hosmer, Samuel	H, 4th H. A.	Private.		with regiment.	
Hughes, Richard	Navy, 4th H. A.			with regiment.	
Hartwell, A. J.	A, 36th Regt.	Private.	Disease, Camp Nelson, Ky		Deserted.
Heard, Charles H.	A, 36th "	Private.			
Humes, Joseph	A, 36th "	Private.	Killed, Coal Harbor.		
Howard, Wm.	I, 6th N. H.	Private.	Killed, Spotsylvania, Va		
Hill, Henry K.	G, 2d H. A.	Private.	Disease, Florence, S. C.		Prisoner, starved.
Hayden, Wm. H.	Navy, "Hatteras."		Died in Prison.		Starved, Galveston.
Hosmer, Samuel L.	H, 4th H. A.	Private.		with regiment.	
Haskins, Albert	E, 25th Regt.	Private.		with regiment.	
Hayden, George L.	B, 1st H. A.	Private.		with regiment.	
Huntley, Elisha A.	G, 2d H. A.	Private.		for disability.	
Holman, Alvin	B, 5th Regt.	Private.		with regiment.	
Johnson, Windsor C.	A, 36th "	Corporal.		for disability.	
Joslin, Henry L.	B, 15th "	Private.	Disease, Virginia,		
Jaquith, Asa S.	D, 21st "	Sergeant.		for disability.	Wounded.
Jaquith, Azro B.	D, 21st "	Private.		for disability.	
Jaquith, Isaac P.	A, 53d "	Sergeant.		for disability.	
Jaquith, Levi L.	B, 53d "	Private.		with regiment.	
Joice, David	K, 36th "	Private.			Deserted.
Joice, Bartholomew	K, 36th "	Private.			Deserted.

NAMES.	COMP. & REGT.	RANK.	DEATH.	DISCHARGED.	REMARKS.
Jewett, George	10th & 51st.	Surgeon.			
Jewett, George C	H, 4th H. A.	Private.		with regiment.	Prisoner.
Johnson, Charles H.	H, 4th H. A.	Private.		with regiment.	
Jordon, John S.	H, 4th H. A.	Private.		with regiment.	
Jones, Frank N. P.	Conscript.	Private.			
Jewett, Forestus M.	A, 53d Regt.	Private.		with regiment.	
King, Ostian M.	D, 2d "	Private.		with regiment.	
Kinsman, Frederic	" "	Hospital Steward.		exp. of service.	
Kimball, John W.	B, 15th, & 53d	Colonel 53d.		with regiment.	Wounded.
Kempton, Elias J.	D, 21st "	Private.		for disability.	Wounded.
Kinsman, Geo. W.	F, 25th "	Private.		with regiment.	Wounded.
Kendall, Gilbert B.	A, 53d "	Sergeant.		with regiment.	
Kempton, Alphonso	A, 53d "	Private.		with regiment.	
Kendall, J. Henry	A, 53d "	Private.	Wounds, Port Hudson.		
Kemp, John	B, 53d "	Private.			
Keyes, Geo. F.	A, 36th "	Sergeant.	Killed, Petersburg, Va.	with regiment.	
King, Daniel	A, 36th "	Private.		for disability.	
Knight, Geo. F.	A, 36th "	Sergeant.	Disease, Nicholasville, Ky		
Kavanaugh, Michael	C, 28th "	Private.	Wounds, Antietam, Md.		
Kendall, J. L.	H, 22d "	Private.	Killed, Wilderness.	for disability.	
Kielty, Daniel	F, 57th "	Private.			
Knapp, John	H, 4th H. A.	Private.		with regiment.	
Killdall, John	22d Regt.	Private.		with regiment.	
Kington, Lewis M.	D, 26th "	Private.	Killed, Wilderness.		
Lakin, Jefferson C.	D, 2d "	Private.	Killed, Winchester.		
Lane, Phillip	14th "	Private.		exp. of service.	
Lavan, Patrick	C, 28th "	Private.		exp. of service.	

Name	Regt.	Rank			Notes
Leahy, John	22d Regt.	Private.		with 4th regt. for disability.	Wounded.
Livermore, Thomas	1st & 4th H. A.	Corporal.			
Lawless, John	F, 57th Regt.	Private.		with regiment.	
Lawrence, Ivers W.	H, 4th H. A.	Private.		with regiment.	
Lesure, Henry A.	H, 4th H. A.	Private.		with regiment.	
Litch, Charles C.	H, 4th H. A.	Private.		with regiment.	
Loverwell, Lyman S.	L, 25th Regt.	Private.	Disease, Newbern, N. C.		
Lamson, John L.	G, 15th "	Private.		for disability.	Lost an arm.
Lannon, Patrick	A, 14th "	Private.	Killed.		
Lane, Phillip	35th "	Sergeant.		with regiment.	Substitute.
Luther, N.	B, 15th "	Private.		with regiment.	Wounded.
Leach, Flavel	D, 2d "	1st Lieut.		with regiment.	
Lakin, Crosby	G, 1st "	Private.		exp. of service.	First Fitchburg man to enlist for three years.
Lawrence, Geo. L.	G, 25th "	Private.		for disability.	
Lobdell, Thomas J.	G, 25th "	Private.		with regiment.	
Lobdell, Thomas J. Jr	B, 15th "	Private.		for disability.	Wounded and Prisoner.
Litchfield, Albert	B, 15th "	Drummer.			
Lawrence, Amos W.	D, 21st "	Corporal.	Disease, Washington.	for disability.	
Lamb, Levi L.	F, 25th "	Captain.	Disease, at home.		
Lowe, George	E, 25th & 57th.	Corporal.		with regiment.	Wounded.
Lawrence, Levi	A, 53d, 4th H.A.	Private.		with regiment.	
Lesure, Thomas G.	A, 53d Regt.	Corporal.		for disability.	
Livermore, Ozro J.	B, 53d "	Private.		with regiment.	
Leonard, Elbridge G.	A, 36th "	Private.		with regiment.	
Lamb, Chester F.	A, 36th "	Corporal.			
Larkin, Michael	A, 32d "	Private.	Wounds, Gettysburg Pa.	with regiment.	Deserted.
Long, Michael	1st H. A.	Private.		with regiment.	
Lamb, Alvin W.	21st "	Private.		with regiment.	
McCue, Patrick				with regiment.	
Miller, James A.					

NAMES.	COMP. & REG'T.	RANK.	DEATH.	DISCHARGED.	REMARKS.
Mitchell, Wm. C.	B, 15th Regt.	Private.		for disability.	
Marshall, Edward T.	4th H. A.	Private.		with regiment.	
Manteas, Albert W.	4th H. A.	Private.		with regiment.	
Mahoney, John H.	1st H. A.	Private.		with regiment.	
McIntire, James	A, 21st Regt.	Private.			
Markham, John	1, 70th N. Y.	Private.	Disease, Newbern, N. C.		
Maynard, George F.	E, 25th Reg't.	Private.	Wounds, Williamsburg, Va		
Makepeace, F. A.	A, 33dd	Private.		for disability.	
Merriam, Newell A.	28th "	Musician.		for disability.	
Morris, John	B, 25th	Private.		for disability.	
Moran, Thomas	C, 32d	Private.		exp. of service.	
McIntire, Albion C.	F, 57th "	Private.		exp. of service.	
Miles, Michael	F, 57th "	Private.	Killed, Petersburg, Va.	for disability.	
McCarty, Patrick		Private.	Killed, Petersburg, Va.		
Mack, John	H, 4th H. A.	Private.		with regiment.	
Marsh, Palmer A.	H, 4th H. A.	Private.		with regiment.	
McCoy, John	H, 4th H. A.	Private.		with regiment.	
McInlay, James A.	H, 4th H. A.	Private.		with regiment.	
Morrison, James	H, 4th H. A.	Private.		with regiment.	
Marshall, Simon F.	3d Cavalry.	Private.	Wounds, Baton Rouge, La		
Marsh, John	B, 15th Regt.	Private.	Killed, Gettysburg, Pa.		
McMahon, Michael	E, 25th "	Private.	Killed, Cold Harbor.		
McCarty, Michael	D, 26th "	Private.		with regiment.	
McIntire, Albert	A, 53d "	Private.		with regiment.	
Marshall, Theo.	Navy, 'Susquehanna.'				Wounded.
Mecorney, John L.	B, 53d "	Corporal.		with regiment.	
Marsh, Thomas	B, 53d "	Private.		with regiment.	

Name	Regiment	Rank	Notes	Status
Miller, Charles E.	B, 53d Regt.	Private.	with regiment.	
Marshall, Geo. P.	B, 53d "	Private.	with regiment.	
Minot, Edwin H.	B, 53d "	Private.	with regiment.	
Morse, Wm. G.	B, 53d, 4th H.A	Private.	with regiment.	
Minot, Hiram P.	B, 53d Regt.	Private.	with regiment.	
Mace, Henry W.	B, 53d & E 5th	Private.	with regiment.	
Mack, G. W.	A, 36th "	Sergeant.	invalid corps.	
Mahan, Thomas	A, 36th "	Private.	Disease, Annapolis, Md.	
Marshall, James A.	A, 36th "	Private.	for disability.	Wounded.
May, Thomas	A, 36th "	Sergeant.	with regiment.	
Mills, Hamilton A.	A, 36th, 4th H.A.	Private.	for disability.	
Murphy, Patrick W.	A, 36th Regt.	Private.	exp. of service.	
Murphy, Maurice	K, 36th "	Private.	with regiment.	
McIntire, Geo. H.	A, 36th "	Private.	with regiment.	
McIntire, Levi	36th "	Private.	transferred.	
Marvin, J.	K, 6th N. H.	Corporal.	for disability.	Deserter.
Moulton, Ansel A.	D, 2d Regt.	Private.	exp. of service.	
Minnehan, Cornelius	H, 20th "	Private.	for disability.	Wounded.
Morgan, John	D, 22d "	Private.	exp. of service.	
Moran, Dennis	D, 25th "	Private.	exp. of service.	
Marshall, Joseph A.	B, 15th & 36th.	Captain.	with regiment.	Wounded.
Morse, John E.	B, 15th "	Private.	with regiment.	Wounded and Prisoner.
Moody, Joseph L.	B, 15th "	Private.	exp. of service.	Prisoner.
Marshall, Frank S.	B, 15th "	Private.	for disability.	
May, James	B, 15th "	Captain.	exp. of service.	Wounded and Prisoner.
Murkland, John	B, 15th "	Captain.	Killed, Gettysburg, Pa	
Monroe, Charles D.	B, 15th "	Sergeant.	Killed, Ball's Bluff, Va.	
McIntire, Herbert D.	B, 15th "	Private.	with regiment.	Wounded.
Marsh, Alphonzo	D, 21st "	1st Lt. Col'd Regt.	Resigned.	

NAMES.	COMP. & REG'T.	RANK.	DEATH.	DISCHARGED.	REMARKS.
Marsh, Timothy S.	D, 21st Regt.	Private.		with regiment.	
Marshall, Joseph F.	D, 21st "	Private.		for disability.	
Montjoy, Charles F.	D, 21st "	Private.	Killed, Spottsylvania, Va.		
May, Simon	D, 21st "	Sergeant.	Killed, Petersburg, Va.		
Miles, Eugene T.	A, 53d "	Captain.		resigned.	
Marshall, Geo. E.	40th "	Lieut. Colonel.	Killed, Coal Harbor,		
Merriam, David H.	Provost Marshal 9th Dist.	Captain.		exp. of service.	
Nason, Edwin F.	D, 2nd Regt.	Private.		exp. of service.	
Nixon, Nahum	F, 25th "	Private.		for disability.	Wounded.
Nutting, Geo G.	A, 53d "	1st Lieut.	Killed, Bisland, La.		
Nutting, J. Q. A.	B, 53d "	Sergeant.		with regiment.	
Noonan, Morris	A, 36th "	Private.		for disability.	
Noonan, James	Navy, "Conemaugh."				
Nourse, Stephen H.	F, 57th Regt.	Private.		for disability.	Wounded.
Noonan, Mathew	D, 1st H. A.	Private.		with regiment.	
O'Donnell, Michael	C, 28th Regt.	Private.		for disability.	
O'Donnell, Pat.	C, 32d "	Private.		exp. of service.	
Osborne, Ai D.	B, 15th "	Private.	Wounds, Ball's Bluff, Va.		
O'Herne, James	B, 53d "	Private.			Deserted.
Osborne, J. W.	A, 36th "	Private.		with regiment.	Wounded.
Oake, Thomas	A, 36th, "	Private.	Killed, Petersburg, Va.		
O'Brien, Wm.	A, 36th "	Private.		from hospital.	
O'Brien, Thos.	30th "	Private.			
O'Donnell, Michael 2d	F, 57th "	Private.		for disability.	Wounded.
O'Brien, Jerry	F, 57th "	Private.	Killed, Petersburg, Va.		
Osborne, Samuel	A, 36th "	1st Lieut.		with regiment.	
Osgood, George D.	F, 4th Cavalry.	Private.		with regiment.	

Name	Regiment	Rank	Notes	Status	Remark
O'Brien, John	M, 1st Cavalry	Private		with regiment.	
Partland, Pat	F, 57th Regt.	Private		with regiment.	Wounded.
Patch, Isaac	4th Cavalry	Private		with regiment.	Prisoner.
Putnam, Cyrus	F, 25th Regt.	Private	Wounds, Richmond, Va.	with regiment.	
Packard, George	B, 25th "	Private		with regiment.	
Perry, Fred D.	3d Cavalry	Private		with regiment.	
Partridge, Harlan P.	B, 53d Regt.	Sergeant Major.		with regiment.	
Pratt, Henry T.	A, 53d "	1st Lieut.		with regiment.	
Parkhurst, Boardman	A, 53d "	Private		with regiment.	
Parker, Alonzo	B, 53d "	Private		with regiment.	
Powers, Fred W.	B, 53d "	Private		with regiment.	
Phelps, Charles	A, 26th "	Private		with regiment.	
Pollard, Augustus	A, 26th "	Private		with regiment.	
Prew, A. G.	A, 36th "	Private		for disability.	
Parks, Fred W.	F, 57th "	Private	Killed, Petersburg, Va.		
Peabody, Wm. T.	E, 57th "	Private	Prison, Salisbury.		Starved.
Parker, Alden W.	H, 4th H. A.	Private		with regiment.	
Parkhurst, James H.	H, 4th H. A.	Private		with regiment.	
Payne, George A.	H, 4th H. A.	Private		with regiment.	
Priest, Willard	H, 4th H. A.	Private		with regiment.	
Proctor, Clarence D.	H, 4th H. A.	Private		with regiment.	
Putnam, Fred A.	H, 4th H. A.	Private		with regiment.	
Perkins, Francis H.	A, 36th Regt.	Private		with regiment.	
Pierce, Henry O.	D, 2d "	Private	Disease at home.	exp. of service.	
Phillips, George C.	C, 10th "	Private		exp. of service.	Prisoner.
Persons, Wm. H.	B, 30th "	Corporal.	Wounds, Spottsylvania.		
Page, Horace T.	B, 15th "	Private	Disease, at home.		
Phillips, George W.	B, 15th "	Private			
Pratt, Joel	B, 15th "	Private		exp. of service.	
Plaisted, Amos C.	B, 15th "	Private		with regiment.	

272   FITCHBURG IN THE REBELLION.

NAMES.	COMP. & REG'T.	RANK.	DEATH.	DISCHARGED.	REMARKS.
Pratt, Cyrus W.	G, 25th Regt.	Private.		exp. of service.	
Prichard, John H.	B, 15th and C 2d H. A.	Private.	Andersonville prison.		Starved.
Pierce, Daniel R.	B, 15th Regt.	2d Prin'l Musician.		with regiment.	
Patch, Henry J.	D, 21st "	Private.		with regiment.	
Parkhurst, Emmons M.	D, 21st "	Private.		with regiment.	
Phelps, W. W.	F, 25th "	Private.		with regiment.	
Phelps, Phineas.	F, 25th "	Private.		with regiment.	
Partridge, Wm. H.	F, 25th "	Captain Col'd Regt.	Killed, Drury's Bluff.		
Proctor, George B.	E, 25th "	Sergeant.		resigned.	
Putnam, Thomas F.	E, 25th "	2d Lieut.		with regiment.	Wounded.
Putnam, Daniel C.	E, 25th "	Private.		with regiment.	
Parker, George H.	E, 5th "	Private.		with regiment.	
Ryan, Martin	F, 57th "	Private.	Killed, Petersburg, Va.		
Reynolds, Julius F.	H, 4th H. A.	Private.		with regiment.	
Rockwood, George W.	A, 15th, and H, 4th H.A.	Captain.		with regiment.	
Rockwood, Chas. H.	K, 3d and 4th H.A.	Drummer.		for disability.	
Robbins, Solomon.	A, 36th Regt.	Private.		transferred.	
Raymond Owen T.	F, 57th "	Private.	Killed, Wilderness.		
Rice, Aug. M.	G, 3;51 F, 1st Cav.	Corporal.		exp. of service.	
Ring, John R.	B, 15th Regt.	Sergeant.		with regiment.	
Rich, Harrison.	B, 15th "	Private.		with regiment.	Wounded.
Rugg, Daniel W.	D, 21st "	Private.		for disability.	
Rice, George W.	F, 25th "	Private.		for disability.	
Rogeh, Wm.	F, 25th "	1st Lieut.	Killed, Petersburg, Va.		
Richardson, J. Henry	F, 25th "	Corporal.		with regiment.	
Russell, Charles F.	A, 53d "	Corporal.		with regiment.	
Ray, Frank N.	A, 53d "	Corporal.		with regiment.	

Name	Regt.	Rank			
Roach, John	A, 53d Regt.	Private.			with regiment.
Rock, Chas.	A, 53d "	Private.			with regiment.
Robinson, Amory	A, 53d "	Private.			with regiment.
Russell, Francis C.	A, 53d "	Private.			with regiment.
Robinson, Elbridge L.	F, 28th "	Private.	Killed, Port Hudson, La.		
Roy, Michael	F, 28th "	Private.			for disability.
Regan, Michael	G, 22d "	Private.			exp. of service.
Silk, Jeremiah	G, 19th "	Private.			for disability.
Sullivan, Daniel	G, 57th "	Private.			for disability.
Stevens, Almond G.	C, 31st "	Private.		Wounded	
Smith, Lewis	C, 32d "	Private.			
Simonds, George B.	B, 15th "	1st Lieut.	Killed, Spottsylvania, Va.		
Simonds, Clark S.	B, 15th "	Captain.	Killed at Antietam, Md.		
Scollay, Thomas	B, 15th "	Private.	Disease.		
Simonds, Alvin A.	B, 15th "	Corporal.		Wounded & Prisoner	with regiment.
Simonds, George F.	B, 15th "	Private.			for disability.
Scott, Frank	B, 15th "	Sergeant.			exp. of service.
Stone, Luman W.	B, 15th, 4th Cav.	Sergeant.		Prisoner.	exp. of service.
Stevens, Robert	A, 36th Regt.	Private.			
Sweeney, Andrew	Navy, "Gemsbok."				
Sibley, Fred. H.	B, 15th & 36th.	2d Lieut.	Disease, Louisville, Ky.		
Spooner, Henry A.	B, 15th Regt.	Sergeant.			for disability.
Swift, John	D, 21st "	Private.		Wounded.	with regiment.
Skinner, Orin E.	D, 21st "	Corporal.			for disability.
Stewart, Wm. M.	D, 21st "	Private.		Wounded.	with regiment.
Simonds, John	F, 25th "	1st Lieut.			with regiment.
Savaria, Louis	F, 25th "	Private.		Wounded.	with regiment.
Spaulding, J. Calvin	F, 25th "	Sergeant.			for disability.
Sylvester, George F.	F, 25th "	Private.			for disability.
Sylvester, Atwood G.	F, 25th "	Private.			

NAMES.	COMP. & REG'T.	RANK.	DEATH.	DISCHARGED.	REMARKS.
Shehan, Timothy	F, 25th Regt.	Private.	Disease, Newbern, N. C.		
Simonds, Putnam	F, 25th "	Private.		with regiment.	
Simonds, Wm. H.	A, 53d	Sergeant.	Disease, New York.		
Spencer, Edward H.	A, 53d and H, 6th H.A.	Sergeant.		with regiment.	
Sawyer, Alvin M.	A, 53d "	Private.		with regiment.	
Sawyer, George A.	A, 53d "	Private.		with regiment.	
Spaulding, Josiah	A, 53d "	Private.		with regiment.	
Stickney, Alvin O.	A, 53d "	Sergeant.			
Stewart, Charles W.	A, 53d "	Private.	Killed, Bisland, La.		
Shattuck, William H.	A, 53d "	Private.	Disease, at New York.		
Stevens, Samuel	B, 53d, F, 57th	Corporal.		with regiment.	
Sabin, George F.	B, 53d	Sergeant.		with regiment.	Wounded.
Spooner, Solon W.	A, 36th "	Private.	Disease, at home.		
Sheridan, Barney	A, 36th "	Corporal.		with regiment.	
Siner, W. H.	A, 36th "	Private.		for disability.	Wounded.
Smith, Henry R.	A, 36th "	Private.		for disability.	Wounded.
Smith, George M.	A, 36th "	Sergeant.			
Smith, O. F.	K, 36th "	Corporal.		with regiment.	
Smith, Albert A.	A, 36th "	Private.	Wounds.		
Stockwell, Orwell L.	A, 36th "	Private.	Disease, Alexandria, Va.		
Sullivan, John	A, 36th "	Corporal.		with regiment.	Wounded.
Shattuck, Mark	24th "	Private.			Deserted.
Spencer, Michael	28th "	Private.	Killed at Antietam, Md.		
Sprague, J. W.	I, 12th "	Private.		exp. of service.	
Sullivan, Patrick C.	K, 28th "	Private.	Killed, Chantilly, Va.		
Sawyer, Edgar F.	F, 57th "	Private.		with regiment.	
Skye, Wm.	F, 57th "	Private.	Wounds.		

Name	Regiment	Rank	Notes	Status	Remarks
Southey, John	F, 57th Regt.	Private.		with regiment.	
Stevens, Alden W.	F, 57th "	Private.		with regiment.	Wounded.
Stafford, Edward	H, 4th H. A.	Private.		with regiment.	Wounded.
Stearns, Samuel	B, 15th Regt.	Corporal.	Killed, Bristoe Station.		
Sheldon, Henry L.	B, 15th "	Corporal.		with regiment.	Wounded, Prisoner.
Smith, Otis B.	B, 1st H. A.	Private.		with regiment.	
Swain, Oliver	Vet. Reserves.	Private.		with regiment.	
Sullivan, Daniel	F, 57th Regt.	Private.		with regiment.	
Sawtell Wm.	G, 32d "	Private.	Disease, at home.		Conscript, Prisoner.
Shattuck, Danforth	D, 2d "	Private.		exp. of service.	
Sweeney, Robert	Navy, "Vermont."				
Sheldon, H. T.	F, 4th Cavalry.	Private.		with regiment.	
Shippee, Melzard		Private.			Substitute.
Shay, Edward	A, 1st H. A.	Private.		with regiment.	
Steinberg, Bernard	5th Battery.	Private.		exp. of service.	
Sullivan, Michael	K, 61st Regt.	Private.		with regiment.	
Samson D. H.	54th "	Private.		with regiment.	
Sanderson, Henry	10th "	Private.		with regiment.	
Sampson, Robert W.	F, 12th U. S. I.	Private.	Disease, Salisbury, N. C.		
Safford, Frank	D, 21st Regt.	Private.		exp. of service.	Deserted.
Sawyer, Henry W.	F, 4th Cav.	Corporal.		exp. of service.	
Tarbox, Charles	D, 2d Regt.	Sergeant Major.		with regiment.	
Thurston, Thomas B.	D, 2d "	Private.	Killed, Fair Oaks, Va.		Wounded.
Tohman, Thos.	D, 22d "	Private.		for disability.	
Taylor, Thomas P.	B, 15th "	Private.			Wounded, Prisoner.
Tenney, James H.	B, 15th "	Sergeant.	Killed, Ball's Bluff, Va.		Wounded.
Taylor, George G.	B, 15th "	Private.	Killed, Chantilly, Va.		
Tolman, Calvin E.	D, 21st "	Captain.	Wounds, Port Hudson.		
Tait, Jerome K.	A, 53d "	2d Lieut.		for disability.	
Tuttle, Daniel W.	A, 53d "				

NAMES.	COMP. & REGT.	RANK.	DEATH.	DISCHARGED.	REMARKS.
Tourtellot, Albert D.	A, 53d Regt.	Sergeant.		with regiment.	
Thomas Orin A.	A, 53d "	Private.		with regiment.	
Thompson, Lysander F.	A, 53d "	Private.		with regiment.	
Tolman, Thomas W.	A, 53d "	Private.		with regiment.	
Tucker, Richard	B, 53d "	Private.		with regiment.	
Tileston, George F.	B, 53d "	Private.		with regiment.	
Taylor, Henry	A, 36th and 9th H. A.	Private.		for disability.	
Thompson, H. A.	A, 36th Regt.	Private.		with regiment.	
Thornton, John J.	A, 36th & 56th	Private.	Disease, Harrison's Landing, La.		
Townsend, James	A, 32d Regt.	1st Lieut.			Wounded.
Thompson, Gilbert	4th Cavalry.	Ensign.		exp. of service.	
Trask, Brainard P.	Navy, Congress.	1st Lieut.	Killed, Petersburg, Va.	exp. of service.	
Upton, Charles E.	F, 25th Regt.	Private.		for disability.	
Upton, Thomas	25th "	Colonel.		resigned.	
Upton, Edwin		Private.		with regiment.	
Underwood, Edwin M.	A, 53d "	Private.			
Upham, N Bradlee	A, 53d "	Private.	Killed, Port Hudson, La.		
Underwood, George H.	H, 4th H. A.	Private.		with regiment.	
Underwood, James M.	M, 2d Cal. Cav	Musician.	Drowned, Utah Ter.		
Vanderford, James	B, 53d Regt.	Private.	Wounds, Winchester, Va.		
Vose, Edwin F.	D, 2d "	Private.	Disease, New Orleans.		
Winchester, George G.	A, 53d "	Private.		for disability.	
Wyman, Jackson	A, 53d "	1st Lieut.		with regiment.	
Wilson, Carlos B.	B, 53d "	Private.		with regiment.	
Wheeler, Henry M.	B, 53d "	Private.		with regiment.	
Wheeler, Erastus O. Jr.	B, 53d "	Private.		with regiment.	
Willard, Herbert	B, 53d "	Private.		with regiment.	

Name	Regt	Rank	Notes	Status
Whitney, James D.	21st Regt	Private.	exp. of service.	
Wright, Amasa	B, 53d	Private.	with regiment.	
Wheeler, Francis S.	B, 53d	Private.	with regiment.	
Wright, Levi S.	B, 53d	Private.	with regiment.	
Wyman, Brad. H.	B, 53d	Private.	with regiment.	
Wright, George W.	B, 53d	Private.	with regiment.	
Wilsey, Albert C.	B, 53d	Private.	Disease, New Orleans.	
Wiley, Benj. K.	B, 53d	Private.	Disease, Baton Rouge, La.	
Webb, R. F.	A, 36th	Private.	Killed, Petersburg, Va.	
Wetherbee, Aaron F.	A, 36th	Sergeant.	with regiment.	Wounded.
Wheeler, James M.	36th	Private.		
Whittemore, Chas. F.	A, 36th	Private.	with regiment.	
Winch, Caleb.	A, 36th	Private.	with regiment.	
Wood, F. A.	A, 36th	Private.	for disability.	
Wood, Aaron W.	A, 36th	Private.	for disability.	
Whitney, D.	1st Cavalry.	Private.		
Whittemore, N. G.	I, 18th N.Y.	Private.	exp. of service	
Warner, W. B.	H, 2d Regt.	Private.		Deserted.
Whitney, Sidney	H, 11th	Private.	for disability.	
Watson, Benj.	H, 21st	Private.		Wounded. Reg. Service.
Warren, Wm. T.	H, 23d	Private.	exp. of service.	
Whitney, Daniel	K, 26th	Private.		
Whittemore, Henry F.	B, 15th	Private.	for disability.	Prisoner.
Wetherbee, Orlando	B, 15th	Private.	with regiment.	Wounded and Prisoner.
Wheeler, Charles A.	B, 15th	Asst. Surgeon.	exp. of service.	
Wheelock, Samuel	D, 21st	Private.	for disability.	
Whitcomb, George A.	D, 21st	Private.	with regiment.	
Warren, Thomas A.	D, 21st	Private.	with regiment.	
Warren, Preston	D, 21st	Private.	for disability.	Wounded.
Warren Henry A.	D, 21st	Private.	with regiment.	Wounded.

NAMES.	COMP. & REGT.	RANK.	DEATH.	DISCHARGED.	REMARKS.
Wright, Walter S.	D, 21st	Private.		for disability.	
Whitney, Julius	D, 21st	2d Lieut.		with regiment.	
Whitney, Charles M.	D, 21st	Private.	Killed, Chantilly, Va.		
Whitcomb, Charles A.	D, 25th	Private,		with regiment.	
Whittemore, Oliver H.	F, 25th	Private.	Disease, Newbern, N. C.		
Withington, Alonzo	A, 2d H. A.	Com. Sergeant.		exp. of service.	
Willis, Wm. M.	F, 25th Regt.	Private.		with regiment.	
Wait, Milan B.	F, 25th	Hospital Steward.	Killed, Petersburg, Va.		Wounded.
Whitney, Chas. H.	F, 25th	Private.		with regiment.	
Ware, German F.	F, 25th	Adjutant.		for disability.	
Willis, Henry A.	53d	Private.		with regiment.	
Wetherbee, Wm. H.	A, 53d	Private.		with regiment.	
Wheeler, Horace E.	A, 53d	Private.		with regiment.	
Wheeler, Wm. C.	A, 53d	Private.		with regiment.	
Whitcomb, Henry F.	A, 53d	Private.		with regiment.	
Whitman, Waldo	A, 53d & 4th H.A.	Private.		with regiment.	
Whittemore, Alfred	A, 53d Regt.	Private.		with regiment.	
Wiley, Robert G.	A, 53d	Private.		with regiment.	Deserted.
Waite, Fred E.	D, 21st	Private.		with regiment.	
Woodbury, Hurlbert W.	A, 53d	Private.		with regiment.	
Woodbury, Oscar F.	A, 53d	Private.		with regiment.	
Woodward, Fred F.	A, 53d	Private.		with regiment.	
Works, George F.	A, 53d	Private.	Disease, Baton Rouge.		
Woodbury, Henry S.	A, 53d	Private.	Wounds, Port Hudson, La.		
Woolridge, Wm.	A, 53d	Private.			
Works, Fred. L.	A, 53d	Private.	Disease, Opelousas, La.		
Watts, George	E, 57th	Private.	Disease, City Point, Va.		

Name	Co., Regt.	Rank	Status	Notes
Wilkins, Henry A.	F, 57th Regt.	Private.	with regiment.	
Wetherbee, Warren S.	F, 57th "	Drummer.	with regiment.	Wounded.
Wilkins, Aaron	F, 57th "	Private.	for disability.	Wounded.
Webber, Amos A.	H, 4th H. A.	Private.	with regiment.	
Wheeler, Henry M.	H, 4th H. A.	Private.	with regiment.	
Waters, Silas C.	H, 4th H. A.	Private.	with regiment.	
Whitcomb, Gilman W.	H, 4th H. A.	Private.	with regiment.	
Winch, William J.	H, 4th H. A.	Private.	with regiment.	
Woolson, Isaac M.	H, 4th H. A.	Private.	with regiment.	
Whittemore, John M.	Navy.	3d Asst. Engineer.	Killed, Port Royal, S. C.	
Worcester, John E.	A, 36th Regt.	Private.	for disability.	
Waterman, Henry	54th "	Private.	with regiment.	
Wilder, Fred A.	H, 4th H. A.	Private.	with regiment.	
Wright, Thos. H.	58th Regt.	Private.	with regiment.	
Watson, Howard	Engineer Corps.	Private.		In Service.
Wood, Tim	D, 1st H. A.	Private.	for disability.	
Wilkins, Ambrose	7th Battery.	Private.	Disease, Louisiana.	
Wallace, Charles	E, 5th Regt.	Private.	exp. of service.	
Whittemore, Hervey M.	F, 4th Cav.	Private.	exp. of service.	
Yott, Charles	H, 4th H. A.	Private.	for disability.	

SUBSTITUTES CREDITED TO FITCHBURG.

COLORED RECRUITS.

Alfred Sawyer,	George Horton,	Gross Harvey,	Madison Stewart,
Thomas Black,	Taswell Helm,	Theodore Warren,	Benj. Smith,
Peter Carr,	Andrew Jackson,	Anthony Newserville,	John Strother,
		Robert Skurlock.	

SUBSTITUTES FOR DRAFTED MEN.

Patrick Flynn,	Ireland.	Randall Meigs,	Virginia.	Wm. J. Cornish,	Virginia.	Thomas Jimmirson,	Canada.
Darsey Sandy,	Hayti.	James Brady,	Ireland.	Charles H. Greene,		Wm. Johnson,	"
Chauncy Lowe,	Canada.	Samuel Borchard,	Canada.	John Jines,	"	John Russell,	England.
Wm. Dunlap,	Virginia.	Frederick Northup,	"	Wm. Gray.	Canada.		

SUBSTITUTES FOR ENROLLED MEN.

Chas. S. Granger,	Canada.	Wm. Big Fire,	Canada.	Daniel McDonald,	Canada.	George W. Waldron,	Canada.
George Jimmirson,	"	James Upshur,	Kentucky.	John Pearson,	"	John F. Remmington,	England.
John J. Ellis,	"	John O'Brien,		Andrew Jones,	Boston.	Joseph Thompson,	Florida.
George Wilson,	Virginia.	John Burns,		Jacob Stone,	England.	John Allen,	Sweden.
Edward Gill,	Ireland.	Michael White,	New Brunswick	John H. Lee,	Virginia.	Joseph Gill,	Canada.
George Chapman,	Canada.	H. Michael Hinsland,		Francis Foster,	New Brunswick	Jule Mortel,	"
George Duncan,	"	Patrick Farmer,	Ireland.	James Notaway,	"	G. H. Edgerley,	N. Brunswick
John Kelly,	"	Charles Bauer,	France.	Wm. Russell,	Canada.	Andrew J. Rider,	"
Chicken Big Fire,	"	Peter Masson,	"	Thos. McKenzie,	Scotland.	Henry Moonshine,	Germany.

CONTENTS.

OPENING SCENES AND ACTION OF THE TOWN,	7
HISTORY OF THE SECOND REGIMENT,	15
" " " FIFTEENTH REGIMENT,	22
" " " TWENTY-FIRST REGIMENT,	36
" " " TWENTY-FIFTH REGIMENT,	47
" " " THIRTY-SIXTH REGIMENT,	62
" " " FIFTY-THIRD REGIMENT,	71
" " " FIFTY-SEVENTH REGIMENT,	91
" " " FOURTH HEAVY ARTILLERY,	99
CALL FOR THREE MONTHS TROOPS, 1862,	102
THE DRAFT,	106

Draft of 1863, Draft of 1864, Substitutes, Representative Recruits, &c.

RELIEF TO SOLDIERS AND FAMILIES, ... 114

Soldiers' Aid Society, Soldiers' Relief Committee, After Ball's Bluff, After Roanoke Island, After Antietam, After Fredericksburg, After Gettysburg, The Wilderness, Petersburg, Correspondence.

OUR PATRIOT DEAD, ... 148

Roll of Dead, Obituary Notices of F. A. Hildreth, C. S. Simonds, John Murkland, Geo. C. Taylor, Ai D. Osborne, Geo. B. Simonds, John M. Whittemore, Henry A. Beckwith, C. E. Tolman, C. E. Upton, F. H. Sibley, Geo. E. Marshall, Geo. G. Nutting, F. L. Works, H. S. Woodbury, Geo. H. Bailey, E. P. Farwell, J. H. Kendall, Joseph W. Gird, S. F. Marshall, Joseph Lowe, Josiah C. Trask, Fred. Kimball.

SOLDIERS' FUNERALS, ... 178

Capt. C. S. Simonds, Lieut. H. A. Beckwith, Lieut. George G. Nutting, Lieut. Fred H. Sibley, Captains Bailey and Taft, Sergt. Marshall, Privates Farwell, Stuart and Kendall, Lieut. Col. G. E. Marshall.

CONTENTS.

IN PRISON, ... 189
 Notices of John H. Prichard, Chas. E. Goodrich, Wm. T. Peabody
  H. K. Hill, Geo. P. Cotting, W. H. Hayden, Cyrus Putnam,
  "Recollections of Andersonville." "Life in the South."

RECEPTION OF REGIMENTS, ... 203
 Reception of Fifty-third, Reception of Fifteenth.

TOWN ACTION, PUBLIC MEETINGS, INCIDENTS, CORRESPONDENCE, &c., 211
 Resolutions, Summary of Expenses, Soldiers' Monument, Rejoicing
  and Mourning, Public Meeting. "The Escape." Correspondence, &c.

CONCLUSION, ... 244

ROSTER OF COMMISSIONED OFFICERS, ... 250

ROLL OF FITCHBURG SOLDIERS. 253

ACKNOWLEDGEMENTS.

To the Adjutant General of the State for the use of the Reports and records of his office; to the proprietors of the "Sentinel" and "Reveille," for free access to their files; to Captain Miles of the Board of Selectmen, for valuable assistance, and to many officers, soldiers and others who have given important information, the compiler tenders his grateful acknowledgements.

www.ingramcontent.com/pod-product-compliance
Lightning Source LLC
Chambersburg PA
CBHW032116230426
43672CB00009B/1752